Global Challenges, Local Responses in Higher Education

Higher Education Research in the 21st Century Series

Volume 6

Series Editors:
Barbara M. Kehm, INCHER, Kassel University (Germany)
Christine Musselin, CNRS and Science Po Paris (France)

This new series provides overviews about state of the art research in the field of higher education studies. It documents a selection of papers from the annual conferences of the Consortium of Higher Education Researchers (CHER), the world organisation of researchers in the field of higher education. This object and problem related field of studies is by nature interdisciplinary and theoretically as well as methodologically informed by disciplines such as sociology, political science, economics, history, philosophy, law and education. Each book includes an introduction by the editors explaining the thematic approach and criteria for selection as well as how the book can be used by its possible audience which might include graduate students, policy makers, researchers in the field, and practitioners in higher education administration, leadership and management.

Please email queries to kehm@incher.uni-kassel.de

International Editorial Advisory Board:

Patrick Clancy, University College Dublin (Ireland)
Creso Sà, University of Toronto (Canada)
Pedro Teixeira, Centre for Research in Higher Education Policies, University of Porto (Portugal)
Jussi Välimaa, University of Jyväskylä (Finland)
Don F. Westerheijden, Centre for Higher Education Policy Studies, University of Twente (The Netherlands)

Global Challenges, Local Responses in Higher Education

The Contemporary Issues in National and Comparative Perspective

Edited by

Jelena Branković
Ghent University, Belgium & Centre for Education Policy, Serbia

Manja Klemenčić
Harvard University, United States of America

Predrag Lažetić
Centre for Education Policy, Serbia & University of Bath, United Kingdom

and

Pavel Zgaga
University of Ljubljana, Slovenia

SENSE PUBLISHERS
ROTTERDAM/BOSTON/TAIPEI

A C.I.P. record for this book is available from the Library of Congress.

ISBN: 978-94-6209-579-3 (paperback)
ISBN: 978-94-6209-580-9 (hardback)
ISBN: 978-94-6209-581-6 (e-book)

Published by: Sense Publishers,
P.O. Box 21858,
3001 AW Rotterdam,
The Netherlands
https://www.sensepublishers.com/

Printed on acid-free paper

TABLE OF CONTENTS

Introduction

Global Challenges, Local Responses in Higher Education: An Introduction   3
Pavel Zgaga, Jelena Branković, Manja Klemenčić & Predrag Lažetić

Part 1: Academic Profession

Coarsely Ground: Developing the Czech System of Research Evaluation   15
Mitchell Young

Knowledge Society/Economy and Managerial Changes: New Challenges for
    Portuguese Academics   35
Rui Santiago, Teresa Carvalho & Andreia Ferreira

Croatian Academics and University Civic Mission Integration:
    Possibilities and Constraints   59
Bojana Ćulum

Crossing the Borders: Investigating Social and Economic Forces Shaping
    International Academic Mobility International Academic Mobility   79
Michele Rostan & Flavio A. Ceravolo

Part 2: Research Training

A Career Outside the Academy? Doctorate Holders in the Finnish
    Professional Labour Market   107
Arja Haapakorpi

Early Career Researchers Training: The Construction and Maintenance
    of Academic Prestige in Changing Environments   127
Emilia Primeri & Emanuela Reale

Participation as a Form of Socialisation How a Research Team Can Support
    Phd Students in Their Academic Path   149
Viviana Meschitti & Antonella Carassa

Part 3: Institutional Governance

Strategic Actor-Hood and Internal Transformation: The Rise of the
    'quadruple-helix university'?   171
Rómulo Pinheiro & Bjørn Stensaker

The Permanent Liminality Transition and Liminal Change in the
Italian University: A Theoretical Framework and Early Evidences   191
Massimiliano Vaira

Between Western Ideals and Post-Conflict Reconstruction: Meaning and
Perceptions of Higher Education in the Western Balkans   209
Klemen Miklavič & Janja Komljenovič

Mapping Portuguese Institutional Policies on Access Against the European
Standards and Guidelines   229
Orlanda Tavares, Sónia Cardoso & Cristina Sin

INTRODUCTION

PAVEL ZGAGA, JELENA BRANKOVIĆ, MANJA KLEMENČIĆ &
PREDRAG LAŽETIĆ

GLOBAL CHALLENGES, LOCAL RESPONSES IN
HIGHER EDUCATION: AN INTRODUCTION

I

History of the social sciences could be followed via keywords that characterize each period of its development. *Globalization* is a term that suddenly appeared at the end of the last century pushing its brand in the forefront where it still insists. Depending on the viewing angle it is invoked once as a "solution" and other time as "destruction." At the same time it opens up yet other perspectives; one of them is articulated as *glocalization*. The dialectic of the *global* and *local* is very prominent in contemporary social science debates and has had a significant impact on higher education studies. Last but not least, the recent debates on the *glocalization* of education have confirmed that this is a fertile field of comparative education.

These discussions are more or less consensual in that the following two or three decades the focus of higher education was transferred from the national to an international or global level. Since the 19th century, national systems of higher education and national universities were promoted by the dynamics of national markets and required to develop a nation-building scope; now they are challenged by the global market and the requirement for a much broader scope. However, this transition has been neither linear nor simple: the process of globalization is accompanied by a parallel process of localization. Every day we can read about an increasing global competition within the higher education sector. This competition pressures on institutions in two – at first glance opposite – directions: to be "globally competitive" and to serve the needs of local economy, i.e., to be "locally engaged" (OECD, 2007). This seemingly paradoxical relationship is well translated into political discourses. For example, the European People's Party Group reported a few months ago: "Higher education institutions should act locally to compete globally".[1]

This is an inventive rephrasing of an older saying, by substituting the verb "to think" into "to compete". "How cute," someone would sigh (and we need to comment by saying how indicative it is for the *Zeitgeist* of our time). However, even the original saying – "act locally, think globally" – is just one of those that are nice to hear but do not really say much. In today's world, "thinking globally" can quickly dissolve into Platonic abstractions and "acting locally" can turn into egotistic rescue of the self. Therefore, it is much better if the passion of inventing sympathetic sayings is replaced with an analysis of the world around us. If we follow this path,

J. Branković et al., Global Challenges, Local Responses in Higher Education, 3–11.

we can see soon that the global and local do not shake hands but are characterized with a much more complex relationship.

Therefore, what should be considered carefully from the perspective of comparative education is the very paradox of this relationship. Around the world we are faced with common, global challenges and we respond to them individually, locally. In the recently published monograph on the dialectic of the global and the local in the lens of comparative education we could read that "the workings of a global economy and the increasing interconnectedness of societies pose common problems for education systems around the world" but "regional, national and local responses [...] vary" (Arnove, Torres, & Franz, 2013, p. 1). Of course, there are efforts to respond to global challenges with common responses; however the "happy end" scenarios obviously do not work in the world around us. Most often, they resemble either a utopia or a dystopia.

Therefore, we need to analyze common problems in the perspective of their possible variations. To understand global, common problems we need to study variations and to make comparative analyses. At the same time it also should not be overseen that "cross-national comparisons of national patterns" by themselves do not explain the global dynamics, as "global forces are not so much analyzed or theorized as they are identified." For serious analyses we need a "glonacal agency heuristic" (Marginson & Rhoades, 2002, p. 281).

II

Europe has a special position in this respect. The idea and the gradual development of the European Higher Education Area (EHEA) have put all of these issues in a double perspective: on one hand, the EHEA has been an innovative "European response" to the "global challenges"; on the other, "global" and "local" face one another in many different ways within Europe itself. Europeanisation is but just "the regional version of internationalisation or globalisation" (Teichler, 2004, p. 4). The idea of building a "common" higher education area has faced from the outset with an overwhelming diversity. Fifteen years of building a common space has certainly contributed to the creation of some "common solutions," while the EHEA today faces also many interpretations of what it was supposed to be. Besides "common solutions," a considerable part of the old diversity has been preserved within the EHEA and has been partially reinforced and partially renovated in the process.

Two decades after the beginning of major reforms the EHEA is facing the dynamics of global and local in a new light. Development of national systems of higher education does not have the same pace; greatly enhanced mobility is far from the ideal of balanced flows; it seems that the crisis of recent years in some countries hit the higher education sector in an especially hard way. Attention should not only be aimed at the "full implementation" of the principles of the EHEA but also at "locally defined" factors. Last fall the first European Access Network (EAN) World

Congress was held in Montreal and according to University World News one of the major issues was that access to post-secondary education is "locally defined." For example: "Who is excluded and how they are excluded differ across countries and continents." (Atherton, 2013).

Of course, this is not only a European but a global issue. A whole series of factors – and many of them are only accessible with cultural and ethnological research – explain why it is so difficult to defend generalized answers. Brave new common global world is a world that is cut across by many fault zones, such as those which delimit the famous "World Class Universities" from unknown "local" colleges or higher education "centres" from higher education "peripheries," etc. These fault zones do not only delimit developed and developing countries; they are fault zones also within them.

The EHEA is not divided only in the context of mobility: surveys show that there is a dominant flow of students and staff from the (south)east to the (north)west. This division seems to be influenced mainly by economy. However, there is also a division which can be attributed to culture. For example, hegemony of the English language requires a paradigm shift from local academic communities, and this is not just a problem of the "third" world, but increasingly of Europe itself. World, as well as the European higher education is faced with "academic discrimination of locality," which is particularly clearly demonstrated, for example, by the "SSCI Syndrome in Higher Education": by "degrading local journals" and "accelerating academic stratification" (Chou, 2013, p. xi) in global frames. Global vs. local is not the only dichotomy which characterizes universities in a globalized world; no less important is the dichotomy of "centres" vs. "peripheries" which, last but not least, draws attention also to the "academic inequality" (Altbach, 2010, p. 10).

This is just another reason why only focusing on differences may help to identify and understand what is – or should be – common (Zgaga, Teichler, & Brennan, 2013, p. 14). A lot of research has been done over the past two decades and a lot more we know today about the European and global higher education. Nevertheless, many questions remain insufficiently treated, especially from the perspective of "centres" and "peripheries," and new ones are also opening.

This book seeks to contribute to filling the gaps in this area. It offers a series of contributions in the intersection of university governance, academic profession and internationalisation and reflects the profound interest of contemporary researchers in the questions of how the contemporary higher education reforms across Europe affect university governance and especially the roles and functions of academics. Twenty authors from all over Europe – from South to North and from East to West – deal with some specific aspects of "global challenges" and "local responses" in eleven chapters. Their papers are divided into three parts: the first dealing with issues of academic profession, the second dealing with changes in research training and doctoral studies and the third dealing with changes in the organization of higher education and higher education institutions in different parts of Europe.

III

Ever since the prominent projects Condition of academic profession (CAP) and Academic Profession in Europe (EUROAC) research on academic profession has proliferated. The present book reflects this rising interest in conditions of academic work and the impact of contemporary higher education reforms on academic profession. The book opens with a chapter by Mitchell Young in which the author analyses governance changes in the Czech Republic's research policy over the past decade according to New Public Management (NPM) principles. Young claims that Czech Republic has developed what is arguably the most radically quantitative and retrospective performance-based research evaluation system in Europe, known locally as the "coffee grinder." This policy tool has come under heavy criticism from both local academics and international experts as not fit for purpose. Young presents year by year evolution of the research evaluation as a policy tool and outlines the shift in research policy ideas, and concludes by examining the distorting effects of an extreme NPM agenda.

Based on the experience of the Czech Republic in developing the Evaluation Methodology author identifies three sets of dangers which should be considered as research policy reforms are carried out: the first set are the dangers in allowing a single doctrine to dominate a policy debate; the second set is that of the abstraction of policy discourse, as policy and policy innovation become more transnational especially though the use of entirely abstracted models or prototypes as promoted by supranational bodies like the EU and OECD; lastly, the third set is that of using purely quantitative measures to analyse and judge research quality, excellence, and relevance: terms which are rooted in a qualitative understanding of what is good and desirable.

In chapter 2, Santiago, Carvalho and Ferreira discuss the new challenges for Portuguese academics with regards to the issue of knowledge society/economy and managerial changes. The starting point of the chapter is the 2007 higher education act in Portugal which was implemented with the aim to (re)configure higher education institutions to make them more corporate and to impose a more competitive and efficient environment. The authors then analyse how academics in Portugal are positioned in relation to these changes and whether they view changes as affecting their professional group. The chapter draws empirical data from a survey of academics with management responsibilities (which are in the extended research project compared to physicians and nurses).

The authors first confirm the findings from previous research that the majority of academics overall still identify the mainstream "traditional" academic values and beliefs as the core reference of their professionalism. Further, they expose some important differences and qualifications to these findings. The authors point out that academics in managerial positions perceive a dramatic change in institutional objectives which have predominantly turned to market and managerial concerns. The knowledge society is substantially present in their day-to-day professional practices, at least discursively. Next, they suggest that surveyed academics in leadership positions perceived strengthening of their influence over key institutional decisions. In turn, academic boards and individuals emerge as the actors who have been losing more power over the main institutional decision-making processes. Finally, the authors conclude that their respondents were in agreement suggesting that the academic profession has been losing social prestige and power compared with other social groups.

In chapter 3 Ćulum engages with the question of the role of academics in the university civic mission and university engagement in local community as "to embody university purpose, objectives, priorities and academic pillars, meaning teaching and research, with the needs and problems of their neighbouring (local) communities." Drawing on the existing literature, Ćulum suggests that the most sustainable way of integrating civic mission is its incorporation into teaching and research, thus exposing a crucial role of the academics. The chapter further discusses some possibilities and constraints of the civic mission integration into Croatian universities. It focuses on three key determinants of successful integration: (a) academics' readiness to introduce change into their everyday teaching and research, (b) attitudes that academics take toward the civic mission and (c) models of institutional support that would encourage academics to integrate community engaged learning in their everyday teaching and research.

In addition, Ćulum develops a typology of Croatian academics in relation to their willingness to accept changes in their daily teaching and research. Ćulum finds that in Croatia academics working in humanities and social sciences as well as in arts, women, associate and tenured professors and those academics aged from 41 to 50 years appear to be more willing to accept changes and new ideas, and to integrate the university civic mission in their teaching and research activities. Finally, the least likely to bring change in daily teaching and research are the youngest respondents up to 31 years of age in the associate status.

Another highly relevant subject in the domain of academic profession is discussed in chapter 4. The authors Rostan and Ceravolo present an analysis of the international academic mobility based on the *Changing Academic Profession* international survey (CAP) data. Descriptive analysis of the CAP sample indicates that there are five main types of academic mobility based on the duration and purpose of mobility, named by authors as: 1) early circulation for study; 2) late short job circulation; 3) late long job circulation; 4) early migration for study and 5) late job migration. In the subsequent analysis authors use multinomial regression modelling for the analysis of different factors influencing different types of academic mobility. The primary focus of the analysis is the influence of macro factors like country size, level of economic development in the country, presence of English as one of the official languages etc, while controlling for individual and organisational characteristics and dimensions.

The results confirm the importance and relevance of macro level social and economic characteristics of the countries of origin and current residence for academic mobility, confirming the theoretical models of brain-drain and brain circulation which exist in various shapes in different contexts. Rostan and Ceravalo show that countries' linguistic traditions, size, economic status and regional location do have an impact on international mobility, although in different ways according to different types of mobility. Finally, data confirm the existence, or the persistence, of inequalities between English speaking and non-English speaking countries, more developed and less developed countries, smaller and larger countries, and the existence of differences between China, other Asian countries and Western countries.

IV

The second part of the book addresses the changes in research training and doctoral studies. The rising interest in doctoral training and careers of doctoral graduates has two main causes. One certainly is in the rising numbers of doctoral students. The other is in the interest of governments to promote research excellence, of which training of doctoral students, and their employment inside and outside of academia are central parts. In chapter 5, Arja Haapakorpi takes on the issue of doctoral education and careers of doctoral graduates in Finland, in particular those employed outside academia. The empirical basis of the analysis represents the combination of quantitative data from the survey of doctoral degree holders in Finland who completed their doctoral examinations in the academic year 2004/05 and qualitative data collected through interviews with the managers of the employer organisations employing doctoral graduates outside academic institutions. Firstly, Haapakorpi analyses careers, job descriptions and hierarchical status at work of doctoral holders employed outside academia and compares them with employees in the same organisations who have a lower higher education degree. Secondly, based on the employer interviews, the author studies the reasons to employ doctorate holders and competence requirements required for their work.

Haapakorpi finds out that although there was no particular labour market niche for doctorate holders outside the academy, doctorate holders had special tasks or positions, for which the degree was regarded as appropriate. At work sites outside the academia, the industry-specific competence was considered important, which, however, did not invalidate the value of the highest academic degree. The membership in the academic community appears to be a good reason to employ doctorate holders for the purpose of reinforcing collaboration with universities, while the doctorate holders themselves were rather satisfied with their jobs. Finally, the author concludes that in order to improve the matching process of competences required through doctoral training and education and job requirements outside academia, doctoral qualifications have to be translated into industry-specific and organisation-based doctoral competences.

Moving to Italy, in chapter 6, Primeri and Reale look into the subject of doctoral training as the process of acquiring academic norms, values, and rules, as well as the behaviours, attitudes, and know-how within specific scientific community. Primeri and Reale discuss several factors are changing the way in which PhD students and early career researchers are selected and trained. Among these, a key element is the increasing competition and pressure to gain a better position in international rankings – considered a visible measure of academic excellence – and to improve prestige and reputation. Authors present the findings from two case studies (two departments of different disciplines within a large, comprehensive Italian university). The analysis highlights changes concerning three main features: selection and training habits; modifications in the relationships between students and supervisors; and research practices. Authors conclude that the specific characteristics of the disciplines play an important role in shaping how PhD students and early career researchers are trained, but other factors seem to be more relevant: external competition for excellence, evaluation of academic research and performance, size of research groups, and the national features of the HE system.

The discussion on the doctoral training is further complemented by the contribution of Meschitti and Carassa. In chapter 7, the authors explore the process of doctoral students' socialisation into their own disciplinary community, to the role of PhD student, to the department and the research group, and to the academic profession. Inspired by situated learning theory, the authors use ethnographic method of direct observation and interviews to gather data on daily academic routines of PhD students belonging to the same research team at a Swiss department of informatics. The authors make several important findings. First, they observe that the research team represents a peculiar community of practice, with a strong mutual engagement among its members, which is considered a good condition to facilitate socialisation. In terms of particular activities which affect trajectory of new PhD, they observed that team meetings were particularly important, as well as invited lectures for fostering disciplinary knowledge. They also highlight the role of team leader in fostering socialisation. Finally, the authors propose a model of PhD student socialisation, highlighting the role of the department, the specific work conditions, and the relationships with peers and supervisors, arguing for the need to create open spaces for discussion to foster socialisation.

V

In the last two decades we have witnessed dramatic changes in the organization of higher education and higher education institutions in different parts Europe. In Chapter 8, Pinheiro and Stensaker address the way in which external possibilities and strategic initiatives lead to internal transformation process of universities. Looking into the empirical account from a Danish university, Pinheiro and Stensaker tentatively conclude that the European university is gradually but steadily moving towards the notion of a unified, strategic, organisational actor: pro-active, more financially self-reliant, increasingly sensitive to the needs and expectations of various stakeholders and more accountable to society. In conclusion, it is suggested that the extent to which the ambitions of the university will be realised depends on the extent to which organisational culture will be changed in the processes of systematic human resource management.

In chapter 9, Vaira addresses the issue of reforms in higher education by applying the concepts of liminality and transition to organisational change and reflects on it from theoretical and empirical perspective. The author offers a general theoretical model built on these two concepts which is then applied to an empirical case – the Italian university, to show in what way organisational change is hindered. The author argues that the Italian university is a paradigmatic example of an organisation being trapped in a liminal state, given that despite the four different waves of reform in the last twenty years, the organisational change appears to be chronically impeded.

The debate on reforms in different national context is complemented by chapter 10 in which Miklavič and Komljenovič identify the ideational bases – the topics and meanings – underpinning higher education reforms in the Western Balkans. As such it contributes to a much needed research on this little known area of Europe. The main focus of the chapter is on regional idiosyncrasies as expressed through narratives of interviewed regional actors. These narratives are complemented to the data from a large-scale survey of academic staff in the region. The authors apply an inductive approach and to a highly beneficial effect combine both sources. The authors expose several major narratives surrounding the development of higher education systems in the region. One such narrative is the idealisation of the West and in turn a self-imagined peripheral identity which stimulates the discourse of emulation. Another powerful narrative is that of nation-building, especially in the countries that emerged from the armed conflict or delayed transition (as in the case of Albania). Yet another is the difference between the discipline faculties in their perception on the role of higher education. The authors conclude that the reconstruction of society, formation of intellectual elites and nation building are often given priority and importantly shaping higher education reforms.

In the final chapter in this volume, Tavares and Santiago analyse the initiatives of Portuguese higher education institutions in the domain of student access and the extent to which these align with the European Standards and Guidelines (ESG). In specific, the analysis focuses on three issues: the data on different student cohorts, the institutional mechanisms in place to support the admission and progression of distinct cohorts of students and the variation of such mechanisms by academic programme, as well as the changes in the last decade with regards to the enrolments pattern. The authors conclude that with regards to the ESG 1.1 and 1.6, there is only partial compliance, and while the HEIs in Portugal are in principle aligned with the national legal framework, they do have an extent of autonomy within which they develop their own specific institutional policies on access, as well as strategies and initiatives to attract students aside the national competition. However, as authors further suggest, the notion of quality in the eyes of institutions appears to be much more along the lines of the academic quality of students, rather than the quality culture, procedures and instruments in place with the aim to assure the quality of the institution and its academic content.

VI

This book contains the revised version of some of the papers presented at the anniversary 25th Conference of the Consortium of Higher Education Researchers (CHER) on "Higher Education and Social Dynamics" which took place in Belgrade in early September 2012. The eleven contributions were selected by editors from about one hundred papers presented at the Conference. Overall, the contributions confirm again that the higher education research landscape is a diverse and rich one. At the same time, these diverse cases have at least one commonality – the fact that even though they are located in different higher education systems, they address issues that, albeit as a rule context-specific, can be found in all parts of Europe and beyond. Certainly, the local responses to the hereby addressed global challenges represent a mere snapshot of a broader landscape the European higher education dynamics is.

NOTES

[1] 14 November 2013; see http://web.cor.europa.eu/epp/News/Pages/13-11-14_Boroboly-higher-education.aspx#.Uv9vArQwAT4.

REFERENCES

Altbach, P. G., Reisberg, L., & Rumbley, L. E. (2010). *Trends in global higher education. tracking an academic revolution.* Rotterdam: Sense.

Arnove, R. F., Torres, C. A., & Franz, S. (Eds.) (2013). *Comparative education. The Dialectic of the global and the local.* Lanham, MD: Roman and Littlefield.

Atherton, G. (2013, October 11). Time for a global movement for higher education access. *University World News.* Retrieved from http://www.universityworldnews.com/.

Chou, P. C. (Ed.) (2013). *The SSCI syndrome in higher education. A local or global phenomenon.* Rotterdam: Sense.

Marginson, S., & Rhoades, G. (2002). Beyond national states, markets, and systems of higher education: A glonacal agency heuristic. *Higher Education, 43*(3): 281–309.

OECD (2007). *Higher Education and Regions: Globally Competitive, Locally Engaged.* Paris: OECD.

Teichler, U. (2004). The changing debate of internationalisation of higher education. *Higher Education, 48*(1), 5–26.

Zgaga, P., Teichler, U., & Brennan, J. (Eds.) (2013). *The globalisation challenge for European Higher Education: Convergence and diversity, centres and peripheries.* Frankfurt: Peter Lang.

PART 1

ACADEMIC PROFESSION

MITCHELL YOUNG

COARSELY GROUND

Developing the Czech System of Research Evaluation

INTRODUCTION

The Czech Republic has developed what is arguably the most radical performance-based research evaluation system in Europe, the Evaluation Methodology (EM). Locally it is referred to as the "coffee grinder" after its ability to take research outputs from all disciplines and organizations (universities, academy of science and research institutes) and reduce them to a common numerical point system. This combination of a universal system that uses only one dimension of measurement and that is intended to be used to allocate all of the institutional funding for research on a yearly basis, has brought forth significant criticism. A recent international audit of the Czech Research system commissioned by the Ministry of Education called it "inappropriate" in regards to its intended objectives of improving the quality of research and "threatening" in regards to its potential to irreversibly deform the research environment (Arnold, 2011, p. 5). However, the EM appears to have solid roots in broadly accepted values and principles which are supported by supranational organizations such as the OECD and the EU and are central elements in what is labelled New Public Management (NPM). This paper aims to examine governance changes in Czech research policy, particularly the development of the EM, to see if they correspond with NPM discourse, and further, to explore how such a problematic tool developed. Is the EM is a model NPM-type policy instrument or some sort of a perversion?

THE ROLE OF NPM IN UNIVERSITY-BASED RESEARCH POLICY

Despite recent claims that NPM is finished (Dunleavy et al., 2006) or that we are now in a post-NPM period (Christensen & Laegreid, 2007), there is still ample evidence of NPM reforms occurring in the research policy area. This is perhaps because research policy, like much of higher education policy, didn't become a central focus of policymakers until the late 1990's. It may also be that this is part of the general trajectory of NPM reforms, which show a tendency to move from one area of the state administration to the next, following the basic template of a 'solution looking for a problem.' However, neither by itself is a fully satisfying argument. I will argue that there are strong forces shaping the discourse on research and higher education

J. Branković et al., Global Challenges, Local Responses in Higher Education, 15–33.

at both a national and supranational level, which have brought research policy into the NPM fold, and which have shaped the problem definition in a way that leads to NPM-type policy solutions.

The conceptual understanding of the university's role in contemporary society is undergoing dramatic change driven by an underlying shift in the way in which countries compete in a globalized world. Economic competitiveness has become the primary mode of measuring competition between nations, and the university is being re-evaluated and re-envisioned in light of this. The university is recast in a way that emphasizes its role as a knowledge creator and disseminator that plays a central part in national innovation systems and hence directly supports economic development. The concept of the knowledge economy has been fully embraced by the European Union and with the establishment of the Lisbon strategy in the early 2000s, the EU has acted through both policy and institutional means to promote reform in the university sector.

The strong promotion of the knowledge economy narrative as a key driver of national economic competitiveness, has meant that the basic societal contract with the university is being rewritten. Universities are no longer being treated as a special type of institution, but are being seen as generic public institutions that can and as the logic goes, should, be treated in the same way as any other public service (Christensen, 2011). When we bring together these two lines of argument, the idea that universities' main role is to support economic competitiveness, and the belief that they should be treated as any other part of the state apparatus, we find fertile ground for NPM reforms.

NPM is a difficult concept to pin down with precision (Dunleavy, 2006). The term itself appears in the early 1990's as way to make sense of policy reforms that began in the 1980's and which continued to develop and expand over time. The result is that there are a wide range of often disparate tools and policy reforms that are characterized as NPM. We also find a debate over what in fact NPM actually is: a philosophy, a policy, a narrative, a reform movement, a discourse, or a set of tools. The identification of NPM reforms thus follows more of a family resemblance model, in other words, by drawing on a significant subset of generally agreed upon elements, the reform becomes recognizable as NPM. A very broad definition of NPM comes from the OECD document *Governance in Transition* (1995): "A new paradigm for public management has emerged, aimed at fostering a performance-oriented culture in a less centralised public sector (OECD, 1995 p. 8)." This definition highlights the key elements of what is generally understood to be constituent of NPM, performance-orientation and decentralization. The term paradigm is also worth noting as it suggests that NPM is an archetype or worldview rather than a policy alternative. These two basic elements listed by the OECD can be further unpacked. Christopher Hood in his seminal 1991 article *A Public Management for All Seasons?* defines NPM as a doctrine for public administration and identifies seven overlapping components (see Table 1). As explained above, it should be noted that for Hood these seven components are not necessarily found in equal measure in each reform, nor must all of them be present at once. A more recent definition by Pollitt and Bouckaert (2011) sees NPM as a two-level concept that in addition to being a general theory or doctrine, can be understood "a bundle of specific concepts and practices" (Pollitt & Bouckaert, 2011, p. 10). These are listed in Table 1.

Table 1. The two streams of NPM elements

	Managerial Theory	Liberal Economics
OECD	Performance-oriented	Less centralized
Hood	'Free to manage' 'Hands-on professional management' in the public sector; Explicit standards and measures of performance; Greater emphasis on output controls; Stress on private-sector styles of management practice	'Free to choose' Shift to disaggregation of units in the public sector; Shift to greater competition in public sector; Stress on greater discipline and parsimony in resource use
Pollitt and Bouckaert	Greater emphasis on 'performance,' especially the measurement of outputs; An emphasis on treating service users as 'customers' and on the application of generic quality improvement techniques such as Total Quality Management	A preference for lean, flat, small, specialized (disaggregated) organization forms over large, multi-functional forms; A widespread substitution of contracts for hierarchical relations as the principle coordinating device; A widespread injection of market-type mechanisms including competitive tendering, public sector league tables, and performance-related pay

Hood (1991) argues that the sources of NPM come from two quite distinct disciplinary streams, a "marriage of opposites (p. 5)," which brings together liberal economics with managerial theory. Hood characterizes this as a difference between "free to choose," with its implications of promoting competition between more autonomous and responsible actors and "free to manage," with its ideas of performance management and control. While this hybrid may seem commonplace in today's world and while the values and interests of the two areas may dovetail in many situations, there is also an inherent tension between the two streams. Table 1 separates the elements of the above mentioned definitions according to which stream they fall under.

A less often cited section of Hood's (1991) article is the one which connects NPM ideas with administrative-cultural values. Hood identifies three major cultural value types: sigma-type, "keep it lean and purposeful," theta-type, "keep it honest and fair," and lambda-type, "keep it robust and resilient" (p. 11). He hypothesizes that it is possible to satisfy two of these three sets of values, but it is unlikely that any given policy solution can satisfy all three. He argues that NPM is predominantly rooted in sigma-type values, where the standard of success is frugality in an output controlled system, and that theta-type values are implied as NPM "assumes a culture of public service honesty as given (p. 16)." Further, the theta-type values could also be supported in terms of the arguably non-discriminatory nature of markets. If his hypothesis that only two value sets can be satisfied is correct, it would suggest that the lambda-type values will not be satisfied by NPM tools. Those lambda-type values of diversity, resilience, reliability, and robustness are oriented towards emergent goals and are nevertheless extremely important for a research system seeking to create a stable platform for scientific progress and innovation, objectives which are not prone to predictability.

How can NPM be recognized in research policy? I will begin with a sub-question: is there a relationship between NPM and the power dynamics between the university and the state? The area of university dynamics has been well mapped. Burton Clark's (1983) seminal publication laid out a typology with three basic relationship models upon which most of the later research has developed: state control, academic oligarchy, and market. Subsequent works contain slight variations, but the essential elements are consistent and transparent across the newer theories (Gornitzka & Maassen, 2000; Maassen & Olsen, 2007; Dobbins, 2009). For the purpose of examining these dynamics within the context of NPM, a variant developed by de Boer, Enders, & Schimank (2007) is used in this paper. It identifies five dimensions of governance that shape the university-state relationship and that in certain patterns are indicative of NPM-type reform. These five dimensions are not meant to be mutually exclusive, quite the opposite: the authors claim that they are often all present to varying degrees. The government can increase and decrease each of the five dimensions semi-independently as you might turn the dials on an equalizer (de Boer, Enders, & Schimank, 2007).

The five dimensions are: state regulation, managerial self-governance, academic self governance, stakeholder guidance, and competition. *State regulation* refers to direct influence exerted by the state over the university in all areas. This corresponds directly to Clark's state control model, and can be seen clearly in terms of a lack of formal autonomy for the university to set its human resources policies, control its real estate, determine student numbers, etc. Each of these areas is managed by the state. Managerial self-governance and academic self-governance refer to the other two points on Clark's triangle. *Managerial self-governance* fits into the entrepreneurial or market based model of the university. This model suggests that universities should run like businesses and that they need professional management in order to run effectively. Managerial self-governance gives the university autonomy to make its own decisions, but these decisions are made by a powerful administration staffed by professional managers. This is directly opposed to the *academic self-governance* model, which describes the classic collegial model of university in which the faculty makes all the major decisions. The states' role in this model is often seen as protecting the university from outside interference so as to allow academics the freedom to pursue their research and teaching agendas without manipulation. While the first three dimensions are focused on the management of the university and who holds the power to make strategic decisions, the final two dimensions look at the formal inclusion of influence from external forces which have been given the ability to shape the university. *Stakeholder guidance* refers to external groups or institutions which have a role in university governance. The stakeholders can be industry representatives which play an increasing role on university boards, as well as other organizations which represent the social interests of society and correspond to what is referred to as the third mission of the university. The state can also be a stakeholder in a system where formal autonomy has been given to the university and the state is no longer directly involved in its management. The fifth and final dimension, *competition*, refers to the overall environment in which the university acts. Competition in the university sector typically revolves around money, personnel, students, and prestige. These markets do not necessarily act as financial markets, but often as quasimarkets where citations, recognition, and influence play a higher role than finances. Competition can be seen at both a national and a global level, and becomes explicit in the search for both funding and prestige, through league tables and global rankings systems, as can be demonstrated through the remarkably rapid rise of the global rankings systems since 2003.

The authors argue that each of these five dimensions can be turned up or down like the dial of an equalizer. By looking at the configuration of all five dials, we can identify certain patterns which reflect different types of public administration systems. When there are reductions in state regulation and academic self-governance and increases in stakeholder guidance, managerial self-governance, and competition we are likely to find NPM-type governance.

UNIVERSITY DYNAMICS IN THE CZECH REPUBLIC

In the past two decades, the Czech Republic has undergone dramatic reforms which generally been driven by transition politics and the entry to the EU. While that change has been incremental and piecemeal (Verheijen, 2003; Bouckaert et al., 2011) rather than following a deliberate and explicit NPM agenda, nevertheless new policies are influenced and borrowed from countries which are following NPM reform agendas. Therefore, we can identify specific policies in the Czech Republic as NPM-type in hindsight, without insisting that they were initiated with NPM as an explicit agenda or part of an overall administrative reform.

In the area of higher education and research policy, is there evidence of NPM-type reform in the Czech Republic? Using the metaphor of the equalizer: where are the dials set in the Czech Republic with regards to university dynamics and how have they been adjusted over the past 20 years? Since the fall of communism in 1989 we find a clear move away from the state regulation model in the Czech Republic, as was also the case in most of the formerly communist countries (Dobbins & Knill, 2009). The role of students in the 'velvet revolution,' the overarching value of freedom, and abuses of the communist years in using the university system for ideological indoctrination and screening, deeply affected the 1990 higher education act. This first major post-communist reform of the university sector resulted in a system characterized by extremely high levels of autonomy through academic self governance. It ended the state's central control over universities and established institutional autonomy under the model of a 'representative democracy' (Pabian, 2009). The institutional autonomy covered staff recruitment, establishment of study programs, enrollment numbers, conditions of access, and as of 1992, budgetary autonomy with the establishment of formula based lump-sum funding rather than line-item funding. The reform also strengthened the academic senate and the individual faculties at the expense of the rector and the university's central administration as a whole. The level of autonomy in Czech universities was arguably the highest in Europe (Pabian, 2009), but in terms of the dials, it was not a NPM type system. Although the state control dial was turned way down, in its place the academic self-governance was turned up, but the other three dials were not turned on at all.

With the second major post communist reform of the higher education act in 1998, those dials get turned, even if only slightly. The major thrust of the 1998 act was to promote quality assurance, and it required that all programs be accredited by the newly formed accreditation commission. Quality assurance had previously been solely within the purview of the university itself. The act's other major change was to allow for the accreditation of private institutions. Further changes were more minor, but are ones that concern NPM. The act strengthened the university vis-à-vis the faculties, which were no longer given the status of a legal entity, a turn of the managerial self-governance dial. Also boards of trustees were created, with members appointed by the minster. Though the boards had few real powers, they did have a role in any capital expenses or real estate dealings and were able to review and comment on strategic plans and the direction of the institution. Primarily though, they were to be appointed "with the view of associating representatives of public life, municipality as well as state administration (Government, 1998, Article 14.1)" with the university. In other words, they turned on the stakeholder dial.

The third period of reform witnesses a split between the education and research areas in terms of policy activity. A third major higher education act has been under discussion, but has been repeatedly delayed due to protests and government turnover. The key issues in that proposal have to do with student funding, and the possible introduction of tuition fees. In the area of research policy, however, reform has gone forward with an act passed in 2008. The reform act of 2008 defines it primary vision in this way: "To create an innovative environment through reforming the system of research, development and innovation in the Czech Republic in order to be held true that 'Science makes knowledge from money, innovation makes money from knowledge' (Government, 2008, p. 1)." The embedded quote comes from the 2007 comparative analysis of Czech research report, where it serves as the "motto" which introduces the preface signed by the Prime Minister and head of the Council of Research, Development and Innovation, Miroslav Topolanek of the center-right ODS party (Council, 2007b). The role of these yearly analyses will be examined in the following section of this paper. For now we can note from the quotation above that the prime minister is clearly attuned to the conceptualization of the university as an economic driver within a global arena. Money, or less crudely, economic gain or competitiveness, is the central issue. More specifically the reform identifies seven main objectives which correspond with many of the NPM elements and EU policy recommendations.

The 2008 reform (Government, 2008) builds on the government resolution which established the Evaluation Methodology in 2004 and subsequent comparative analyses of Czech and international research results, particularly the 2007 analysis mentioned above. The reform addresses both institutional research funding, which it proposes to move entirely to a performance based model, based on data from the EM, and targeted research funding, which it proposes to simplify into two central bodies: the Grant Agency of the Czech Republic which is focused on basic research and the Technological Agency of the Czech Republic which will fund applied research. There are a few additional sources of funds for which exceptions are allowed, but the basic principle is to allocate virtually all the institutional funding ex-post as determined by the EM and all the ex-ante project type funding through these two bodies. The support of excellence in research is to be achieved through the establishment of centers of excellence, and also to the use of the ex-post evaluation of research results for the purpose of funding. Simply put, it seeks to realign the Evaluation Methodology as a performance based funding system.

There are also efforts in the 2008 reform to connect universities more closely with industrial research by externalizing research funding to independent bodies, comprised of academic, industry, and state representatives which allocate funds on a competitive basis. These can be interpreted as increases in the stakeholder and competitiveness dials.

NPM reform is a process and over the three periods of Czech research policy development we can find reforms that emerge from the two root sources of NPM reforms, the managerial and the economic, as well as conforming to the expected pattern of increases and decreases on the governance equalizer. The EM, with its emphasis on performance and measurement of outputs but simultaneously displaying a quasi-market like approach, brings together both the 'free to manage' and the 'free to choose' aspects of policy. The following section will analyze its development more systematically.

THE DEVELOPMENT OF THE EVALUATION METHODOLOGY

The "coffee grinder" or Evaluation Methodology (EM) system for evaluating research results was first implemented in 2004. Each year, the EM has been revisited and adjusted; the accumulation of those changes has led to the current version of the EM which is highly controversial. To quote the European experts who were invited by the Ministry of Education to conduct an audit of the Czech research system in 2011: "Our conclusion is that the existing Evaluation Methodology is inappropriate for both the evaluation of research quality and the allocation of institutional funding. For this reason, we recommend discontinuing it. (Arnold, 2011, p. 5)"

The EM did not start out as a particularly radical tool, but over time developed into one. At what point in time did this happen? Was it influenced by debates that were going on in other European countries over how to improve research results?

The research reform agenda in the Czech Republic is rooted in problems which have been demonstrated in yearly reports using OECD and EU indicators. These reports, which have been produced since 2003, and sporadically before that, show a gap between both the inputs and outputs of the Czech system of research in comparison with other developed countries. The strong desire to be above the European average in the Czech Republic allows this demonstrated gap to become a relevant policy concern. The historical position of the Czech Republic as a leading industrial power of the interwar period in the 20th century and its geographical position in regards to its German speaking neighbors support the general acceptance of this aim.

Comparing the yearly *Analysis of the Existing State of Research, Development and Innovation in the Czech Republic and a Comparison with the Situation Abroad* (hereafter: State of Research) reports can show us how the political and policy context changes over time. For this purpose, the preface, which is signed by the chairman of the Council of Research and Development, is particularly valuable. As the chairman since 2007 has been the Prime Minister and prior to that was a Vice-Minister, this can be used to demonstrate how the political leadership is framing research policy issues. The 2007 motto mentioned in the previous section was followed in 2008 with this one "'we will only do what we are number one or number two at in the world' Jack Welch (Council, 2007b, p. 6)." By using a quote that sums up the basic business philosophy of Jack Welch, the CEO of General Electric (GE) company, the document shows the clear importation of business models to public management as promoted by NPM ideas. The statement from Welch served as the guiding strategic philosophy for GE, and was used to justify the disposal of any businesses within GE that was not leading its category. Welch's philosophy was extremely popular in the 2000's but fell out of favor after his departure and subsequent corporate difficulties at GE. It is unlikely that the Prime Minister meant to enact this philosophy literally, as it would have required dismantling most of the science system in the country, but abstractly as a threat to underperforming areas, the message was clear. Here we see as well the tenuousness of bringing business-like practices to public administration as management is not a static field and what is considered good practice at one time can quickly fall out of favor.

In the 1999 analysis, the policy problem is depicted more as an input than an output problem. This corresponds with the general European argumentation at the time which suggest that increasing funding levels to 3% of GDP, the so called Barcelona target, was the solution to improving research results. By 2008, the thinking had reversed: "The one percentage point we need to meet the EU target of investing 3% of GDP in research can be bridged by drawing on private resources, primarily in the field of innovation. A more fundamental problem is making sure they are used effectively (Council, 2008b, p. 6)." The effective use refers to obtaining what are deemed sufficient outputs in relation to the government investment in research.

The understanding of the economic role of the university also undergoes clear changes during this decade-long period. In 2011, the "Motto: Even in this difficult economic and budget situation the research and development remains a priority for this government (Council, 2011, p. 4)," is followed by an economic justification for the importance of research to national competitiveness:

> Apart from traditional characteristics such as independence, rationality and objectivity other values are coming into the forefront nowadays due to the changes in the science policy, such as usability, excellence, interdisciplinarity, international cooperation and mobility. These new values contribute to the improvement of our country's competitiveness, which is also one of the main priorities of the government (Council, 2011 p. 4).

This is in distinct contrast to the 1999 documents which was skeptical of the connection:

> There is no theoretical justification indicating whether support extended to research and development is the reason for or consequence of economic growth. The success of dynamically developing countries (Ireland, Finland, Israel, etc.) proves that increased support extended to research and development must either precede or at least accompany economic restructuring (Council and Ministry 1999 summary).

The 1999 document also demonstrates a skepticism towards bibliometric analysis: "Bibliometric analysis was performed for the first time in connection with a material for the Czech government; although it is commonplace in official foreign documents, in the Czech Republic it has been so far considered doubtful or downright deprecated (Council and Ministry 1999 summary)." But by 2003, this has already changed due apparently in large part to the overall acceptance of such methods in the broader global discourse: "In the last years the bibliometric analysis, i.e. evaluation of the number of publications and their citations, despite all reservations against its objectivity, methodology and other aspects, became an integral part of documents evaluating the level of research in the member countries of OECD, as well as in the European Union (Council, 2003 p. 65)."

Nationally, the anti-corruption discourse gained traction during the time period, if not in terms of aggressive political action to stamp out corrupt practices at the highest levels, at least in terms of a growing awareness and concern over the issue. Generally options are that the Czech Republic has a high level of corruption supported by evidence from Transparency International's Corruption Perceptions Index (Transparency International, 2012). There is also a low level of trust in society as can be seen in studies such as the World Values Survey[1]. We see all of these concerns addressed in the rational for the Evaluation Methodology. The quantitative objectiveness of the system is strongly supported. It is seen as a way to counteract the favoritism and cronyism which is seen as endemic in the country and which was seen to have dominated the dissemination of research funds prior to the EM. The idea of a peer-review based evaluation system has been consistently rejected both as regards the cost and also over the fears of favoritism, which are more pronounced in a small country such as the Czech Republic. As complex as the EM is, it does produce results that are transparently obtained, and in that way the points and the formulas for developing them are objective.

Tracking the Yearly Changes

The EM changes dramatically over time. From its introduction in 2004 to the version of 2012, it displays strong staying power as an institution while at the same time being adapted to various purposes. This section will trace the year-to-year developments of the EM in terms of its aims and mechanisms for valuing research outputs, that is, attributing points. Table 2 below provides a summary of the changes in the point system.

Table 2. Point system for selected outputs

	Journal Article – Impact (WoS)	*Journal Article – Non Impact (Erih, Scopus, Czech list)*	*Book*	*Patent*
2004	1	1	1	1
2005	$10\times$(factor [a])	$1/2^b$	$5/10^b$	25
2006	$1+(10\times$(factor [a])$/4+(10\times$(factor [a])$)^b$	$1/4^b$	$5/20^b$	$50/100^f$
2007	$5+(15\times$(factor [a])	$1/2^b/4^{bc}$	$12.5/25^b/50^{bc}$	$50/500^f$
2008	$5+140\times$(factor [c])	$4/8^b/10^c/12^{bc}$	$20/40^b/40^c$	$40/200^g/500^f$
2009	$10-305$ $(10+295\times$(factor [c]) $/500^d$	$4/8^b/10^c/12^{bc}$	$20/40^b/40^c$	$40/200^g/500^f$
2010– 2012	$10-305$ $(10+295\times$(factor [c])$/500^d$	$4/10^b/10^c/11^b/ 12^b/12^c/20^c/30^c$	$20/40^b/40^c$	$40/200^g/500^f$

a based on journal impact factor and median impact factor of field; b international language; c based on the ranking of the journal in its field and the overall number of journals in the field; d prestige journal; e fields of humanities and social sciences; f international patent; g licensed patent

Overall we will find that there have been four significant shifts over the lifetime of this instrument, some occurring gradually as year-to-year adjustments to correct for perceived weaknesses in the system, while others are abruptly introduced. The objective and measurement dimension shifts from being informational, intended to measure the effectiveness of research spending, to distributional, measuring outputs as a means to re-distribute research funds. There is a shift in responsibility for the tool in 2007, which moves it from being jointly developed by the Research Council and the Ministry of Education to being solely developed under the Research Council. The final two shifts are more gradual and deal with the complexity and differentiation factor of the instrument. In terms of complexity, the EM begins with a proposal for three categories of output and by 2010 has 26 categories and more complex systems and rules that can be seen in the ever increasing size of the document which in 2004 was six pages and by 2012 has grown to 45. The differentiation factor between outputs, meaning the range of possible points for different types of output, has also dramatically increased, from a proposed factor of four to a factor of 500.

The EM was established in 2004, the same year as the Czech Republic joined the EU, as a tool to evaluate the effectiveness of funds spent on research in the Czech Republic. The ground rules for the evaluation are laid out in the government resolution number 644/2004 (Government, 2004), and are part of a larger discussion which includes the results of the 2003 comparison of Czech and international research results as well as the development of a new phase of the national research and development policy for the years 2004 to 2008 (Government, 2004a) which called for creating a "complex proposal" for the evaluation of research results that will "respect global trends" and "follow best practices" of EU and OECD member states.

The tool which was created in 2004 was intended as a preliminary tool. The measurements were kept simple, one point for each output for all outputs between 1999 and 2003. The very short timeframe which was given by the government for the implementation of this tool, did not allow for a complex discussion of methodology, but that was planned for the following year. The document does include a basic outline for what it envisions as the future system: there would be a three tiered categorization of outputs: high impact articles and patents at the top, mid-level impact articles, books, other applied outputs in the middle tier, and low-impact articles at the bottom. A suggested point system of 2.0, 1.0, 0.5 was proposed for the three levels. Overall, the EM 2004 was short document, six pages, which was signed by the representatives of the two bodies which developed it: the Ministry of Education and the Council for Research and Development (Council, 2004).

The 2004 EM was intended to determine effectiveness and this was done by creating the State Budget Index. The index value for each research provider was determined by dividing the output points for a given project by the amount of funding that went into the project, at this time all the research funding was organized around ex-ante research projects, so called research intentions. Though these did have some of the formal appearance of a competitive grant proposal, in reality they functioned more as mechanism for organizing the provision of institutional funding. The results of the state budget index evaluation were made public and the research units, the faculties, departments, and small research organizations, were divided into four color coded groups which corresponded to 'well below average', 'below average', average, and 'above average' results. It was stated that the funding for those groups would be reduced for the below average performers or increased for the above average ones. Several thousand projects were indexed in this manner. Different reports were created to show the effectiveness of the funders (i.e. ministry of education, other ministries with research budgets, academy of science, etc.) and the effectiveness of the projects and the organization or university which was responsible for them (Council, 2004a). What was actually measured by this system is debatable; however, the objective was clear: create a system which quantitatively measures the effectiveness of government expenditure on research so that in the future, the government could revise the overall funding system to produce both more and higher quality results.

The 2005 version of the Evaluation Methodology (Council, 2005), rather than follow the relatively simple three tiered system as proposed, established a seven tier system, with additional sub-tiers for foreign language publications. Also, rather than using pre-determined whole numbers, the points given for impact journal articles were calculated based on a formula. The journals which did not meet the criteria allowing them to be categorized as impact journals were all lumped together and given a small number of points. A footnote explains that there would not be an attempt to develop specific list of acceptable journals as had been attempted in the prior year, so all journals counted. The report goes on to say that a great deal of discussion had gone into how to come up with such a list, but that in the end it was decided to go without, presumably for lack of agreement on any specific method. Attempts at steering research towards more international publications can be seen in the provision of double points to publications in languages other than Czech or Slovak in the categories of non-impact articles, books, chapters in books, and articles in collections. As well, for applied research two additional categories, patents and specific applied outputs, were created.

The EM for 2006 was a vastly expanded document which ran 36 pages in length. The document stresses that this version was produced by a consensus working group between the Council for Research and the Ministry of Education (Council, 2006). It aims to move towards a system for dividing the research budget between institutions based on "objective criteria." It was developed in preparation for the new law on higher education and research policy that was planned for 2008, and which was expected to revise the funding system for universities and research. In the introduction it states that the previous methodologies were "counterproductive" and justifies this argument with evidence that the level of funding had increased but the outputs had not (ibid). In reality, the research outputs of the Czech Republic were increasing steadily, and had been since the mid-1990s. They remained, however, below the world average (Arnold, 2011). This simplistic argument may have been influenced by EU policy recommendations focused on the funding input level as a means of improving research results (European Commission, 2003). The EU's Barcelona target of increasing the level of research funds to 3% of GDP was by 2006 well established. This comment also shows the conflicting aims that the Council has for the EM. Is it a tool to observe or to steer? If it is a steering tool, then it should provide transparency so that researchers know what will earn them points and are thus able to adjust their behavior accordingly. Alternatively, if it is supposed primarily to observe and measure, then how can the council have expectations that it will improve the research environment?

The aims of the EM in 2006 were widened (Council, 2006). In addition to evaluating the effectiveness of government spending on research and development, there are two new aims. The first is that the system and the results of Czech Research should be brought as close as possible to international standards and the results of other countries as indicated by the OECD and EU. It is important to note the direct and prominent mention of these two bodies in the text. The second new aim is that the Council for Research and Development should recommend, on the basis of the research results adjustments to the division of funding for research and development.

The point system in 2006 is yet again revised and the values are increased. To further encourage the hoped for steering effect, the differential between Czech and Slovak results and foreign language ones is increased to quadruple the value, rather than double. The formula for impact articles has been adjusted, and two new applied research categories have been created by splitting national, European and world patents and adding the sale of a license (ibid).

Finally the report acknowledges, though does not offer solutions to, several issues with the past EMs which were of concern to parts of the academic community. Specifically mentioned is the issue of academic disciplines, which refers to the way in which different disciplines are advantaged or disadvantaged by the point system due to their emphasis on different types of outputs, for example, the social sciences and humanities which tend to focus more on monographs than journal articles. Also mentioned is the issue of how to further categorize different non-impact journal articles which still does not have a resolution.

The 2007 system which was expected to be in something of a holding pattern before the major educational system reform of 2008, instead brings a whole new set of issues to the table. Here we find the impact of a decided shift in the political leadership of the Czech Republic from the election in 2006. During the years 1998 until 2006, the government was led by left-leaning and pro-EU social democrat governments. In 2006, the right leaning parties returned to power with a coalition government of centrist to center-right parties that had a strong neoliberal program. First, we can note that the group of policy entrepreneurs has been expanded to include members of the university community and the academy of sciences whereas before the development was only through the Ministry of Education and the Council for Research and Development. Secondly, it backtracks on the goals set out in the 2006 EM due to a legal difficulty. It states that the EM cannot be used to distribute funds according to the current laws, so that that aim was officially dropped and replaced with the aim that the Council should develop a system by which the funds could be reallocated, presuming that amendments to the higher education act will provide for this possibility. The aim of approaching international standards has been removed (Council, 2007).

The point system has again been subdivided and modified in an attempt to resolve the disciplinary bias acknowledged in the previous year. The major change in this version is the addition of a new category for the social sciences, which is defined to include humanities. Within that category books, articles in non impact journals and chapters are given twice as many points as for those in the sciences category. The differences between Czech and foreign language publications remain. A slight increase in the impact factor calculations has been made, patents have been increased to 500 points and articles in collections have been reduced to fractional points (ibid).

The 2008 EM brings about significant further changes (Council, 2008). The most prominent change is that what had up to this point been the primary objective, evaluating the 'effectiveness' of government spending on research, has been dropped. Now the aim is only to provide comprehensive information on the results of research to the government and secondly to provide the basis of a system which will be used for a future proposal on the funding of institutional research and development. Secondly, the ministry of education is no longer involved in the development of the methodology. The government is now the sole policy entrepreneur, and its role is exercised primarily through the Council for research, development and innovation, which is chaired by the prime minister. An official subcommittee, the Commission for evaluation of the results of research organizations and finished programs is established to develop and propose changes to the EM. According to its statute, it is comprised of between 7 and 15 members from the academic community who must come from a range of disciplines and may not hold high positions in other academic bodies.

The points system in this version again sees an increase in impact journal points and another new formula. There are also refinements in the area of social sciences and languages. The column for social sciences has been renamed to "National reference framework of excellence" (NRRE) and includes 10 disciplinary areas, but no longer includes all the social sciences, for example, economics and psychology are not part of the category. The "other languages" category which provided for increased points, has been renamed "world languages" and includes only English, Chinese, French, German, Russian, and Spanish (ibid).

In the 2009 EM (Council, 2009), a new point system is introduced, but is only to be used for the 2008 results. The calculations for years 2004 to 2007 were to remain as calculated under the old system, thereby eliminating the need to recalculate past results. The point system in this version provides a range for impact articles from 10 to 305 points, and adds a special category for prestigious impact journals, in which a publication is worth 500 points. There are three such journals: Nature, Science, and the proceedings of the National Academy of Science USA. For non impact journals there is a further division. Points will be given for articles published in journals that are listed in Scopus or ERIH. Points will also be given for articles published in Czech peer reviewed journals which are on an official list. Publications not falling under any of these sources are given no points.

The EMs for the years 2010 through 2012 use the same document (Council, 2010). The point system itself remains similar to the one in 2009. In the prestige journals, only Nature and Science remain. The document has again been expanded to pave the way for its use in funding research. It now includes a major section on the verification of results. Due to the plan that all institutional funding for research is to be allocated by this tool, there is an even stronger reason to be concerned over the attempts to cheat or manipulate the system. Although the EM did call for all institutional funding to be distributed according to the EM results, in the end, it was only used to influence the distribution of a smaller percentage at the discretion of the Council for Research Development and Innovation.

Over time we see that the EM has increased dramatically in complexity as the result of an ongoing attempt to make the quantitative system work more effectively. Problems uncovered in one year would be addressed by tinkering with the formulas, points, categories and definitions in the next. It has also transformed from being a tool that measures effectiveness to one that simply provides information. But that information has gone from being a source of evaluation to being an integral, even mechanical, element in system by which research funding is allocated. The system as of 2012 has a very detailed structure with 26 categories of output each with a different point value. However, it is not clear what justifies the differential in points between the outputs. The system distributes points ranging from 4 to 500, a hundred and twenty five fold interval, which is well beyond the originally proposed fourfold interval. This stretching of results, in a winner-take-all manner as well as simply the very large numbers that the system uses, makes comprehension and steering more difficult. The reliance on journal impact factors to determine the influence of specific articles is a rough estimation at best. It is also extremely difficult to pre-judge the points that one is likely to obtain. Those that do have a good grasp on the system, can "game the system" and there are examples of how lower impact journals can bring more points than their more respected counterparts. Daniel Munich, a member of the Commission, demonstrates on his blog how the points that could be obtained by publishing in several less known Lithuanian economics journals would be significantly higher than for publishing in what are broadly considered the top journals in those fields (Munich, 2012).

While the EM does aim at objectivity, there are nevertheless significant politics inherent to the system. Concerns over the gaming of the system only reinforce the existence of the overall problem. Such a system, if it is supposed to steer research, should intend for researchers to attempt to maximize their results and hence maximize their rewards. This would indicate an effective steering system. The assumption being that the change in behavior is seen in a positive light. However, the concept of gaming the system, implies that people can use the system in ways that are seen in a negative light. That is, they can obtain high points for outputs that are not qualitatively judged as desirable. This presents a fundamental problem for the quantitative system, which is that the qualitative critique appears to trump the quantitative results. The consequence is a cat-and-mouse game of tinkering to get the quantitative to match the qualitative ideas of what constitutes good research. It is, however, unlikely that a perfect quantitative system will ever be possible.

CONCLUSION

The experience of the Czech Republic in developing the EM suggest several dangers which should be considered as research policy reforms and more generally NPM type reforms are carried out. First, what I would call NPM run amuck. The way in which this reform was developed demonstrates the dangers in allowing a single doctrine to dominate a policy debate. The NPM sigma-type values which were identified by Hood have clearly come to dominate this policy tool, to the exemption of lambda-type values as predicted. Some sort of balance in these three types of administrative values is desirable, but it is understandable that particularly under periods of economic uncertainly, the sigma-type values of avoiding waste come to dominate. Also, it is clear that the theta-type values are quite different in the Czech case than what Hood imagines. Trust is not inherent in the participants, but there is an attempt to implement it formally through a quasi-market system. The EM focuses on process, in this case the mechanistic process of allocating points, with the aim of creating a fair system.

A second danger is that of the abstraction of policy discourse, as policy and policy innovation become more transnational. The use of entirely abstracted models or prototypes as promoted by supranational bodies like the EU and OECD in the Czech system is likely a consequence of how these policies are presented in a global context. In order to make them more attractive and applicable, they are stripped of most of their national context, but some context is intended to be re-implemented in national discourse as these policy ideas are translated into national policies. However, we can see in the Czech Republic something like an attempt to implement an ideal-type policy, one in its abstract, global form, without translation. Note that there has been nationalized justification for the policy in the way it fits the political debates, but the policy idea itself still follows a very abstract philosophy.

Finally, the third danger is that of using purely quantitative measures to analyze and judge quality, excellence, and relevance: terms which are rooted in a qualitative understanding of what is good and desirable. While indicators and other quantitative tools may help in making this judgment, it is not likely that there can be an effective system that does not include some degree of qualitative judgment. The resulting system in which everything is formalized, means that the definition of a good book is one which is at least 50 pages long, has an index, bibliography, registration number, and at least one expert review. It is worth recalling that the original proposal in the UK for the REF was to create a quantitative system, conceivably like what has appeared in the Czech Republic. "The Government's firm presumption is that after the 2008 RAE the system for assessing research quality and allocating QR funding from the DfES will be mainly metrics-based (HM Treasury, 2006, p. 10)." In the end, the REF system has remained mainly a peer-review based system, but the trends of the mid-aughts were to push for quantification even in the country with the most known and respected peer-review based system.

The trends and values inherent in NPM are not likely to disappear anytime soon; however, it is important to see where they can lead if there isn't some emphasis on competing values. NPM holds partially contradicting arguments at its heart, and these lead to paradoxes in the way in which values like autonomy engage the policy debates. A balanced approach between the three types of administrative values which Hood identifies, means that process and inputs should not be ignored in the quest to improve the outputs of research, as these alternative values promote diversity, resilience, and emergence, which are important drivers of creativity and innovation.

ACKNOWLEDGEMENTS

This research was supported by the Grant Agency of Charles University (GAUK 910988).

NOTE

[1] See for example the World Map of Interpersonal Trust which is based on the World Values Survey data (http://www.jdsurvey.net/jds/jdsurveyMaps.jsp?Idioma=I&SeccionTexto=0404&NOID=104)

BIBLIOGRAPHY

Arnold, E. et al. (2011). *International audit of research, development and innovation in the czech republic. final report 3: The quality of research, institutional funding and research evaluation in the czech republic and abroad*, Brighton: Technopolis.

Bouckaert, G., Nakrošis, V., & Nemec, J (2011). Public administration and management reforms in CEE: Main trajectories and results, *NISPAcee Journal of Public Administration and Policy, 4* (1).

Christensen, T. (2011). University governance reforms: potential problems of more autonomy?, *Higher Education, 62*, 503–517.

Christensen, T., & Laegreid, P. (2007). *Transcending new public management*. Surrey: Ashgate

Clark, B. (1983). *The higher education system: Academic Organization in Cross-National Perspective*, Berkeley: University of California Press.

Council for Research and Development (2003). *Analysis of the existing state of research, development and innovation in the czech republic and a comparison with the situation abroad – 2003*. Prague: Office of the Government.

Council for Research and Development (2004). *Methodology for evaluating research and development and their results*. Prague: Office of the Government.

Council for Research and Development (2004a). Zpráva o výsledcích hodnocení výzkumu a vývoje a jeho výsledků v roce 2004.

Council for Research and Development (2005). *Methodology for evaluating research and development and their results for the year 2005*. Prague: Office of the Government.

Council for Research and Development (2006). *Methodology for evaluating research and development and their results for the year 2006*. Prague: Office of the Government.

Council for Research and Development (2007). *Methodology for evaluating research and development and their results for the year 2007*. Prague: Office of the Government.

Council for Research and Development (2007b). *Analysis of the existing state of research, development and innovation in the czech republic and a comparison with the situation abroad in 2007*. Prague: Office of the Government.

Council for Research and Development (2008). *Methodology for evaluating research and development and their results for the year 2008*. Prague: Office of the Government.

Council for Research and Development (2008b). *Analysis of the existing state of research, development and innovation in the czech republic and a comparison with the situation abroad in 2008*. Prague: Office of the Government.

Council for Research and Development (2009). *Methodology for evaluating research and development and their results for the year 2009*. Prague: Office of the Government.

Council for Research and Development and Innovation (2010). *Methodology for evaluating the results of research organizations and evaluating the results of completed* programs (for 2010 and 2011). Prague: Office of the Government.

Council for Research and Development (2011). *Analysis of the existing state of research, development and innovation in the czech republic and a comparison with the situation abroad in 2011*. Prague: Office of the Government.

Council for Research and Development and Ministry of Education, Youth, and Sport (1999). *Analysis of previous trends and existing state of research and development in the czech republic and a comparison with the situation abroad*.

de Boer, H., Enders, J., & Schimank, U. (2007). On the way towards new public management? the governance of university systems in England, the Netherlands, Austria, and Germany. In D. Jansen (Ed.) *New Forms of Governance in Research Organizations*. Dordrecht: Springer.

Dobbins, M., & Knill, C. (2009). Higher education policies in central and Eastern Europe: Convergence Toward a Common Model?. *Governance, 22*(3), 397–430.

Dunleavy, P., Margetts, H., Bastow, S., & Tinkler J. (2006). New public management is dead-long live digital-era governance. *Journal of Public Administration Research & Theory, 16*(3), 467.

European Commission (2003). *Investing in Research: an action plan for Europe*. COM (2003) 226, Brussels.

Gornitzka, A., & Maassen, P. (2000). Hybrid steering approaches with respect to European higher education, *Higher Education Policy, 13*(3): 267–286.

Government of the Czech Republic (1998). Act 111/1998: *Higher Education Act*. Prague: Office of the Government.

Government of the Czech Republic (2002). Act 130/2002: *Research and development support act*. Prague: Office of the Government.

Government of the Czech Republic (2004). Resolution 644/2004: *Evaluation of the results of research and development*. Prague: Office of the Government.

Government of the Czech Republic (2004a). Resolution 5/2004: *National research and development policy of the czech republic for 2004–2008*. Prague: Office of the Government.

Government of the Czech Republic (2008). *Reform of the research, development and innovation system in the Czech Republic, Part III of document Ref. No. 346/08*. Prague: Office of the Government.

Government of the Czech Republic (2009). Act 211/2009: *Complete amendment of the research and development support act*. Prague: Office of the Government.

HM Treasury (2006). *Science and Innovation Investment Framework 2004–2014: Next Steps*. Norwich: HMSO.

Maassen, P., & Olsen, J. (Eds.) (2007). *University dynamics and European Integration*. Dordrecht: Springer.

Munich, D. (2012). Citacni bratrstva, O hodnoceni a financovani vedy, http://metodikahodnoceni. blogspot.cz/2012/05/citacni-bratstva.html. Accessed on 28.8.2012.

OECD (1995). *Governance in Transition*. Paris: OECD.

Pabian, P. (2009). Europeanisation of Higher Education Governance in the Post-Communist Context: The Case of the Czech Republic. In A. Amaral, et al. (Eds.), *European Integration and the Governance of Higher Education and Research*. Dordrecht: Springer.

Pollitt, C. & Bouckaert, G. (2011). *Public Management Reform* (3rd ed.). Oxford: Oxford University Press.

Transparency International Corruption Perceptions Index 2012, http://www.transparency.org/cpi2012/results. Accessed on 23.10.2013.

Verheijen, A. J. G. (2003). Public administration in post-communist states. In G. B. Peters, & J. Pierre (Eds.), *Handbook of Public Administration*, London: Sage.

AFFILIATIONS

Mitchell Young
Charles University in Prague
Faculty of Social Sciences
Institute of International Studies
Department of West European Studies

RUI SANTIAGO, TERESA CARVALHO & ANDREIA FERREIRA

KNOWLEDGE SOCIETY/ECONOMY AND MANAGERIAL CHANGES: NEW CHALLENGES FOR PORTUGUESE ACADEMICS

INTRODUCTION

In Portugal, reforms in higher education (HE) have been mainly conducted under the influence of a new political rationality. The dominant global trace of this rationality is the extension of economic and managerial logics to the set of HE activities, as well as the way of managing them and the professionals involved in their achievement. New Public Management (NPM) emerged in this context both as a set of narratives and a key managerial technology used to operate these reforms. It entails distinct facets according to its adaptation to national contexts (Pollit & Boukaert, 2000). However, there is a convergence in some of its basic principles and recipes (Bezes & Demazière, 2012): centralising policy and strategic power and decentralising implementation and execution; empowering 'consumers' of educational and knowledge services ('consumers sovereignty'); imposing and/or inducing market coordination mechanisms (competition between institutions and collective and individual incentives); enacting entrepreneurial culture; limiting the scope of the bureau/collegial-professional regime by reinforcing executive power; formalising accountability systems; turning teaching, research and knowledge production into more sensible social and economic needs; and using contracts-driven programs as a new mode of organizational control.

Within this NPM-driven environment, academic professional power was viewed as a key problem and as an obstacle to the implementation of those principles. At the international level, numerous studies have analysed changes influenced by market and NPM over the academics working conditions, employment terms and career pathways. Most of these studies conclude that these influences are negative. Academics' professional autonomy is presented as limited by an inextricable array of formal regulatory rules, which transferred their professional power and trust to new instruments of quality and evaluation (Harley, Muller-Carmen & Collin, 2003; Deem, Hillyard & Reed, 2007; Altbach, Reisberg & Rumbley, 2009). Similar conclusions have been drawn in Portuguese studies concerning these topics (Santiago & Carvalho, 2008; Carvalho & Santiago, 2010a; Santiago & Carvalho, 2012). However, although sharing some aspects of this 'pessimistic' diagnosis, some studies also emphasise that academics can develop strategies aimed at maintaining

J. Branković et al., Global Challenges, Local Responses in Higher Education, 35–57.

power and control over their work (Kogan & Bauer, 2000; Carvalho & Santiago 2010a,b; Carvalho, 2012; Santiago & Carvalho, 2012).

By examining the conclusions of these studies, the purpose of this chapter is to analyse how academics in Portugal are positioned in relation to changes in the Portuguese higher education system and institutions, and to consider whether they view changes as affecting their professional group. The analysis starts with the assumption that these complex issues can be better understood if different approaches are combined. Three of them were chosen which were probably the most influential in the potential reconfiguration of the academic profession and professionalism: the new state roles and policies in steering higher education; the changes in higher education institutions' governance and management; and the current political and institutional emphasis on knowledge society.

The empirical data supporting the study was gathered from a survey of academics, physicians and nurses, who have management responsibilities in, respectively, universities, polytechnics and public hospitals. This is part of an ongoing research project aimed at comparing changes in the three professional groups. However, the present study is confined only to academic units.[1] Actually, in higher education, these professionals are, in their key positions, the best witnesses of the potential changes in the academic professional field. They are positioned between the market and managerial logics, which seem to have strongly influenced Portuguese HEIs' top governance and management, and the professional logics emerging from the 'bottom' (Carvalho & Santiago, 2010a,b).

The chapter is structured into three main sections. First, the overall synthesis of changes that emerged in the Portuguese higher education landscape is addressed. Second, the methodological approach in collecting and analysing data is summarised and, finally, in the third section, the main findings and some future research directions are presented.

CHANGES IN THE PORTUGUESE HIGHER EDUCATION INSTITUTIONAL, ORGANISATIONAL AND PROFESSIONAL LANDSCAPE: AN OVERALL VIEW

Higher education and the academic profession were not immune to changes in the state policies, which reconfigured the public sector in most developed countries. These changes translated into a new global mode of steering institutions aimed also at transforming the relationship of the academics with knowledge.

This trend presupposes decentralisation, autonomy and the organic (re) construction of HEIs. It is expected that HEIs, once released from the centralised hierarchical control, will be able to manage market opportunities in a rational way, as well as to achieve accountability and a more efficient mechanism allowing for a better allocation of their financial resources. Additionally, this presupposes the HEIs' (re)conceptualization as more unitary (Carvalho & Santiago, 2010a) or as 'complete organizations' (Enders, De Boer & Leisyte, 2008) towards their organisational identity and professional commitment to self-renovation. These attempts to (re) conceptualise and to reconstruct HEIs' results in a paradigmatic rupture with their previous organisational forms is termed by Mintzberg (1990) as 'professional bureaucracies'. These traditional forms were based on two articulated logics: the bureaucratic logic and the professional logic. It can be said that this articulation has entailed, in a certain sense, an alliance and co-determination mechanism (Bleikie & Michelsen, 2008) between bureaucracy and professionalism, which had reached their uppermost in the welfare state, at least in Europe.

This association has been questioned by NPM assumptions and technologies. HEIs were induced to change their traditional bureaucratic-collegial structures and modus operandi to an entrepreneurial-driven model, based on the idea that they have to act more as 'producers of educative services', targeted to consumers' expectations (Freidson, 2001; Reed, 2002) in the marketplace, than as public entities framed by the public service logic (Bleikie & Michelsen, 2008). In this respect, more than an administrative or technical orthodoxy, NPM emerges in the public sector as a set of beliefs and a system of thought which encompass two main loosely coupled dimensions. The first underlines the need for the public sector to use models and management technologies adopted from the private sector as a way to improve efficiency and to achieve positive results in services delivery. The second is connected to a set of conjectures on the power structures and exercise reshaping the linkage nexus between, on the one hand, the state and the public institutions and, on the other hand, these institutions and their different occupational or professional groups. Trust in professionals was replaced by the credit of the 'right to manage' given to whoever is empowered as the 'principal-agent' in the top governance structures of public institutions (Deem et al., 2007). It was also replaced by the array of technologies of control and regulation of professional work deployed at the macro, meso and micro levels. Knowledge is also a major target of this plot. Global and hegemonic tendencies emerged to impose knowledge society assumptions, increasingly defined as a knowledge economy (Olssen & Peters, 2005), as the main driving force of research activities. Thus, to approach potential changes in the academic profession, it is also essential to understand how academics are positioning themselves in this specific context.

The bureaucratic-collegial regime was also associated with the expert knowledge (Larson, 1977; Brint, 1994) in terms of sustaining the social division of the academic work. The formal and abstract knowledge, certificated with academic credentials, have been largely recognised as a structural dimension of the professionalisation processes of diverse occupational groups including, obviously, academics (Freidson, 1994; 2001). Formal and abstract knowledge, or expert knowledge, was identified in the classical literature in the field as an important condition for the professions' social acknowledgement and legitimacy (Johnson, 1972; Larson, 1977; Brint, 1994). Freidson (1994, 2001), for instance, assigned to formal and abstract knowledge a key role in the legitimacy of professional power together with two others sources – the technical autonomy over the development of work and the credential authority streaming from HEIs (universities and professional schools). Current changes in society imply a set of transformations in the ontological and epistemological conditions under which knowledge is produced and disseminated. This emerged as a powerful force in the deconstruction of the academics' conventional, and mostly long-established, forms of professionalism. As the profession that is more dependent on autonomy, as well as endogenous dynamics of knowledge production and dissemination, academics probably make up the group that is facing more important challenges to maintaining their autonomy and control over their professionalisation processes.

In the Portuguese HE landscape, the influence of NPM in the system and institutions' reconfiguration emerged later than in Anglo-Saxon countries. In fact, this influence began to have an impact on the ground only at the beginning of the twenty-first century (Carvalho, 2012; Santiago & Carvalho, 2012). In the 1990s, it can be argued that this influence was more rhetorical than practical, stressing quite exclusively narrative issues as those organised around efficiency, quality, excellence and accountability. The aim of this rhetoric was to persuade institutions and academics to become more sensitive to market devices and societal needs than to provoke a 'managerial revolution' in HE (Amaral, Magalhães & Santiago, 2003; Santiago, Magalhães & Carvalho, 2005; Santiago, Carvalho, Amaral & Meek, 2006). At the time, trends in Europe moving from direct state control over HEIs to action-at-a-distance (Neave, 2012) favoured the dissemination of the managerial rhetoric as a sort of counterpart to the increased autonomy delegated to institutions.

At the end of the 1990s, the institutional panorama changed radically. The intrusion of NPM in HE became more evident, along with strong political criticism vis-à-vis the corporatist nature of collegiality and the social inefficiency of curricula and knowledge production. More recently, in 2007, a new HE act was approved (Law n°62/2007), bringing about wide ranging transformations in the power structures of institutions. In fact, this new regime has imposed a new institutional power design to the HEIs' governance and management, which were largely inspired by the entrepreneurial culture. The strategic power concentration at the top – a general boards with an impressive representation of external 'stakeholders' – replaced the previous academic senate and the polytechnics assembly. The (re)conceptualisation of rectors and polytechnics presidents as executives, and the implementation of line management structures, all emerge as the more salient traces of that new design implementation. Along with these new organisational traces, other regulatory policies and managerial devices were put forward, being also inspired by the control and regulation apparatus typical of NPM. Among them, the more relevant can be synthetically described as follows: the formalisation of a national accreditation and evaluation system, based on typically regulatory business-oriented principles; micro-systems of institutional evaluation based on students' opinions and in teaching and research production; budget restrictions, which were also taken as an instrument to legitimate increased control over professional practices; research funds allocated on an increased competitive and centralised basis aimed at increasing the system stratification (between research and teaching universities/polytechnics); and strong science and technology policies giving incentives towards the establishment of a close connection between knowledge, economy and the entrepreneurial tissue.

Indubitably, this set of transformations has been increasing the institutions' vertical integration, provoking, as mentioned above, ruptures in the traditional alliance and co-determination mechanisms between bureaucracy and professionalism in place since the 1974 Portuguese democratic revolution. The right of HEIs' self-governance and autonomy, (re)conceptualised through the lens of the market and economic rationalities, seems to have been actively endorsed by the HEIs' top governance and management (Santiago & Carvalho, 2012). This new trend in HE steering can bring important changes to the academic profession. Institutional environments are now structured more in line with the organisation logic than with the professional 'self-constituting' logic (Freidson, 2001). In this context, shifts in academics' work professional control (professional rationalism) to management control (organisational rationalism) can potentially weaken academic professionalism.

In fact, especially after the 2007 new higher education act, Portuguese academics seemed to be losing the power to self-regulate their work. The loss of this political and institutional tool means also that the locus of professional decisions – teaching and researching 'why', 'what' and 'how' – has been increasingly displaced by external forces. However, in spite of the deterioration of academic work conditions and terms, for the majority of the Portuguese academics, the dominant pattern in their professional narratives seems to be related to traditional professionalism, covering, to a certain extent, the legacy of the traditional symbolic and cultural academic capital (Amaral, Magalhães & Santiago, 2003; Santiago & Carvalho, 2004; Santiago & Carvalho, 2008; Carvalho & Santiago, 2010a,b; Carvalho, 2012).

SUMMARISING THE SURVEY METHODOLOGICAL STRATEGIES: DATA COLLECTION AND SAMPLE CHARACTERISTICS

This study is included in a research project aimed at comparing recent changes in three professional groups: academics, physicians and nurses. However, this analysis is only based on HEIs' heads perceptions of changes in the academic profession and professionalism. Actually, they can be considered as the first 'front-line troupes' (Fulton, 2003) of market and NPM-led changes that, since the end of the 1990s, have been introduced into the Portuguese HE system and institutions. Besides, these actors are located between the state, the HEIs' top governance and the 'bottom-up' pressures. That is, they can be considered both as the privileged 'witnesses' of the impact of the current changes in the 'academic heartland' and key-actors involved in its diverse and sensible implications (Carvalho & Santiago, 2010a).

The empirical component of this study is based on an on-line survey, which was structured according to two main themes: changes in society, policies and organisations and changes in professions. A third component was devoted to socio-demographic issues. The survey was mailed (with a message inviting academics to participate in the study) to all the Portuguese heads of academic units in charge of faculties, schools and departments in public universities and public polytechnics institutes (who were temporarily appointed or elected to this position for two or four years, depending on each institution). The respondents completed the survey through the web page of the project. Among the Portuguese heads (400), the response rate was 28% (112). The academics who only partially responded to the survey were not excluded from the sample.

In this sample, 55% of those surveyed are from universities and 45% from polytechnics institutes. Regarding gender, the majority of the heads of the academic units are men (63%). Furthermore, 29% are between 31 and 45 years old, 47% – the majority – between 46 and 55 and 24% are 56 years old or over. Forty percent also have 1–4 years of experience as managers-academics (there is some diversity in the organisational design of the HEIs' units, some of which are based on faculties and others on schools or departments), 31% 5–9 years and 29% have been in charge of academic units for 10–20 years. As regards the degrees held by the surveyed, 83% have a PhD and 17% a Master's degree. Actually, the Portuguese HE can be classified as a binary system with two different career pathways corresponding to each and different subsystem national assignments – more research/academic knowledge focused on universities and more teaching/vocation focused on polytechnic institutes. However, since 2009, in both cases, PhD is the minimum requirement for a first appointment. All the surveyed are full-time and hold a tenured position.

For the empirical purposes of this paper, only the general views of academic units' managers on state, organisational and knowledge changes are presented, leaving aside the survey data related to their individual and more subjective experiences. Data collected were submitted to the usual standardised statistical procedures (descriptive and non-parametric). Additionally, some variables were used – type of institutions (universities or polytechnic institutes), gender, age and experience in academic units management – to analyse potential differences in the surveyed views. However, in almost all the operations of statistical procedures (cross-tabulation and non-parametric tests), no relevant differences were found.

FINDINGS: CHANGES IN THE ACADEMIC PROFESSION: STATE POLICIES, ORGANISATION AND KNOWLEDGE PRODUCTION

As argued above, potential changes in the academic profession and professionalism are better approached if different analytical perspectives are combined. Nevertheless, we started from the assumption that changes in HE were not only focused on the 'deconstruction' of HE institutional and organisational environment, but also on academics' habitus and *modus operandi*. The impact of NPM in institutions and on academics is not linear. As our analysis demonstrates, contradictions, ambiguities, different degrees of acceptance and resistance arise in the academics' views on HE changes at the system and institutional levels.

The Role of the State in Financing and Organising Higher Education

When questioned whether the state has to be committed to and responsible for financing and organising public HE, the great majority (98%) said yes. Unit heads were invited to justify their position with an open question. Their responses were submitted to content analysis according to four categories: social and cultural relevance; economic relevance; regulation and financing; and institutional autonomy. This qualitative data were also quantified in order to find the number of relevant statements produced by the surveyed (this item does not represent the number of the sample cases).

Surprisingly, although diverse, the main reasons given by heads to substantiate their positions (Table 1) were primarily linked to the social and cultural relevance of HE (33%), namely, the view of its intangible value as a social and public good (18%), and of its broader mission as an instrument for the achievement of social equality (10%).

Table 1. Deans' and heads' views on the state's general role in higher education

Categories of content analysis	n° of statements	%
Higher Education social and cultural relevance		
Social equality avoiding inequalities and elitism	15	9.9
Public service and public good	27	17.9
Increase of the universal right to be qualified	7	4.6
Preservation and divulgation of the Portuguese culture	2	0.1
Sub-total	51	32.5
Higher Education economic relevance		
A long term investment and strategic value	4	2.6
Entrepreneurial innovation and entrepreneurs' training	4	2.6
National and regional economic development	7	4.6
Sub-total	15	9.9
Higher Education regulation and financing		
State as the warrant of quality in opposition to market	12	7.9
External funds and fees as insufficient	15	9.9
Sub-total	27	17.8
Higher Education institutional autonomy		
Independence from external pressures (market and entrepreneurial)	14	9.3
Independence of science	8	5.3
Sub-total	22	14.6
Totals	151	100

Source: Survey data base (2012)

For academic heads, the state should be the custodian of system quality, which is a role that the market can never guarantee because it has too many related clients and entrepreneurial private interests. Additionally, the quest for external funds, whether from the sponsors in the private sector (funds for teaching and research), or from increase in fees (10%), will never be sufficient to assure the survival and/ or normal functioning of HEIs. Finally, heads of units' statements emphasised the HEIs' needs for active support from the state as a warranty of institutional (9%) and science production (5%) autonomy from the market and entrepreneurial external pressures.

In general terms, this set of qualitative findings is in line with previous conclusions in studies of the early 2000s (Amaral, Magalhães & Santiago, 2003; Santiago & Carvalho, 2004; Santiago, Magalhães & Carvalho, 2005). In spite of the new state policies in steering HE, the welfare state 'archetypes' seem to continue to have a leading role in shaping academics' views about who should have system control, regulation and financing. Additionally, the unit heads surveyed seem also to have retained a sort of outmoded narrative of higher education missions and functions – social equality, public good and universal right to education – that confronts some 'post-modern' competitive and entrepreneurial discourses of HE ultimate goals.

In spite of this outmoded narrative, unit heads acknowledge that, in the last five years, state policies, especially those concerning the financing of the HE public system, have brought wide ranging changes to their institutions, units and academic work organisation and functioning. According to a large majority, the increasing decline in state public funding of HE (around 30% in the last three years) has been transforming institutions (74%) and units (71%), structuring and functioning (74%), academic work and professional practices (68%) and even institutional management practices (82%). Among such changes, unit heads emphasise those connected to core professional tasks (67%), the reduction of staff (92%), the increase in administrative and bureaucratic tasks (88%), the introduction of flexibility in academic staff management (79%) and the institutions and units concerned with the external search for financial solutions to complement insufficient public funds (94%).

In this context, when questioned whether their work conditions had changed in the last five years, a substantial majority of the unit heads surveyed agree and strongly agree (see Table 2) that there were substantial changes in the following dimensions of academic work: increase in working hours (89%); and increase in workloads (91%). Additionally, during this period, a large majority denied that the general conditions of academic work had improved (93%) or that there were no relevant changes in these conditions (92%). The only topic where responses were more moderated referred to the duration of the contracts, although a slight majority (52%) still has a negative view on this important condition of employment security.

Table 2. Deans' and heads' views on the changes of academic working conditions in the last five years

	Strongly Disagree and disagree	Neither agree nor disagree	Strongly agree and agree	N
Increase in working hours	4,2%	7,3%	88,6%	96 (100%)
Increase in workloads	4,2	4,2%	91,6%	95 (100%)
Diminishing contract duration	28,8%	19,1%	52,0%	94 (100%)
Improvement in working conditions	92,8%	5,2%	1,8%	96 (100%)

Source: Survey data base (2012)

Again, these findings agree with the conclusions of numerous studies from different countries (Askling, 2001; Deem et al., 2007; Musselin, 2008; Altbach, Reisberg & Rumbley, 2009). In general, these conclusions, drawn from empirical and/or theoretical studies, are convergent on the idea that academic working conditions have decreased in the last three decades; at least for academics located on the margins of the academic career structure – non tenured, part-time, young academics, outside of tenure track. As a matter of fact the new Portuguese HE act (2007), together with the new career statute act (2009), has brought more insecurity and flexibility to academics' contractual links. Since 2009, obtaining a PhD has become the minimum requirement to enter an academic career, but this does not guarantee a permanent employment prospective. Newcomers are recruited for a five-year experimental period, and at the end of it, they have to apply for a permanent position. The success of this application and, subsequently, the possibility of securing a tenured appointment, are dependent on a recruitment committee decision (composed by internal and external members), based mainly on scientific productivity. The insecurity of academic employment becomes the norm.

Looking at findings in table 3, it can be seen that the majority of the surveyed have a 'pessimistic' view of the policy objectives assigned to HEIs. When asked about the main institutional and organisational changes promoted by these policies at the professional level, the majority strongly disagree and disagree (63,5%) with the statement that these changes were oriented towards professional satisfaction, as well as improving the academic work conditions (635). A high proportion of the surveyed also have doubts about the relevance of changes for the public mission of HEIs – 46% of the unit heads surveyed strongly disagree and disagree with the idea that changes promoted in HEIs were oriented to improve higher education public services delivery. In comparison, a high proportion of unit heads acknowledge that changes in objectives assigned to HEIs primarily focused on the clients' satisfaction principle (47%) and on the promotion of their external image and visibility (50%). Moreover, a large majority seems persuaded that changes were essentially guided by managerial and economic objectives – getting more external resources (64%) and 'doing more with less' (69%).

Table 3. Deans' and heads' perceptions of the main changing objectives promoted in higher education institutions

	Strongly disagree and disagree	Neither agree nor disagree	Strongly agree and agree	N
Professionals' satisfaction	68.0%	19.8%	15.1%	106 (100%)
Clients' satisfaction	29.8%	24%	46.2%	104 (100%)
External resources	15.1%	21.7%	66.2%	106 (100%)
Increasing productivity with less resources	10.7%	19.6%	69.1%	107 (100%)
Improving academic work conditions	62.6%	22.4%	14.9%	107 (100%)
Improving public services delivery conditions	45.3%	26.4%	28.3%	106 (100%)
Promoting the external image and visibility	23.5%	26.4%	50.0%	106 (100%)

Source: Survey data base (2012)

Among these survey findings, which reveal a clear and articulated response pattern, one has to note that some can illustrate, eventually, the ongoing shift from the internal dynamics and actions in the exploration of the external spaces to a different 'paradigm'. In this 'paradigm', the external market-oriented HE environment has come to dominate the Portuguese institutions' landscape. Barnett (2003) also observed this, for instance, in the UK case – institutions started to live outside themselves and constructed on the shoulders of their external 'clients' and 'stakeholders' Barnett (2003, p.71).

Deans' and Heads' Perceptions of the Changes in the Decision-Making Processes of Higher Education Institutions

Portuguese state policies focused on the changes in the HEIs power structures, which encompassed the expectation that the traditional bureaucratic-collegial regime and academic work self-control have to be deconstructed and the remainder submitted to the organisation and managerial logics. These political intentions, largely endorsed by numerous HEIs' top governance and management, imply the reconstruction of the institutions as vertically integrated (Carvalho & Santiago, 2010a) or, as Enders and colleagues (2008) posit, re-engineered or 'complete organizations'.

Some coercive impositions of the new Portuguese HE act, approved in 2007, appear as a good illustration of this design. The concentration of power at different institutional levels was one of the key expectations of this act, which was mainly visible in three aspects: the political and strategic power assigned to the HEIs' top

Table 4. Units' and heads' perceptions of the academic actors with more influence in the institutional decisions linked to the main governance and management issues

	Government	Rector/ Polytechnic president	Units' managers	Academic boards	Academics	N
Basic unit organisation	13.1%	44.9%	30.8%	8.4%	2.8%	107 (100%)
Institution budget priorities	28%	63.6%	6.5%	1.9%	0%	107 (100%)
Basic units budget priorities	6.5%	48.6%	43%	1.9	0%	107 (100%)
Creation of new units	24.3%	52.3%	12.1%	10.3%	0.9%	107 (100%)
Definition of rules related to the distribution of the academic activities and tasks	0.9%	6.6%	64.2%	15.1%	13.2%	106 (100%)
Programmes and projects approval	4.7%	36.7%	27.4%	18.9%	12.3%	106 (100%)
Selection, appointment and/or election of rectors/polytechnics presidents	3.7%	22.4%	10.3%	31.8%	31.8%	107 (100%)

Source: Survey data base (2012)

governance through the replacement of the academic senate (or the polytechnic assembly) by a more restricted general board with a strong representation of external stakeholders; the reinforcement of executive power assigned to the rector and the polytechnic president; and the operational power distributed to the heads of academic units – (re)named 'directors' – within the framework of a line management 'philosophy'.

This new HEIs power design seems to have affected the academics' perceptions of the locus of institutional decision-making processes initiatives and control, since they were different from those found in previous studies (Santiago, Magalhães & Carvalho, 1995; Amaral, Magalhães & Santiago, 2003; Carvalho & Santiago, 2010a, b). In fact, when invited to identify the main locus of influence over institutional decisions, the unit heads' responses were very 'hierarchised' in line with the recent changes in the HEIs' power redistribution and exercise.

As can be observed in the previous table (4), academics identified senior managers (rector/polytechnic president) as influential in the following main issues: the organisation of units (45%); the institution budget priorities (64%); the units budget priorities (49%); the creation of new units (52%). To a lesser extent, rectors and presidents of polytechnics are also considered as the most influential in the programmes and projects approval (37%). At the same time, unit heads were also identified as sharing some of this power in these issues: unit organisation (31%); budget priorities (43%) and the programmes and projects approval (27%). The units' 'academic managers' were perceived, by a large majority, as being the most influential only in the definition of the academics' teaching tasks and agenda (64%). On the other hand, individual academics were perceived as the most influential only in the selection/appointment and/or election of the rectors and polytechnics presidents (32/%), even if they share this influence with the academic boards (scientific and pedagogical boards) (32%).

These response patterns are quite similar to those given by the surveyed when they were asked to identify the most influential actors in the institutional decision-making related to academics and the academics' work (Table 5).

Unit heads referred to rectors and presidents of polytechnics as the most influential in relation to career promotion (46%) and academics' individual assessment evaluation (31%); but their views were not so homogeneous concerning the unit heads' influence over institutional decisions. They are identified as more influential in decisions associated with the recruitment of academics (35%); the general issues concerning academic work (39%); and the organisation on the ground of academic activities and teaching services (63%). Once more, the academics boards (30%) and individuals (38%) are recognised as more influential only in the heads selection/ appointment or election.

Unit heads referred to rectors and presidents of polytechnics as the most influential in relation to career promotion (46%) and academics' individual assessment evaluation (31%); but their views were not so homogeneous concerning the unit

Table 5. Deans' and heads' perceptions of the actors with more influence in the institutional decisions regarding issues related to academics

	Government	Rector/ Polytechnic president	Unit managers	Academic boards	Academics	N
Recruitment of academics	7.5%	32.1%	34.9%	16%	9.4%	106 (100%)
Promotion in academic career	18.9%	46.2%	17.9%	10.4%	6.6%	106 (100%)
Academics' evaluation	1.9%	31.4%	25.7%	22.9%	18.1%	105 (100%)
Teaching activities and tasks	0%	8.5%	63.2%	17.9%	10.4%	106 (100%)
General issues regarding academics' work	1%	25.7%	39%	21%	13.3%	105 (100%
Selection, appointment and/or election of heads	2.9%	20.2%	9.6%	29.8%	37.5%	104 (100%)

Source: Survey data base (2012)

heads' influence over institutional decisions. They are identified as more influential in decisions associated with the recruitment of academics (35%); the general issues concerning academic work (39%); and the organisation on the ground of academic activities and teaching services (63%). Once more, the academics boards (30%) and individuals (38%) are recognised as more influential only in the heads selection/appointment or election.

Regarding the results of the actors' influence over the HEIs' organisation and functioning and over the management of academics and academic work, it can be noted that academic boards and individuals have only a residual power. This seems to be the outcome of the tendency to concentrate strategic power in the top and operational power of the unit heads at the intermediate levels. The academic boards and individuals only seem to have kept the control of the representative democracy mechanisms, which were viewed by the surveyed as the most influential in the selection, appointment and/or election of the rectors/polytechnics presidents and of the deans and heads.

In the face of these findings, the hypothesis can be made that the balance between the participative and the representative democracy, which has characterised the Portuguese HEIs' bureaucratic-collegial regime since the 1974 democratic revolution, at least in rhetorical terms, ended with the 2007 new higher education act. If these results are compared with the conclusions from previous studies in the field (Amaral, Magalhães & Santiago, 2003; Santiago & Carvalho, 2004; Santiago, Magalhães & Carvalho, 2005; Carvalho & Santiago, 2010a, b; Santiago & Carvalho, 2012), it seems that the mechanisms of the representative democracy were more or less preserved, but the participation of the academics from the 'organizational periphery', or the 'operational center' in institutional decisions as Mintzberg (1990) put it, has diminished.

However, this conclusion does not entirely apply to the two Portuguese HE subsystems. Statistical differences become relevant if universities and polytechnics are compared. Surprisingly, polytechnics seem to have resisted changes in the governance and management structures imposed by the new HE act more than universities. In fact, unit heads from polytechnics have emphasised less the influence that the polytechnics presidents have in the decision-making regarding the HEIs' management of academics and of the academic work (statistical differences between sig; 0.055 and sig; 0.005). Compared with those from universities, polytechnics surveyed asserted that top institutional managers have less influence on some decisions linked to promotions in academic career rank (university-45%; polytechnic-37%), the evaluation of academics' work (university-45%; polytechnic-16%), management of academics' professional agenda and tasks (university-72%; polytechnic-51%) and decisions on general academic issues (university-34%; polytechnic-16%). In comparison, unit heads from polytechnics emphasised more than those from universities the influence of the unit heads and the academic boards (scientific and pedagogical boards) on decisions associated with promotion in academic career rank (middle management; university-11%; polytechnic-25%), the evaluation of academic work (middle management; university-20%, polytechnic-33% and academic boards university-13%; polytechnic-35%), the general issues of academic work (middle management; university-36%; polytechnic-43% and academic boards; university-11%; polytechnic-33%) and, finally, the management of academics' professional agenda and tasks (academic boards; university-5%; polytechnic-33%).

To sum up, it is possible to conclude that academics from this subsystem more than those from universities have turned to their advantage the interpretation of the state policies requirements driven to reconfigure the HEIs' governance and management. Against the political expectations of the HEIs' organisational vertical integration (Carvalho & Santiago, 2010a), they seem to have resisted more than universities the power concentration at the top, keeping also more than universities some of the essential features of the bureaucratic-collegial model.

The interpretation of this difference is complex and needs further comparative research. However, it can be argued that polytechnic schools have similar autonomous traditions as faculties in universities. Since the early 1980s, they have also been changed by the 'academic drift', as, at the same time, universities started to be increasingly engaged in the 'professional drift'. Moreover, all the academics from polytechnics were trained in universities, where they obtained their masters and/or PhD degrees. In this sense, the mimetic and normative isomorphism phenomena (DiMaggio & Powell, 1991), as well as their reproduction in time and space, aiming at reinforcing the polytechnics' academic symbolic and cultural capital, can be a useful conceptual tool for further analysis of these differences between the institutions from the two subsystems.

Deans' and Heads' Perceptions of the Influence of Knowledge Society in the Academic Profession

The intersection between the bureaucratic and professional rationalities was a core structural dimension of the academics' careers structuring. Nevertheless, since the beginning of 1980s, this panorama has changed dramatically. Subsequent to Kuhlmann's (2012) arguments for the healthcare sector, it can be suggested that the knowledge society/economy is also used to control academics' professional practices along with the market and managerial rationalities. According to Kuhlmann, "scientific knowledge is turned into 'technologies of control' aimed at controlling the professionals who have produced this knowledge' (p. 152).

In Portugal, the state and the HEIs' science and technologies policies have had a similar tendency to emphasise the knowledge society/economy impact over the economic development and the acquisition of national competiveness advantages (Santiago et al., 2008). Since the beginning of 2000 (after the Lisbon Agenda), Portuguese academics have been faced with strong pressures to change their way of doing research, as well as to change their epistemological and ontological knowledge production assumptions, so that they are more in line with knowledge society/economy. Hence, it is pertinent to analyse how heads responded to this new trend and how they acknowledged its presence in their professional practices.

Table 6. Heads' perceptions of the influence of knowledge society in their professional practices

	Not at all present and not present	Neutral	Very present and present	N
The public access to scientific knowledge	15.6%	22%	62.4%	109 (100%)
A more prompt diffusion of scientific information	7.3%	8.3%	84.4%	109 (100%)
The diversity of the scientific knowledge production locus	10.0%	20.5%	69.0%	109 (100%)
The linkage between the economic development and the scientific knowledge	8.2%	22%	69.3%	109 (100%)
The emphasis in knowledge social utility	7.3%	29.1%	63.6%	110 (100%)
The emphasis in knowledge short-term application	12.1%	30.8%	57.0%	107 (100%)
The increase of scientific knowledge privatisation and commercialisation	20.6%	28%	51.4%	107 (100%)
The scientific knowledge orientation to technological innovation	9.1%	34.9%	55.9%	109 (100%)

Source: Survey data base (2012)

The results in table 6 seem to indicate that, in general, a large majority of the academics surveyed identified the strong presence of some main traces of knowledge society/economy in their professional practices. However, the intensity of this presence is more evident in relation to what is more intrinsically connected to the general rhetoric on the phenomenon than the tangible factors affecting the realm of their everyday professional practices. Indeed, public access to scientific knowledge (62%), a more prompt diffusion of scientific information (85%), the diversity of the locus of knowledge production (70%), the linkage of economic development to scientific knowledge (70%); and the emphasis in knowledge social utility (64%), are all more outlines of knowledge society/ontology – 'why' knowledge – than of knowledge society epistemologies – 'what' knowledge. In this latter sphere, unit heads are less affirmative in acknowledging the presence of the short-term application (57%), privatisation and commercialisation (52%) and the orientation of knowledge to the technological innovation (56%).

This slight difference of surveyed views on the intensity of the knowledge society epistemology and ontology presence in their everyday professional practices seems to be in line with previous national survey results included in the 'Changing Academic Professions' (CAP) international project (Santiago & Carvalho, 2011). In this study, the majority of the Portuguese academics surveyed declared that the external sponsors or clients have no influence over their research activities and that they were not involved in knowledge and technology transfer to the entrepreneurial world, even if their institutions emphasised commercially-oriented research activities. On the contrary, these academics characterised their research activities as being mainly socially-oriented for the betterment of society. These conclusions can help to understand why heads seem to have emphasised more the presence of the 'social side' of the knowledge society in their everyday professional practices than the economic and commercial side.

Unit Heads' Overall View on Changes in the Academic Profession: Autonomy and Social Prestige

In Portugal, the academics' professionalisation was achievable after the 1974 democratic revolution with the approval of the academic career national statute in 1979 (Carvalho, 2012). The academic profession has been released from the stigma of the 'political university' of the totalitarian regime (Torgal, 2012); and, in this regard, it can be argued that academics' autonomy and social prestige increased substantially until the end of the 1990s (Carvalho, 2012). When analysing the extension of market and NPM to HE, some current studies claim that tendencies are emerging for the academic profession to lose its professional power, autonomy and social prestige, even if the resistance on the ground seems relevant (Santiago & Carvalho, 2008; Carvalho & Santiago, 2010b; Carvalho, 2012; Santiago & Carvalho, 2012).

When questioned over this survey topic, unit heads' responses were somewhat diverse and ambiguous (table 7). A large majority of the surveyed acknowledged that the social prestige of the academic profession has been diminishing (62%). A high proportion also recognised that the academics' professional group has lost power when compared with other groups (41%), even if responses are more nuanced and divided (neutral-20%). On the other hand, a high percentage of academics (46%) rejected the idea that managers are the more powerful among the professional groups in HEIs. Additionally, a slight majority believed that academics constitute one of the groups more appreciated by institutions (42%), but once more a notable proportion of the surveyed assumed a neutral position (40%) on this topic. Where the responses emerge as more assertive is the large majority who asserted that they would like to have more professional autonomy (63%).

Unit heads' responses seem to reinforce the hypothesis that the academic profession has been losing its statute and power as a focal profession in Portuguese society (Carvalho & Santiago, 2010a).

Table 7. Unit heads' perceptions of autonomy and the social prestige of the academic profession

	Not at all and not	Neutral	Very much and much	Totals
The social prestige of the academic profession has being diminishing	14.3%	24.2%	61.6%	91 (100%)
Managers are more appreciated than the other professional groups in my institution	46.2%	26.4%	27.5%	91 (100%)
The academic group is one of the more appreciated by institutions	17.8%	40%	42.2%	90 (100%)
Academics lose power in comparison with other professional groups	31.6%%	27.2%	41.3%	92 (100%)
I would like to have more autonomy in professional decisions	17.0%	20.2	62.7%	94 (100%)

Source: Survey data base (2012)

Probably, as in other countries (Reed, 2002; Harley, Muller & Collin, 2003; Musselin, 2008; Meek & Goedgebuure, 2010), Portuguese academics, who until the end of the 1990s enjoyed social prestige and professional autonomy (Carvalho, 2012), may view this 'privileged' position as having weakened. In fact, in the last decade, academics are seen more as intellectual workers, or employees accountable to their institutions that pay their salaries, than as the 'owners' of their expertise (Harley et al., 2003; Santiago & Carvalho, 2012). The academics' wish for more autonomy in their professional decisions is a helpful empirical argument to illustrate the new political and institutional conditions under which academic work is organised and the academics' professional actions are developed. Nevertheless, one needs to remember that this study is mainly based on academics' perceptions. More comparative and even longitudinal studies are needed to conclude on the effects of new governance structures on academics' professional power.

CONCLUSIONS

The 2007 HE act in Portugal was implemented with the aim to (re)configure institutions according to two main axes. The first was to make HEIs more corporate or businesslike, transforming them into unitary organisations, sustained in a new pyramidal power structure with top-down power relations. The second was to impose a more competitive and efficient environment, considering academics as rational optimisers of consumer-led teaching, research and knowledge services.

This political endeavour implies, on the one hand, restrictions on collegial power, viewed as a source of dispersion, slowness and self-interested corporatism; and, on the other hand, the deconstruction and the redesign of the professional spaces of the academics' autonomy, as well as their conceptions of professionalism.

Portuguese state HE policies have been using some political tools typical of the so-called NPM in order to create this new institutional environment. Among these tools a mix up of 'action-at-a-distance' and direct control emerge as the more salient. In the former, greater autonomy was assigned to HEIs, although 'escorted' by an array of regulatory instruments aimed at disciplining and conforming institutions and academics to the political expectations and correlated norms of formal policies framing the system. Concurrently, and paradoxically, the Portuguese state kept the hierarchical control of some key variables to the HE structuring, as, for instance, financing, access (access rules and numerous clauses) and selective science and technology incentives mainly oriented to favour 'blind' productivism and economic utilitarianism. At the present time, this overall context framing the Portuguese HE system and institutions is confronting the academic profession with significant challenges. Over the last decade, national studies on this subject have revealed that the majority of academics although presenting different commitments to change – compliance, neutrality, pragmatism and resistance – still identify the mainstream 'traditional' academic values and beliefs as the core reference of their professionalism (Amaral, Magalhães & Santiago, 2003; Santiago & Carvalho, 2004; Santiago et al., 2006; Carvalho & Santiago, 2010a,b). The results of the present study are congruent with these conclusions. However, when looking carefully at the way unit heads are positioned in relation to institutional and professional changes, some important differences come into view.

First, unit heads stressed, more than before, the state as a key player in assuring the public good, social equality, quality and the autonomy and independency of institutions, professionals and science from external pressures (market and private interests). Conversely, they have the strong feeling that the HEIs' objectives have been changing dramatically. According to their views, these objectives are primarily focused on managerial and market concerns (clients' satisfaction, external resources, increasing productivity and external image and visibility), leaving aside professionals' satisfaction and improvement in the academics' work and HE public services' delivery. Second, more than in previous studies, the academics surveyed recognised that the top academic senior managers have strengthened their influence over key institutional decisions connected to the organisation of the main HEIs' governance and management areas – the structuring of units, budget priorities (at the institutional and units levels), the creation of new units and the programmes and projects approval. In a similar way, top institutional governance and management actors have gained more influence over academic career promotions and evaluations. In a certain sense, this power concentration is shared with the unit heads, but around issues more associated with the definition of units' budget priorities and academic staff recruitment. The latter seem to be more influential in operational tasks as the organisation of the teaching timetables and the general issues related to academics' tasks and activities.

Within this general context, academic boards and individuals emerge as the actors who have been losing more power over the main institutional decision-making processes (they only exercised a major influence in the selection, appointment and election of the rectors/polytechnics presidents and of the unit heads). This seems not to be the case for polytechnics where the unit heads' views are more nuanced – the top institutional managers-academics are less influential in decisions associated with academic management (promotions, evaluation, timetables and general issues on academic work). It seems that polytechnics have resisted the market and managerial changes in the institutional set more than the universities. This may be explained by the independence of the polytechnics schools' vis-à-vis the polytechnics institutes' central administration since their creation in the 1980s (in fact, polytechnics institutes were a federation of polytechnics schools), and by the continuity of the 'academic drift' reproduction in time and space (academics from polytechnics were scientifically socialised in universities).

The unit heads surveyed recognised also that the knowledge society is substantially present in their day-to-day professional practices. Nevertheless, the intensity of this presence seems to be more rhetorical than tangible. In other words, acknowledgement of the presence of general assumptions of a knowledge society (public access to knowledge, diffusion of scientific information, diversity in the knowledge production locus, knowledge social utility and the linkage between knowledge and economic development) was more salient than those connected to a knowledge society in action – short-term application, privatisation/commercialisation and orientation to technological innovation.

As a conclusion, a very large majority of the unit heads were quite in agreement, assertively pointing out that the academic profession has been losing social prestige and power compared with other social groups. A strong desire arose for more autonomy in making professional decisions. This last concern of professional autonomy calls attention to the hypothesis that academics, as a professional group, are losing the institutional initiative in the definition of teaching and research of the 'what' and 'how'. Further empirical research is needed to address how far this contingency is representing a decline of the academic profession, metamorphosing it in a manageable skilled profession; or whether the so-called knowledge society/economy is emerging as an opportunity to readdress the academics' legitimacy. The question of who will control knowledge production and use remains an open issue.

ACKNOWLEDGEMENTS

We thank the editors and the anonymous reviewers of this volume for their helpful comments. The authors acknowledge the support of the FCT in sponsoring the project PTDC/CPE-PEC/104759/2008.

NOTE

¹[1]   Unit head is the term used in this chapter to describe all academics whose are in charge of management responsibilities in faculties, schools and departments.

REFERENCES/BIBLIOGRAPHY

Altbach, P., Reisberg, L., & Rumbley, L. (2009). *Trends in global higher education: Tracking an academic revolution.* Chestnut Hill, M.A.: Center for International Higher Education/Boston College.

Amaral, A., Magalhães, A., & Santiago, R. (2003). The rise of academic managerialism in Portugal. In A. Amaral, L. Meek, & I. Larsen (Eds.), *The higher education managerial revolution?* (pp. 101–123). Dordrecht: Kluwer Academic Publishers.

Askling, B. (2001). Higher education and academic staff in a period of policy and system change. *Higher Education, 41,* 157–181.

Barnett, R. (2003). *Beyond all reason: living with ideology in the University.* Buckingham: SRHE and Open University Press.

Bezes, P., & Demazière, D. (2012). Introduction. In P. Bezes, D. Demazière, T. Le Bianic, C. Paradeise, R. Normand, D. Benamouzig, F. Pierru, & J. Evetts, (2012). New public management and professionals in the public sector. What new patterns beyond opposition? *Sociologie du Travail, 54,* Supplement, *1* (0), e1–e52.

Bleiklie, I., & Michelsen, S. (2008). The university as enterprise and academic co-determination. In A. Amaral, I. Bleiklie, & C. Musselin (Eds.), *From governance to identity, a festschrift for Mary Henkel* (pp.57–80). London: Springer.

Brint, S. (1994). *In an age of experts: The changing role of professionals in politics and public life.* Princetown/New Jersey: Princetown University Press.

Carvalho, T. (2012). Shaping the 'new' academic profession. Tensions and contradictions in the professionalisation of academics. In G. Neave, & A. Amaral (Eds.), *Higher education in Portugal 1974–2009. A nation, a generation* (pp. 329–352). Dordrecht: Springer Publishers.

Carvalho, T., & Santiago, R. (2010a). NMP and 'middle management': How do deans influence institutional policies? In L. Meek, L. Gooedgbuure, R. Santiago, & T. Carvalho (Eds.), *The changing dynamics of higher education middle management* (pp. 165–196). London: Springer.

Carvalho, T., & Santiago, R. (2010b). Still academics after all. *Higher Education Policy, 23,* 397–411.

Deem, R., Hillyard, S., & Reed, M. (2007). *Knowledge, higher education, and the new managerialism. The changing management of UK universities.* Oxford: Oxford University Press.

DiMaggio, P., & Powell, W. (1991). *The iron cage revisited: Institutional isomorphism and collective rationality in organizational analysis.* Chicago: The University of Chicago Press.

Enders, J., De Boer, H., & Leisyte, L. (2008). On striking the right notes: Shifts in governance and the organisational transformation of universities. In A. Amaral, I. Bleiklie, & C. Musselin (Eds.), *From governance to identity, a festschrift for Mary Henkel* (pp. 113–130). London: Springer.

Freidson, E. (2001). *Professionalism, the third logic.* Cambridge: Polity Press.

Freidson. E. (1994). *Professional powers: A study of the institutionalization of formal knowledge.* Chicago: The University of Chicago Press

Fulton, O. (2003). Managerialism in UK universities: Unstable hybridity and the complications of implementation. In A. Amaral, L. Meek, & I. Larsen (Eds.), *The higher education managerial revolution?* (pp. 155–178). Dordrecht: Kluwer Academic Publishers.

Harley, S. Muller-Camen, M., & Collin, A. (2003). From academic communities to managed organisations: The implications for academic careers in UK and German universities. *Journal of Vocational Behavior, 64*(2), 329–345.

Johnson, T. (1972). *Professions and power.* London: Macmillan.

Kogan, M., & Bauer, M. (2000). Change and continuity: some conclusions. In M. Kogan, M. Bauer, I. Bleiklie, & M. Henkel (Eds.), *Transforming higher education, a comparative study* (pp. 199–214). London: Jessica Kingsley Publishers.

Kuhlmann, E. (2012). Professionalism matters: Unpacking the knowledge-power nexus in healthcare governance. In T. Carvalho, R. Santiago, & T. Caria (Eds.), *Grupos Profissionais, Profissionalismo e Sociedade do Conhecimento* (pp.151–162). Porto: Edições Afrontamento.

Larson, M. (1977). *The rise of professionalism, a sociological analysis.* Berkley: University of California Press.

Meek, V., Goedegebuure, L., & De Boer (2010). The changing role of academic leadership in Australia and the Netherlands: Who is the modern dean? In V. Meek, L. Goedegebuure, R. Santiago, & T. Carvalho (Eds.), *The Changing dynamics of higher education middle management* (pp. 31–54). London: Springer.

Mintzberg, H. (1990). *Le management – voyage au centre des organisations.* Paris: Les Editions D'Organization.

Musselin, C. (2008). Towards a sociology of academic work. In A. Amaral, I. Bleiklie, & C. Musselin (Eds.), *From governance to identity, a festschrift for Mary Henkel* (pp. 47–56). London: Springer.

Neave, G. (2012). *The evaluative state, institutional autonomy and re-engineering higher education in Western Europe.* Houndmills/Basinbstoke: Palgrave Macmillan.

Olssen, M., & Peters, M. (2005). Neoliberalism, higher education and the knowledge economy: from the free market to knowledge capitalism. *Journal of Educational Policy, 20*(3), 313–345.

Pollit, C., & Boukaert, G. (2000). *Public management reform: A comparative analysis.* Oxford: Oxford University Press.

Reed, M. (2002). New managerialism, professional power and organisational governance in UK universities: A review and assessment. In A. Amaral, G. Jones, & B. Karseth (Eds.) *Governing higher education: National perspectives on institutional governance (*pp. 163–186). Dordrecht: Kluwer Academic Publishers.

Santiago, R., Carvalho, T., Amaral, A., & Meek, L. (2006). Changing patterns in the middle management of higher education: The case of Portugal. *Higher Education, 52*, 215–250.

Santiago, R., & Carvalho, T. (2012). Managerialism rhetoric in Portuguese higher education. *Minerva, 50*, 511–532.

Santiago, R., & Carvalho, T. (2011). Mudança no conhecimento e na profissão académica em Portugal. *Cadernos de Pesquisa, 41* (143), 402–426.

Santiago, R., & Carvalho, T. (2008). Academics in a new work environment: the impact of new public management on work conditions. *Higher Education Quarterly, 62* (3), 204–223.

Santiago, R., & Carvalho, T. (2004). Effects of managerialism on the perceptions of higher education in Portugal. *Higher Education Policy, 17*, 427–444.

Santiago, R., Magalhães, A. & Carvalho, T. (2005). *O surgimento do managerialismo no sistema de ensino superior português.* Matosinhos: CIPES/FUP.

Torgal, L. (2012).University, society and politics. In G. Neave, A. Amaral (Eds.), *Higher education in Portugal. A nation, a generation* (pp.67–87). Dordrecht: Springer Publishers.

AFFILIATIONS

Rui Santiago
CIPES (Center for Research in Higher Education policies)
University of Aveiro

Teresa Carvalho
CIPES (Center for Research in Higher Education policies)
University of Aveiro

Andreia Ferreira
CIPES (Center for Research in Higher Education policies)
University of Aveiro

BOJANA ĆULUM

CROATIAN ACADEMICS AND UNIVERSITY CIVIC MISSION INTEGRATION: POSSIBILITIES AND CONSTRAINTS

INTRODUCTION

University civic mission is a reflection of universities as good institutional citizens that engage in their (local) communities in multiple ways – by researching and providing solutions for significant (local) problems (usually universal problems that are manifested locally, such as poverty, unequal health care, substandard housing, hunger, and inadequate, unequal education, etc.); by conducting research on democracy, civil society, and civic development; by educating students to be active and responsible citizens; by providing forums for free democratic dialogue not only for academics and students, but for (local) community members as well; and by offering its various resources and educational opportunities to the local community – to sum up by paraphrasing Benjamin Barber (1996), by being a 'good neighbour' that cares about and supports the improvement of (civic) life in local communities.

The idea of civic mission and university engagement in local community is to embody university purpose, objectives, priorities and academic pillars, meaning teaching and research, with the needs and problems of their neighbouring (local) communities. Without undermining the importance of the institutional commitment, the most sustainable way of integrating civic mission, as studies consistently show, is its incorporation into teaching and research and their mutual interface throughout models that induce community-engaged learning (Zlotkowski & Williams, 2003; Ostrander, 2004; Macfarlane, 2005, 2007; Zlotkowski et al., 2006; Karlsson, 2007; Laredo, 2007).

Civic mission integration therefore, implies changes in ordinary teaching and research activities that are still unrecognized within the system of evaluation and promotion of the academics (Boyer, 1990, 1996; Glassick et al., 1997; Colbeck, 1998, 2002; Checkoway, 2000, 2001; Calhoun, 2006; Ledić, 2007). For that specific reason, civic mission integration is, to a certain extent, dependent on university teachers: on their attitudes towards (civic) mission of universities; their willingness to (re) define their traditional work patterns; their readiness to import models of teaching and research that are based on the needs and problems of the (local) community and that support students' community-engaged learning. Moreover, it depends on the elements of institutional support that could motivate academics to such a change.

J. Branković et al., Global Challenges, Local Responses in Higher Education, 59–78.

Following this crucial role of the academics in the successful civic mission integration, this chapter discusses some possibilities and constraints of the civic mission integration into Croatian universities with regard to its fundamental determinants of successful integration: (I) academics' readiness to introduce change into their everyday teaching and research, (II) attitudes that academics take toward the civic mission and (III) models of institutional support that would encourage academics to integrate community engaged learning in their everyday teaching and research.

Resting on segments of Rogers's Diffusion of Innovations theory (Rogers, 1964, 2003), additional attention was given to the development of typology of Croatian academics in relation to their willingness to accept changes in their daily teaching and research: (I) ready for a change, (II) neutral, and (III) resistant to changes. In addition, some characteristics of the academics, which according to the research results show a greater willingness to integrate civic mission in their academic activities, were identified. Developed typology is a useful basis, backed up by empirical data, and can contribute to the reflection of further steps in promotion of the civic mission in Croatian universities.

UNIVERSITY CIVIC MISSION AND THE IMPORTANT ROLE ACADEMICS PLAY

University civic mission articulates a separate system of values, principles, standards and various academic activities that encourage community-engaged learning and civic engagement in local communities. Furthermore, it accentuate the university's role in contributing to the education of socially responsible and active citizens, civil society, democracy, and generally improving the quality of life in the community. In that context, the civic mission implies a stronger integration of the university into the local community as it's vital component: the university should advocate and (professionally) address the needs and concerns of the community, develop collaborative relationships and projects with relevant stakeholders in the external environment (e.g. civil society organizations and initiatives, educational institutions, institutions in the field of health and social care, local and regional government), encourage the commitment of academics and students to the community and contribute to the development of socially responsible and active citizens. To paraphrase Ernest Boyer (1996), the civic mission involves creating a special atmosphere in which academics and local communities communicate on a regular basis in a creative way, improving the quality of life for all in the community.

By encouraging a debate on the integration of civic mission into academic activities, the awareness of the importance that academics play is increasing[1]. Accepting the paradigm of the civic mission means to accept the education of professionals and socially responsible citizens who will be able to critically judge, to participate actively in public debates and to engage in various issues of the common good, as one of the fundamental tasks of the university. In that context, the commitment of academics to the community, their public work, collaboration with representatives from the community and especially their contribution to the development of students as responsible members of the society is seen as their responsibility and duty to which they should be more seriously devoted. For this reason, Altman (1996) strongly advocated the idea that higher education institutions include the knowledge that leads to social responsibility in their programs. Moreover, Zlotkowski and colleagues (2006) contributed to the idea by encouraging academics to commit to integration of socially responsive knowledge. As society becomes more complex, the need for students to build an educational environment that will help them understand the social problems, but also realize the responsibility they carry as members of the community, becomes just as important, if not more important than educating (successful) experts.

Specifically, the integration of the civic mission in the university implies the close association of academics with the community, and requires a series of changes that academics should make in their daily teaching and research. The cooperation between academics and various external associates is encouraged in the public and non-profit sectors, with kindergartens and schools, with health and social care institutions and local-community activists, expecting the academic knowledge to directly improve the living conditions of the local communities and to impact the development of democracy and civic society.

Although there are various examples of initiatives that universities undertake on their way to integrating the civic mission (e.g. establishing university centres that provide support for the design and implementation of civic activities in the community, developing adequate models of remuneration and evaluation of civic commitment of academics and students, devising special courses and establishing new study programs based on education for active citizenship, etc.), collaboration of academics and their students in various educational programs and research projects that induce community-engaged learning is, however, the most advocated. Thus, we are witnessing the spread of the academic service-learning model and community based research. These models are not, of course, the only way to integrate the principles of civic missions, but they are certainly among those that are the most studied and that are, at least for now, still the most argued in this context. Most academics and experts agree that the goal of student engagement in the community is to educate them so that in the future, they can be responsible and active citizens, involved in all aspects of everyday life in the community in which they live and work. It is therefore important to observe the civic mission of universities in the context of the civic society and democracy in a local, regional and national framework, especially keeping in mind the tradition of the university and specific characteristics of the local communities in which it operates.

Nowadays, the integration of the civic mission at the university means, primarily, to transform the existing academic activities and actions, rather than develop new ones. Specifically, the present academic overload with multiple roles that academics perceive (Rice, Sorcinelli, & Austin, 2000), as well as high levels of stress, fear and discontent because of the expected results of excellence in all areas they address

(O'Meara & Braskamp, 2005) have prompted many authors to advocate for an integrative paradigm of academic roles and a stronger connection of teaching and research activities, which would be based on the needs of the community (Boyer, 1996; Berberet, 1999; Bloomgarden & O'Meara, 2007; Karlsson, 2007).

Boyer (1996) gave a powerful stimulus and support in arguing for the integration of the civic mission in core academic activities, calling for the *scholarship of engagement* and explaining:

> (...) our universities and colleges remain one of the greatest hopes for intellectual and civic progresses in this country. For this hope to be fulfilled, the academy must become a more vigorous partner in the search for answers to our most pressing social, civic, economic, and moral problems, and must reaffirm its historic commitment to the scholarship of engagement. The scholarship of engagement means connecting the rich resources of the university to existing problems, to our children, to our schools, to our teachers, and to our cities (...) I am firmly convinced that we do not need new programs, but a higher purpose, a stronger sense of mission (...) (Boyer, 1996, 19-20).

Since the integration of the civic mission involves transforming teaching and research, it is clear that its success, to an extent, depends on the academics. After all, they run research projects, manage the curricula and teach the courses that can help prepare students for their own civic roles. Such proposed changes in teaching put academics in front of new challenges in terms of thinking of educational goals (Checkoway, 2001; Harkavy, 2006), the transformation of the curriculum (Nussbaum, 1997; Ostrander, 2004) and of the planning and implementation of teaching in such a way to encourage education of socially responsible and active citizens. Along with the changes in teaching, changes in research are also advocated. Although less than the academic service-learning model, the literature more often advocates community-based research (community-based participatory research), as a contribution to applied research and with a long-term aim of putting the expertise of academics and students (as future professionals) in the service of the local community (Strand, 2000; Stoecker, 2003; Strand et al., 2003).

An important aspect of the changes in teaching and research refers to the development of cooperation with representatives of (local) communities and their involvement in planning, carrying-out and evaluating the teaching and research activities. The success of the implementation of these models of teaching and research, therefore, implies the openness of academics to (un) tested models of teaching and research and their willingness to cooperate in intense teamwork in a triangle of teacher-student-local community representative(s).

As many authors agree, the integration of teaching and research and the contribution of academics to the education of socially responsible and active citizens require academics' long-term commitment[2]. If they opt for this kind of a change, they are expected to be open to cooperation with the community, establishing and managing collaborative (research) projects, designing unconventional curriculum, devising fieldwork, fostering teamwork, adequate documentation of their work, especially of students and their progress, as well as nurturing interdisciplinary work, etc. Bearing in mind that academics rarely have adequate institutional and administrative support for implementing such changes in their daily teaching and research, and that the results of such activities are rarely (if at all) adequately valued in terms of academics' promotion, it is clear why socially engaged teaching and research appeal to the perseverance and dedication of academics. Specifically, involvement in these activities, for which it seems academics are not formally employed, responsible or even evaluated, could endanger important dimensions of their (scientific and professional) academic achievement, as has been evidenced by previous research (Bloomgarden and O'Meara, 2007, Macfarlane, 2007; Karlson, 2007; Ćulum & Ledić, 2010).

Therefore, Kendall (1990) is right when he states that academics play a central role in the promotion and integration of civic mission and they are the only key that can, in the long run, enable universities to make the commitment to community service. Specifically, the success of the development of the university's civic mission and wider use of models that encourage dedication to teaching and research depends precisely on them and their decision of whether they want to 'spend their time' on these activities. The decision is related to their attitudes toward the values and the principles of the civic missions and, not least important, to their willingness to change and reflect the teaching and research activities that would be based on the needs and problems of the community and encourage community-engaged learning aiming at students' civic development.

CROATIAN ACADEMICS AND UNIVERSITY CIVIC MISSION – RESEARCH METHODOLOGY

Accepting civic mission principles and their integration into teaching and research requires persistence, patience and long-term commitment of academics, especially if the *alma mater* university does not show the institutional commitment to the civic mission. That kind of commitment cannot be expected unless academics express the willingness to accept the changes in their everyday work and if their attitudes are consistent with those changes that are, at the same time, required by the civic mission integration (Hassinger & Pinkerton, 1986; Kendall, 1990; McKay & Rozee, 2004; Zlotkowski et al., 2006).

Due to the lack of interest on the part of the Croatian research community in the concept of the civic mission, there is a very little data on what our universities have done in terms of civic mission integration. Moreover, in the university environment in which the civic mission is not institutionalised, promoted and evaluated, as in the case of Croatian universities (Ćulum & Ledić, 2010), it seems that the Croatian academic community has the scope to take a stand towards civic mission depending on personal perception of its importance. Thus, the attitudes of academics towards the civic mission and social responsibility for the (local) communities become even more important to analyze, and raise the main research question: from whom in the Croatian academic community can we expect commitment to the university civic mission, and under what conditions?

Starting from the crucial role that academics play in the successful civic mission integration, this chapter analyses some possibilities and constraints of the civic mission integration into Croatian universities with regard to its fundamental determinants of successful integration: (I) willingness of university teachers to introduce changes into their daily teaching and research, (II) attitudes and dispositions that academics take toward the civic mission and (III) institutional support mechanisms that would encourage them to integrate the civic mission in their everyday teaching and research.

Using the Diffusion of Innovations Theory (Rogers, 1962) as a conceptual base and employing a factor analysis, a typology of Croatian academics in relation to their attitudes towards civic mission and their innovativeness was developed. In this particular context, academics' innovativeness was operationalized as academics' willingness to accept changes in their daily teaching and research (ready for a change, neutral, resistant to the changes). Since it has been supported with the empirical data, this typology can serve as a significant contributor in placing further steps of civic mission promotion among Croatian academics.

The study represents a quantitative research approach. Empirical data were collected by a questionnaire method of a representative sample of 570 examinees[3], academics from all seven Croatian public universities, whereby the network/internet questionnaire, designed specifically for this research purpose, was used.

RESEARCH RESULTS AND THEIR IMPLICATIONS ON POSSIBILITIES AND CONSTRAINTS FOR CIVIC MISSION INTEGRATION AT CROATIAN UNIVERSITIES

Who is (More) Ready for Introducing Change Into Teaching and Research?

As it has been discussed earlier in the chapter, civic mission integration in academic activities brings significant changes for academics and numerous challenges in planning, implementing and evaluating teaching and research that foster community-engaged learning. It is important, therefore, that academics express a willingness to change (traditional) patterns in their daily teaching and research (Kendall, 1990).

In the present study, academics' willingness to accept changes has been examined in accordance with (part of) the Diffusion of Innovations Theory (Rogers, 1962). In a broader sense, this theory seeks to answer the question of how, why, under what conditions and in what time frame the new ideas spread in a culture. Rogers (1962, 2003) defines diffusion as a process in which, over a certain period of time, an innovation is introduced and spread among the members of a specific social system, organization or culture through selected channels of communication. In this particular study, the innovativeness stands for academics' willingness to accept changes and new ideas in their daily teaching and research. The construct of innovation/ willingness to accept changes and new ideas in daily teaching and research was operationalised through twenty-one variables. Using a scale from 1 ("never applies to me") to 5 ("always applies to me"), respondents were asked to mark how a certain argument applies to them and their behaviour in everyday teaching and research.

Rogers (1962, 2003) makes a significant contribution to the development and popularization of the Diffusion of Innovations Theory by developing a grouping of members of a particular social system on the basis of their innovation, defining it as willingness to accept new ideas relatively earlier than other members of the same social system. According to Rogers (1962, 2003) the distribution of these groups in the population follows the principle of normal distribution and the proposed five groups occur as follows: innovators (2.5%), early adopters (13.5%), early majority (34 %), late majority (34%) and laggards (16%)[4].

Diffusion of innovations and adoption process begins with a tiny number of visionary and imaginative *innovators*. They often lavish great time, energy and creativity on developing new ideas. Innovators are willing to take risks. Usually, but not necessarily, they are younger in age. They are very social and have close contact to scientific sources and interaction with other innovators. As no change program can thrive without their energy and commitment, it is quite important to 'track them down'. Once the benefits start to become apparent, *early adopters* jump in. They are on the lookout for a strategic leap forward in their lives or businesses and are quick to make connections between innovations and their personal needs. They are eager for getting an advantage over their peers, and have the highest degree of opinion leadership among the other adopter categories. Early adopters tend to be well connected, well informed and hence more socially respected. They are an 'easy audience', meaning they do not need much persuading because they are on the lookout for anything that could give them some kind of (usually social or economic) edge. Their natural desire to be trendsetters actually causes the "take-off" of an innovation. What early adopters say about an innovation determines its success, and that is why they are also called "change agents." Individuals in the *early majority* category adopt an innovation after a varying degree of time. Their time of adoption is significantly longer than in the case of the innovators and early adopters. Early majorities are pragmatists, comfortable with moderately progressive ideas, but will not act without solid proof of benefits. They are followers, usually influenced by mainstream fashions. Individuals in the *late majority* category will adopt an innovation after the average member of the society. These individuals approach an innovation with a high degree of skepticism and will accept it only after the majority of society has already adopted it. They are portrayed as conservative pragmatists who are not likely to take any risk and are uncomfortable with new ideas. What drives them most is usually the fear of not fitting in; hence they will follow mainstream fashions and established standards. Acceptance of certain ideas is also driven by economic reasons or frequent pressure from colleagues and/or superiors. *Laggards* are the last to adopt an innovation. They are people who see a high risk in adopting a particular innovation, whether it is a product or certain behaviour. Unlike some of the previous categories, individuals in this category show little to no opinion leadership. These individuals typically have an aversion to change agents and tend to be advanced in age. Laggards typically tend to be focused on "traditions" and are often portrayed as conservatives.

Personal characteristics and interactions among the groups presented above explain the domino effect present in the process of diffusion of innovations. Rogers' analysis suggests that the spread of a particular innovation, or acceptance of certain changes and implementation of new ideas, depends on a very small group of members of a system, or on the so-called "Tipping Point" (Rogers, 1971, 2003; Gladwell, 2002). Simply put, the success of innovations depends on the early adopters' (change agents) acceptance and their influence and ability to play an important role in encouraging other groups to accept. Thus, the power of persuasion into the benefits of a particular innovation and the need for its implementation should not, as Rogers says, be spent on those who resist change. Instead, support should be provided to those who are really prone to changes and new ideas, and who are trusted by a majority of their colleagues. Given that this group of people is crucial to the successful implementation of innovation, Rogers (1983, 2003) claims that the organisational efforts in achieving the change should be focused on identifying those groups of academics that will impel a specific change and facilitate its implementation. Additionally, it is necessary to provide those academics with an adequate institutional support to ensure full potential in their role of change agents.

Although Rogers developed his theory by creating a system of five categories in relation to the innovation factor (willingness to accept new ideas), he himself also points to some of the common characteristics of individual groups and the possibility of their conjugation for the purpose of better interpretability of data (Rogers, 1971, 2003). The combination of the innovators and early adopters in general indicates the proportion of individuals who could be 'change agents' developing the momentum needed to assure the adoption of changes in the next category, the early majority. On the other hand, the late majority and laggards, show the greatest degree of resistance to new ideas and changes. Their need to retain the *status quo* position and provide resistance to change makes the (social) system more inert and thus hampering the integration of new ideas and change. Some other researchers (Lozano, 2006) decided to merge the categories in their research as well.

Following this explanation for conjunction, three groups according to the factor of innovation were created for the survey presented, and determined among the survey respondents. Research results show that among academics in Croatia, 14.2% are those who accept the changes in teaching and research (innovators and early adopters), 33.7% are neutral (early majority) and 46.8% resist change (late majority and laggards).

Study results show that innovators and early adopters in Croatian academic community are predominantly associate and tenured professors (75,3%), and academics ranging from 31 to 50 years of age (59,5%). They are rarely found among the youngest academics up to the age of 31 (7,4%). More than a third of academics in the group of late majority and laggards are teaching assistants and junior researchers and more than half of them are the younger respondents, up to 40 years of age (56.2%).

The youngest age group (up to 31 years of age) consists of 62,9% late majority and laggards – results show that this age group of youngest academics is the least willing to accept new ideas and changes in their (daily) teaching and research activities.

Distribution of the groups according to the factor of innovation makes the age group of 41 to 50 years of age the most open to the changes in teaching and research, since there is an equal proportion of early majority and late majority and laggards. On the other hand, the analysis of all three groups according to the factor of innovation/ willingness to accept changes and new ideas in the different age groups suggests that the youngest age group (up to 31 years of age) is 62.9% late majority and laggards, compared to just 6.7 % of innovators and early adopters. This means that among the youngest respondents there are almost ten times as many late majority and laggards (which resist changes and new ideas) compared to the innovators and early adopters, and two times more compared to the early majority.

Although respondents from this youngest age group (up to 31 years of age) are in the associate status, in most cases working as teaching assistants and junior researchers whose daily teaching and research is interdependent with their senior colleagues and supervisors with whom they work, what is worrisome is the domination of late majority and laggards, thus describing the youngest academics at the university as the least likely to introduce innovations in teaching and research. Comparison of the age groups, according to the factor of innovation / willingness to accept change, indicates that the members of this age group are the least open to experimenting with new approaches in their work and changes in the classroom. They are not willing to make changes in their work earlier than other (senior) colleagues, and ultimately, they are at least willing to continuously monitor and apply new trends in teaching and research. Although in some aspects, this age group also points to a lower degree of sensibility toward the concept of the civic mission - which will be discussed later in the chapter - they assess the civic mission and the importance of commitment to the common good of the community as less important than all other age groups. Moreover, they estimate addition to salary as a significantly greater motivational factor that would encourage them to integrate their mission into the regular academic activities.

Academics' Reflection on the Civic Mission

Besides the willingness of academics to introduce changes and new ideas into their daily teaching and research, the integration of civic mission depends on the consistency of their attitudes with the system of values and principles that articulate the concept of the civic mission. Hence their willingness to integrate the civic mission into their core academic activities has been examined in relation to their attitudes towards different aspects of civic mission[5]:

– appreciation of the civic mission and its principles as an important purpose of higher education
– attitudes toward civic commitment

- appreciation of the responsibilities of universities and academics in encouraging civic commitment of students and education of socially responsible and active citizens
- commitment to the educational objectives that seek to educate socially responsible and active citizens
- attitudes towards the integration of the civic mission in regular and elective courses and research projects.

Attitudes denote that most academics in Croatia, regardless of the institution they work at, recognize civic mission and its principles as an important purpose of higher education. In doing so, academics from social sciences and humanities as well as arts, estimate the civic mission with the highest central value (M=4.5). Moreover, it was noted that the civic mission gets significantly higher marks from women. It is important to point out that the civic mission gets significantly lower marks from the youngest age group, up to 31 years of age. This group of junior academics identifies itself significantly more with other two missions presented in the questionnaire - the education of experts and university research mission.

Croatian academics express positive attitudes towards civic engagement and respect the responsibility of universities and academics in promoting the civic engagement of students and education of socially responsible and active citizens. A significant proportion of academics believe that commitment to the general good of the community should be a fundamental personal and dominant value in the society (86.4 %) and that the anomalies in society can be reduced via active participation of citizens in public life (76.4 %). Regardless of the responsibility of the power holders, they believe that the citizens should further strive to resolve the issues in the community (69.5%) and in this regard they recognise the importance of the academic community: 81% of them believe that academics should be a model and an exemplar of socially responsible and active citizens who are expected to regularly be involved in public debates (68%) and have special contributions to community development (67.9%). Academics express positive attitudes toward a possible influence of volunteering and philanthropic activities in addressing the needs and problems of the community, which is important given that the integration of academic service-learning model assumes, among other things, the development of similar community initiatives (volunteering) in collaboration with academics, students and associates in the community.

More than two thirds of academics (71.3%) support the important role of universities in fostering civic commitment and empowering citizens to become active in the community. Surprisingly, they find it more important to educate students to be socially responsible and to be active citizens than to teach them the basics of scientific disciplines (67.2%). While 40.6% of academics feel that it is not too late to encourage education for active citizenship in the university and that academics need to transmit the contents and values that transcend the domain of their profession (62%), more than half of academics feel that education for active citizenship should still be implemented at previous levels of education, considering it is too late to 'deal with it' at the university level. Although strongly oriented toward the civic mission as the primary mission of the university, half of academics feel that the activities that contribute to the realization of the civic mission should not be part of the criteria of their advancement. With regard to Croatian academics who can hardly be expected to stimulate debate about the (re) definition of the criteria for academic promotion or advocating for the introduction of specific criteria to track the integration of the civic mission, such an attitude can have a significant impact on the perception of the importance of these activities in the academic community.

The concept of civic mission seems to be weakly associated with the contribution of universities to local community development. Educational goals which are indicators of the civic mission of universities and are associated with the stimulation of the community-engaged learning and students' civic commitment ((I) encouraging students to critically observe and analyze current social issues, (II) development of knowledge and skills for identifying problems in their local communities and contributing to their resolution, and (III) motivating students to develop knowledge, skills and attitudes necessary for acting upon the common good), compared with other educational goals[6], are estimated as less important in everyday teaching and research. Educational objectives associated with the development of motivation and the knowledge and skills of students to solve problems in their local communities are estimated as the least significant. Academics working in the field of social sciences and humanities as well as in arts, estimate the educational goals that serve as indicators of the civic mission, more significant than academics in other disciplines. Similarly, women estimate most of the educational goals to have greater relevance to their daily work than men do, especially the three goals mentioned above that served as indicators of university civic mission[7].

Study results indicate that academics have a positive attitude toward encouragement of the students' civic engagement, but they also point to certain limitations in the context of integration in regular activities. Most academics are inclined to promote civic commitment of students in regular educational programs and research projects (63.8%). They believe that student organizations cannot be the sole factor in the promotion of active citizenship and encouraging civic commitment of students and, ultimately, more than half of them state that encouraging civic commitment of students does not hamper their development as future professionals (57.7%). In doing so, the academics from social sciences and humanities as well as arts, estimate the integration of the civic mission in regular activities as more significant than academics from other disciplines do[8]. The same finding exists with women as compared to men[9].

Assessing the possibility of promoting community-engaged learning and civic engagement in teaching and research activities, academics prefer elective and specifically designed courses, which can have major implications on promotion of the mission in our universities. Specifically, the process of the integration of the civic mission, as already highlighted in the chapter, encourages the introduction of an experiential community-engaged learning model in regular or existing teaching and research programs. The opinion of the majority of the respondents on the impossibility of promoting community engagement through teaching regular courses, as reported in this study, indicates the importance of the promotion of this model for the purpose of enabling academics to get a better understanding of the concepts and possibilities of integrating teaching, research and student engagement in the community. Bearing in mind that the civic mission in Croatian universities is a completely neglected concept, this finding could be a powerful incentive for designing elective courses that would encourage community service-learning, with the aim of promoting the concept of the civic mission.

Incentives: Institutional Support as Motivation for Civic Mission Integration

Integrating the civic mission in academic activities leads to the modification of the traditional work patterns and habits of the academics. However, it is important that possible institutional (re) sources for supporting academics that engage into community service-learning teaching and research activities are organized to follow the academics' professional development opportunities and their (real) possibility of introducing changes in teaching and research (Zlotkowski, 2000). The study presented in the chapter examines the motivational potential of eleven factors, mainly related to the possibility of providing administrative, logistical, institutional support to academics.

In assessing the potential motivational factors that would encourage them to integrate the civic mission in everyday teaching and research work, the highest proportion of academics emphasizes the interest of students (78.2%). This factor is followed by the provided administrative support and infrastructure (73.8%), flexible workload and evaluation of various academic activities (64.9%), financial support for the costs of designed activities (66%) and providing training opportunities (62.6%). The above listed factors make five most important motivators.

The results of this research support previous studies (Hammond, 1994; Abes et al., 2002), given that the largest share of the respondents, 78.2% of them, states that students' interest would motivate them the most to integrate the civic mission into everyday teaching and research (M=4.0). A slightly lower proportion of academics, 73.8% of them, stress the importance of administrative support and infrastructure, which puts this motivational factor in second place (M=3.9). High ranking of these factors is in the accordance with the results of international studies that indicate how academics need additional administrative support due to the complexity of the process of planning, preparation, implementation and evaluation of community-engaged teaching and research activities, which often involves a large number of stakeholders outside the university whose work should also be monitored (Ward, 1996; Rice & Stacey, 1997; Abes et al., 2002). A significant proportion of respondents, 64.9% of them, stated that flexible workload and evaluation of the different academic opportunities would motivate them to integrate the civic mission, which puts this motivating factor in third place (M=3.7).[10]

Table 1. Incentives for introducing civic mission into teaching and research (percentage of respondents*)

	Incentives for introducing community-engaged teaching and research	1+2%	3%	4+5%	M	sd
1	The interest of students	7.2	14.5	78.2	4.0	0.972
2	Administrative support and infrastructure	11.6	14.6	73.8	3.9	1.057
3	Flexible workload and adequate evaluation of various academic activities	13.3	21.9	64.9	3.7	1.085
4	Financial support for the costs of designed activities	15.2	18.8	66.0	3.7	1.091
5	Training and learning opportunities	12.7	24.7	62.6	3.7	1.029
6	Interest of colleagues and their support	15.4	24.0	60.6	3.5	1.062
7	Contributions to the community included as a criterion for promotion	22.6	25.9	51.4	3.4	1.155
8	Defining the civic mission as fundamental aspect of the university mission	19.8	30.3	49.9	3.4	1.055
9	Integrating civic mission in the university acts (statute, strategy etc.)	20.3	32.1	47.6	3.3	1.057
10	Additional income to salary	33.9	26.8	39.3	3.0	1.216
11	Symbolic, non-formal appreciation and evaluation	34.8	32.2	33.1	2.9	1.143

* *Responses on a scale from 1 = Strongly disagree to 5 = Strongly agree*

The importance of financial support for the costs of the designed activities is mentioned by 66% of the respondents (M=3.7), training opportunities by 62.6% of them (M=3.7), and the interest of colleagues and their support for the work by 60.6% (M=3.5). Morton and Tropp (1996) pointed out the importance of professional training and support of colleagues back in the 1990s, and their importance have been recognized as important motivators in recent international studies as well (Abes et al., 2002; Harwood et al., 2005). The results of their research show that academics are ready to engage in the process of the community service-learning model if their respected colleagues do it too. Moreover, the opportunity to acquire new knowledge and skills is also of a great importance. Professional training programs are an important motivator, not only because they allow the academics to explore and better understand the community service-learning concept, but because participating in such educational programs often results in creation of an academic community that share values, interests and similar principles of working with students in wanting to educate socially responsible and active citizens (Abes et al., 2002; Harwood et al., 2005). By creating such a *think tank* community, academics can share ideas and experiences, reflect on the improvement of existing models, build networks and create new opportunities for cooperation. Such support is particularly important given that academics are often faced with the challenges of implementation of such activities due to the lack of time and especially because of the insufficient administrative and financial support in developing activities that encourage civic engagement (Stanton, 1994; Driscoll et al., 1996; Ward, 1996; Abes et al., 2002). Abes et al. (2002) have pointed out the importance of having support, especially for younger colleagues. Connecting with peers who are at different stages of an academic career has proven to be a successful model of mutual tutoring and strengthening interdisciplinary work.

Slightly more than half of the respondents in the study presented would be motivated to integrate the civic mission if contributions to the community would be included as a criterion for their promotion (51,4%). While the burgeoning literature strongly favours (re) definition of the current criteria for the promotion of the academics who contribute to the community development and education of socially responsible and active citizens (Boyer, 1990; Blackburn & Lawrence, 1995; Bloomgarden & O'Meara, 2007; Driscoll, 2007; Ledić, 2007), and while studies indicate that the still system of promotion in the academia is the biggest obstacle in the motivation of university teachers to integrate the civic mission (Hammond, 1994; Stanton, 1994; Morton & Tropp, 1996; Ward, 1996), it is interesting to note that recent studies, although rare, are arguing the opposite.

The results of this study also show that Croatian academics do not recognize the system of the academic promotion as the most important incentive. Although half of the respondents would be motivated to integrate the civic mission if contributions to the community would be included as a formal criterion for promotion; this is a factor, due to its score, in seventh place. Abes et al. (2002) got similar results in their study, so we can say that the finding of this study differs significantly from the dominant position in the current academic debate and the existing literature. These findings, obviously, do not imply that (re) defining the criteria of promotion should stop being advocated, but that it is clearly less important factor in the decision of academic on the integration of civic mission, unlike, for example, institutional support, training opportunities and financial support. Bearing in mind that Croatian academics estimate personal influence on the design and adoption of key academic policies as insignificant, especially at the university level (Rončević & Rafajac, 2010), it can be said that they estimate the possibilities of personal impact on changing the criteria of evaluation of scientific and educational advancement just the same, meaning (very) low. It is therefore more optimal, in this (Croatian) case, to point out those ways of integrating community-engaged learning that can support and enhance teaching and research activities that are already valued in the current system of promotion, rather than putting the emphasis on the change and encourage university teachers to advocate (re) definition of these criteria.

In the context of the motivation for civic mission integration in academic activities, defining the tasks of the civic mission as fundamental aspects of the mission of university (49.9%) and the involvement of the tasks of the civic mission in the basic legal acts of universities and colleges (47.6%) are estimated as less important. Although this finding positions these two factors in eighth and ninth place, it is in compliance with the thesis of numerous authors who state that the university's civic mission must be recognized at the highest governing and managing structures, and its principles integrated into relevant legal and organizational regulations and strategic guidance in order to send a clear message to the academics, and other members of the academic and general public about its importance (Boyer, 1990; Blackburn & Lawrence, 1995; Bloomgarden & O'Meara, 2007). In addition to salary (39.3%), symbolic evaluation and rewarding (33.1%) have the smallest motivational potential for civic mission integration. Junior academics find administrative support, financial support and salary supplements as more important motivational factors than their senior colleagues[11]. Women rank all aspects of (institutional) support as more significant than men do.[12]

FINAL REMARKS

On the way to integrating the civic mission into their regular academic activities, academics should be guided by the principles of social responsibility of universities as well as their personal and public responsibility to the community in which they live and work. It is important that academics recognize the (local) community as a place of learning that can provide sufficient educational opportunities to their students. In cooperation with relevant stakeholders in the community, academics should commit themselves to the analysis of the needs and problems of the community and to the planning, developing and implementing of activities that can contribute to finding solutions. Together with their students, academics should be involved in the dynamic and dialectical process. When designing activities that support students' community-engaged learning and their civic engagement, academics should take into account their students' personalities to provide them with qualitative educational opportunities for professional and personal development. This way of cooperation should act as an example to students for their future work and civic roles and strengthen their sense of responsibility for the community. Integrating the civic mission implies that students are educated in an environment that is aware of its responsibility towards others members of the community in which all members are making efforts aimed at improving the quality of life in the community and bringing positive change.

Results of this study indicate some specific characteristics of Croatian academics whose attitudes are close to the above described elements of the civic mission: (I) academics working in humanities and social sciences as well as in arts, women, associate and tenured professors and those academics aged from 41 to 50 years seem to be more willing to accept changes and new ideas, and to integrate the university civic mission in their teaching and research activities. Thus, they can be placed in the group of potential change agents or engaged base of academic. On the other hand, the least likely to bring change in daily teaching and research, with a reported less sensitivity toward the concept of the civic mission, are the youngest respondents up to 31 years of age in the associate status (teaching assistants and junior researchers). This finding should be kept in mind as a significant barrier to the integration of the civic mission, given that it is unlikely that this group will be the change agents, conveyors of the civic mission concept. To the contrary - the result of the study, according to which the youngest age group consists of 62.6 % late majority and laggards (in the recent literature called conservatives), implies that it is the youngest academics that would resist changes and new ideas in their teaching and research the most.

Nevertheless, the conducted study, bearing in mind the stated (positive) attitudes toward the concept of the civic mission, and with respect to the assessment of individual potential incentives for civic mission integration, identifies some available development opportunities for the university civic mission at Croatian universities.

NOTES

[1] Discussing the responsibilities of universities and academics to educate socially responsible and active citizens, Wellman (2000) points to the frequent assumption that the learning skills of active citizenship is a collateral effect of the study and the years spent at the university, a product of the fusion of students with other students, academics, programs of study and other activities in the university. Education of socially responsible and active citizens, as Wellman (2000) states, is the responsibility of everybody, but in fact is nobody's job.

[2] What worries a growing number of authors who advocate change of traditional patterns of teaching and research is the possible (unfair) association of the civic mission with the moral obligation of academics, and moral development of students as well. Proponents argue for stronger integration of civic engagement activities in teaching and research, because of their potential to help (I) students in their better and deeper understanding of their chosen profession and professional and civic roles they have, and (II) universities and community cohesion and their joint efforts to provide solutions to the needs and concerns of different social groups in the community (Boyer, 1996; Harkavy and Benson, 1998; Thomas, 2000; Checkoway, 2000, 2001; Gamson, 2001; Ramaley, 2001; Ostrander, 2004; Harkavy, 2006; Karlsson, 2007; Ćulum and Ledić, 2010).

[3] Population in this study consisted of all senior and junior academic staff in the Republic of Croatia employed at seven public universities, under full-time contract. According to the Croatian Central Bureau of Statistics, in the academic year 2008/2009 there were 7934 senior and junior academic staff employed that fit into this described category. From this database, a sample was created, randomly stratified by university and field of discipline, and altogether 3654 e-mails were sent to academics. During the process of data collection the research team sent two reminders for the respondents. The final sample of 570 respondents indicates a somewhat low response rate of 15.59% (previous on-line surveys conducted in Croatia indicate a most common response rate of 10%).

[4] For a detailed analysis of all five categories according to three variables: (i) socioeconomic status, (ii) personal values, and (iii) communication skills, it is recommended to read Rogers, E. M. (2003). *Diffusion of Innovations* (Fifth Edition). New York: Free Press (p. 287-299).

[5] The analysis included a comparison of the results on the type of institution, discipline, academic status, age, gender, and membership in working groups, professional associations and/or civil society organizations in the local community.

[6] Some of the other educational goals identified in the questionnaire were: encouraging the development of knowledge and skills needed for the labour market, encouraging the development of knowledge and skills relevant for the advancement in particular discipline, encouraging the development of knowledge and skills relevant for students' future work in the chosen profession.

[7] $p<0,001$; $t>2,59$ in all three cases.

[8] $p=0,014$; $t>1,96$ (in relation to natural sciences in both cases), $p<0,001$; $t>2,59$ (in relation to technical and medical/biomedical/biotechnical sciences in both cases).

[9] $p<0,001$; $t>2,59$ in both cases.

[10] In situations of high teaching loads, academics do not have enough time to study and analyze the appropriate application of models that promote community-engaged learning (Harwood et al., 2005, Hammond, 1994; Ward, 1996) because it takes away time that should be, according to the current system of academics' promotion, invested in a "major" academic activity (Morton and Tropp, 1996). This challenge has been evidently recognized among Croatian academics, as well – results show that integrating academics' contributions to the community development in the criteria of their promotion and advancement, would serve as an incentive to integrate civic mission into everyday teaching and research for half of the respondents (51.4%).

[11] $p<0,05$; $t>1,96$ in relation to all other age groups for administrative support; $p=0,005$; $t>1,96$ in relation to all other age groups for financial support; $p<0,001$; $t>2,59$ in relation to all other age groups for salary supplements.

[12] $p<0,001$; $t>2,59$ in eight, out of eleven variables. In their study, Abes et al. (2002) indicated a greater willingness of women for the community service-learning integration in everyday teaching and research activities, if they are provided with adequate administrative and logistical support.

REFERENCES

Abes, E. S., Jackson, G., & Jones, S. R. (2002). Factors that motivate and deter faculty use of service-learning. *Michigan Journal of Community Service Learning, 9*(1), 5–17.

Altman, I. A. (1996). Higher education and psychology in the millennium. *American Psychologist*, 51, 371–378.

Astin, A., & Vogelgesang, L. J. (2003). Comparing the effects of community service and service-learning. In Campus Compact's Introduction to service-learning toolkit: readings and resources for faculty (2nd Ed.). RI: Campus Compact.

Astin, A., Vogelsgang, L. J., Ikeda, E. K. & Yee, J. A. (2000). *How service learning affects students*, Los Angeles: Higher Education Research Institute, UCLA.

Berberet, J. (1999). The professoriate and institutional citizenship: Toward a scholarship of service. *Liberal Education*, 85(4), 32–39.

Blackburn, R., & Lawrence, J. (1995). *Faculty at work*. Baltimore: John Hopkins University Press.

Bloomgarden, A. H., & O'Meara, K. A. (2007). Faculty role integration and community engagement: Harmony or cacophony? *Michigan Journal of Community Service Learning, 13*(2), 5–18.

Boyer, E. L. (1996). The scholarship of engagement. *Journal of Public Service and Outreach, 1*(1), 11–20.

Boyer, E. L. (1990). *Scholarship reconsidered: priorities of the professoriate*. Stanford, CA: The Carnegie Foundation for the Advancement of Teaching.

Calhoun, C. (2006). The university and the public good. *Thesis Eleven, 84*, 7–43.

Checkoway, B. (2001). Renewing the civic mission of the american research university. *The Journal of Higher Education, 72*(2), 125–147. Special Issue: The Social Role of Higher Education.

Checkoway, B. (2000). Public service: Our new mission. *Academe, 86* (4), 24–28.

Colbeck, C. L. (2002). Integration: Evaluating faculty work as a whole. *New Directions for Institutional Research. 114*, 43–52.

Colbeck, C. L. (1998). Merging in a seamless blend: How faculty integrate teaching and research. *Journal of Higher Education, 69*(6), 647–671.

Ćulum, B., & Ledić, J. (2010). *Civilna misija sveučilišta – element u tragovima?* Filozofski fakultet u Rijeci: Rijeka.

Driscoll, A. (2007). Review Essay on Kecskes, K. (Ed.). (2006). Engaging departments: Moving faculty culture from private to public, individual to collective focus for the common good, *Michigan Journal of Community Service Learning*, 75–79.

Driscoll, A., Holland, B., Gelmon, S., & Kerrigan, S. (1996). An assessment model for service learning: Comprehensive case studies of impact on faculty, students, community, and institution. *Michigan Journal of Community Service Learning*, 3, 66–71.

Eyler, J. S., Giles, D. E., Stenson, C. M., & Gray, C. J. (2003). *What we know about the effects of service learning on college students, faculty, institutions and communities, 1993–2000*. Introduction to Service-learning Toolkit (3rd ed., pp. 15–22). Providence, RI: Campus Compact.

Eyler, J., Giles, D. E., Jr., Stenson, C. M., & Gray, C. J. (2001). *At a glance: What we know about the effects of service learning on college students, faculty, institutions and communities, 1993–2000* (3rd ed.). Nashville, TN: Vanderbilt University.

Eyler, J. S. (2000). What do we most need to know about the impact of service learning on student learning? *Michigan Journal of Community Service Learning*, Special Issue, 11–17.

Eyler, J. S., & Giles, D. E. (1999). *Where's the learning in service learning?* San Francisco, CA: Jossey-Bass.

Gallini, S. M., & Moely, B. E. (2003). Service learning and engagement, academic challenge, and retention. *Michigan Journal of Community Service Learning*, 10(1), 1–14.

Gamson, Z. (2001). Higher education and rebuilding civic life. *Change*, 29(1), 10–13.

Gladwell, M. (2002). *The Tipping point: How little things can make a big difference*. London, UK: Back Bay Books.

Glassick, C. E., Taylor Huber, M., & Maeroff, G. I. (1997). *Scholarship assesses: Evaluation of the professoriate*. San Francisco: Jossey-Bass Publisher.

Hammond, C. (1994). Integrating service and academic study: Faculty motivation and satisfaction in Michigan higher education. *Michigan Journal of Community Service Learning*, 1(1), 21–28.

Harkavy, I. (2006). The Role of universities in advancing citizenship and social justice in the 21st century. *Education, citizenship and social justice*, 1(1), 5–37.

Karlsson, J. (2007). Service as collaboration - an integrated process in teaching and research: A response to Greenbank. *Teaching in Higher Education*, 12, 281–287.

Harkavy, I., & Benson, L. (1998). De-Platonizing and democratizing education as the basis of service learning. In R. Rhodes & J. Howard (Eds.), *Academic service learning: A pedagogy of action and reflection*. San Francisco: Jossey-Bass.

Harwood, A. M., Ochs, L., Currier, D., Duke, S., Hammond, J., Moulds, L., Stout, K., & Werder, C. (2005). Communities for Growth: Cultivating and Sustaining Service-Learning Teaching and Scholarship in a Faculty Fellows Program. *Michigan Journal of Community Service Learning*, 12(1), 41–51.

Hassinger, E. W., & Pinkerton, J. R. (1986). *The human community*. New York: MacMillan.

Howard-Hamilton, M. (2000). Programming for multicultural competences. *New Directions for Student Services*, 90, 67–78.

Karlsson, J. (2007). Service as collaboration - an integrated process in teaching and research: A response to Greenbank. *Teaching in Higher Education*, 12, 281–287.

Kendall, J. (1990). *Combining service and learning: An introduction. Combining service and learning: A resource book for community and public service*. Vol. 1, Raleigh, N. C.: National Society for Internships and Experiential Education.

Laredo, P. (2007). Revisiting the third mission of universities: toward a renewed categorization of university activities? *Higher Education Policy*, 20(4), 441–456.

Ledić, J. (2007). *U potrazi za civilnom misijom hrvatskih sveučilišta*. In Previšić, V., Šoljan, N. N., Hrvatić, N. (Eds.) Pedagogija – prema cjeloživotnom obrazovanju i društvu znanja. Svezak 1, Zagreb: Hrvatsko pedagoško društvo, 123–134.

Lozano, R. (2006). Incorporation and institutionalization of SD into universities: breaking through barriers to change. *Journal of Cleaner Production*, 14, 787–796.

Macfarlane, B. (2007). *The Academic citizen: The virtue of service in university life*, London and New York: Routledge, Taylor & Francis Group.

Macfarlane, B. (2005). Placing service in academic life. In R. Barnett (ed.), *Reshaping the university: New relations between research, scholarship and teaching* (pp. 165–177). Berkshire: Open University Press.

McKay, V. C., & Rozee, P. D. (2004). Characterics of faculty who adopt community service learning pedagogy. *Michigan Journal of Community Service Learning*, Spring, 21–33.

Moely, B. E., McFarland, M., Miron, D., Mercer, S., & Ilustre, V. (2002). Changes in college students' attitudes and inentions for civic involvement as a function of service-learning experiences. *Michigan Journal of Community Service Learning*, Fall, 18–26.

Morton, K., & Troppe, M. (1996). From margin to the mainstream: Campus Compact's project on integrating service with academic study. *Journal of Business Ethics*, 15, 21–32.

Mundy, M., & Eyler, J. (2002). *Service Learning and Retention: Promising Possibilities, Potential Partnerships.* Vanderbilt University.

Nussbaum, M. C. (1997). *Cultivating humanity: A classical defence of reform in liberal education.* Cambridge: Massachusetts and London: England, Harvard University Press.

O'Meara, K., & Braskamp, L. (2005). Aligning faculty reward system and development to promote faculty and student growth. *NASPA Journal*, *42*(2), 223–240.

Ostrander, S. (2004). Democracy, civic participation, and the university: A comparative study of civic engagement on five universities. *Nonprofit and voluntary sector quarterly*, *33*(1), 74–93.

Pribbenow, D. (2005). The impact of service learning pedagogy on faculty teaching and learning. *Michigan Journal of Community Service Learning*, Spring 2005, 25–38.

Ramaley, J. (2001). Why do we engage in engagement? *Metropolitan Universities: An International Forum*, *12*(3), 13–19.

Reinke, S. J. (2003). Making a difference: Does service learning promote civic engagement in MPA students? *Journal of Public Affairs Education*, *9*(2), 129–137.

Rice, R. E., Sorcinelli, M. D., & Austin, A. (2000). *Heeding new voices: Academic careers for a new generation, New Pathways: Faculty Careers and Employment for the 21st Century*, Inquiry #7. Washington, DC: American Association for Higher Education.

Rice, D., & Stacey, K. (1997). Small group dynamics as a catalyst for change: A faculty development model for academic service-learning. *Michigan Journal of Community Service Learning*, 4, 64–71.

Rogers, E. M. (2003). *Diffusion of Innovations* (5th ed.). New York: Free Press.

Rogers, E. M. (1971). *Communication of innovations: A cross-cultural approach.* New York: The Free Press.

Rončević, N., & Rafajac, B. (2010). *Promjene u akademskoj profesiji: komparativna analiza.* Rijeka: Filozofski fakulet u Rijeci.

Root, S., Callahan, J., & Sepanski, J. (2002). Building teaching dispositions and service-learning practice: A multi-site study. *Michigan Journal of Community Service Learning*, *8*(2), 50–59.

Stanton, T. K. (1994). The experience of faculty participants in an instructional development seminar on service-learning. *Michigan Journal of Community Service Learning*, *1*(1), 7–20.

Strand, J. K. (2000). Community-Based Research as Pedagogy. *Michigan Journal of Community Service Learning.* Fall 2000, 85–96.

Strand, J. K., Marullo, S., Cutforth, N., Stoecker, N., & Donohue, P. (2003). Principles of best practice for community-based research. *Michigan Journal of Community Service Learning.* Fall 2000, 5–15.

Tannenbaum, S. C., & Berrett. R. D. (2005). Relevance of service learning in college courses. Accessed 14.01.2009., http://findarticles.com/p/articles/mi_hb3325/is_/ai_n29182843.

Thomas, N. L. (2000). The College and the university as citizen. In T. Ehrlich (Ed.), *Civic responsibility and higher education* (pp. 63–97). Westport: American Council on Education and Oryx Press.

Ward, K. (1996). Service-learning and student volunteerism: Reflections on institutional commitment. *Michigan Journal of Community Service Learning*, 3, 55–65.

Wellman, C. (2000). *The Proliferation of rights: Moral progress or empty rhetoric?* Oxford: Westview.

Zlotkowski, E. Longo, N., & Williams, J. (2006). *Students as colleagues: Expanding the circle of service learning leadership.* Providence: Campus Compact.

Zlotkowski, E., & Williams, D. (2003). The faculty role in civic engagement. *Peer Review,* *5*(3), 9–11.

Zlotkowsky, E. (1998). A service learning approach to faculty development. In R. A. Rhoads, J. P. F. Howard (Eds.), *Academic Service Learning: A Pedagogy of Action and Reflection*. San Francisco: Jossey-Bass.

Zlotkowsky, E. (1995). Does service learning have a future? *Michigan Journal of Community Service Learning*, Fall 1995, 123–133.

AFFILIATIONS

Bojana Ćulum, PhD
University of Rijeka
Faculty of Humanities and Social Sciences
Department of Education

MICHELE ROSTAN & FLAVIO A. CERAVOLO

CROSSING THE BORDERS

Investigating Social and Economic Forces Shaping International Academic Mobility International Academic Mobility

Academics' physical mobility across state borders is not at all a new phenomenon. Since universities have been established, there has always been a certain degree of international mobility of scholars (Welch, 2008). Nowadays, international academic mobility is deemed to be smaller in size compared to international student mobility (Teichler, 2011) and it is considered just as one of the various modes of border-crossing collaboration within the academy (Marginson & van der Wende, 2009; Rostan, 2012). These elements notwithstanding its relevance for both higher education, research and the academic profession itself has been repeatedly asserted.

Looking at higher education we notice some important facts. Firstly, various forms of short-term mobility, such as visits, exchanges and sabbaticals, are seen as a standard feature of the academic career and the well-functioning of both higher education and research systems (El-Khawas, 2002). Doctoral education abroad as well as advanced studies, and post-doctoral training in another country are considered as widespread and involving a considerable proportion of those engaged in these activities (Kehm, 2004; Nerad, 2010). Both national and supra-national agencies and entities – notably the European Union – promote and support the international mobility of academic teachers and researchers at various stages of their career (e.g. Marie Curie Fellowships, Fullbright Program). The proportion of international academic staff has been used for assessing the quality of higher education institutions both by international rankings and national schemes and exercises (Kehm & Stensaker, 2009; Shin et al., 2011).

Although academic labour markets largely remain nationally bounded, and rules regulating academic profession and career are idiosyncratic, a global market for academic labour is considered as emerging and developing (Altbach & Teichler, 2001; Bauder, 2012; Musselin, 2004, 2005). International movements of academics and researchers are also considered as part of wider processes involving increasing international fluxes of highly skilled and highly educated persons (International migration, 2001). The increasing competition between and within higher education and research and innovation systems enhance and feed these fluxes as well as they prompt targeted migration policies aimed either at attracting foreign born scholars or at "bringing back home" native ones working abroad (Hawthorne, 2008; Wildavsky, 2010).

J. Branković et al., Global Challenges, Local Responses in Higher Education, 79–103.

In order to study international academic mobility, all these elements must be placed in the context of the increasingly globalised higher education which has been and continue to be "highly unequal" (Altbach, 2006). As for other aspects of higher education, the economic status of countries, the size of their academic system, the role played worldwide by the English language are considered to have an impact also on the international mobility of academics. Although these views are largely shared, it is less straightforward to support them with worldwide comparable data. Available data from several supra-national and national sources on the international mobility of scholar are considered scare, incomplete, heterogeneous and poorly comparable (Teichler, 2011). In this respect, large scale international surveys are considered an appropriate means to provide more detailed, encompassing and comparable information on international academic mobility.

Thus, we aim at investigating the social and economic forces shaping international academic mobility relying on data provided by one of these surveys, namely the Changing Academic Profession International Survey (CAP). In order to do so, first, we provide some concepts and definitions on international academic mobility; second, we illustrate some characteristics of the CAP survey; and third, we present the results of a set of multinomial regressions elaborated to estimate the effect of selected macro contextual predictors on different types of international academic mobility, controlled by both individual and organizational indicators.

CONCEPTS AND DEFINITIONS

According to the International Organisation for Migration, migration "is a population movement, encompassing any kind of movement of people, whatever its length, composition and causes"; it is "A process of moving, either across an international border, or within a State" (IOM, 2004, p. 41). When people "leave their country of origin, or the country of habitual residence, to establish themselves either permanently or temporarily in another country," and "An international frontier is therefore crossed" (IOM, 2004, p. 33), international migration occurs.

In this chapter, we prefer to use the term "mobility" to refer to any kind of movement of people while reserving the term "migration" to movement of people entailing a change of residence from one place to another with the purpose of settling down elsewhere. Thus, we understand mobility as a more general concept and migration as a more specific one. Further, we focus on international mobility and migration, that is on movements of people across state borders, leaving aside internal mobility and migration. As a consequence, international academic mobility – also including international academic migration – is conceived as a movement of academics across state borders.

In order to use this definition for studying international academic mobility, several specifications must be added (Teichler, 2011). The first concerns the reference population or the target group to be studied. Here, we consider academics as professionals teaching and researching at least part-time in higher education institutes that offer a baccalaureate degree or higher, that is – at least – a Type A of the OECD classification degree or a Level 5A of the ISCED-97 classification degree. Thus, both academics working at universities and other higher education institutions are included, and the whole range of academic disciplines are accounted for. We also acknowledge that, in some countries, doctoral candidates and/or people holding a postdoctoral position are considered as academics while, in others, they are considered as students.

The second specification refers to the temporal dimension of international population movements. In order to study these movements, three aspects are worth distinguishing. First, as international mobility and migration consist of movements across state borders, it is crucial to determine when during the life of migrants or mobile persons the border of their country of origin or habitual residence is crossed for the first time. This helps at determining whether the experience of mobility or migration occurs early or late in people's life. Second, it is also crucial to determine whether the state borders are crossed only once or more times. This helps at distinguishing a one-way movement between country of origin and country of destination from a circular movement back and forth the country of origin or residence. Third, the length or the duration of either mobility or migration must be considered. Although approximately and arbitrarily, it might be possible to distinguish short-term and long-term experiences of mobility or migration[1]. In this chapter, we consider mobility or migration experiences occurring either early or late in academics' life, one-way as well as circular international movements of academics, short-term and long-term experiences of mobility or migration.

Finally, it is necessary to specify the reasons or purposes for being mobile. In the context of the academic profession, there are two main reasons for being mobile. For educational and training purposes, academics-to-be can study abroad possibly earning a degree (from 1st level degree to doctoral degree) and/or can spend periods abroad as part of their advanced studies or early career. For employment and work purposes, academics can spend periods abroad as part of their current job (e.g. visits, sabbatical, exchanges, other assignments) or may find a job abroad. We shall address both these aspects of academic mobility.

THE CHANGING ACADEMIC PROFESSION SURVEY

The Changing Academic Profession International Survey provides data for studying international academic mobility. The survey has been carried out in the year 2007/2008 in 18 countries and the Special Administrative Region of Hong Kong on about 25,000 academics[2].

Although the surveyed countries are not representative of the more 200 countries existing worldwide, they capture a considerable amount of the variation existing across nations. The international sample includes academics from countries located in different continents: 7 in Europe, 1 in Africa, 5 in Asia, 1 in Oceania, 3 in North America and 2 in South America. Besides China, which is the largest country according to total population, there are other 4 large countries (the US, Brazil, Japan and Mexico). There are also 7 medium-size countries (Germany, the UK, Italy, South Korea, South Africa, Argentina and Canada), and 7 small countries (Malaysia, Australia, the Netherlands, Portugal, Hong Kong, Finland and Norway)[3]. These countries have different linguistic traditions. Taking English as reference language because of its international role as the contemporary *lingua franca*, participating countries cluster into three groups. There are 3 countries where English is the only main or official language, 4 countries where English is an official language among others[4] and 12 countries where English is not an official language. Some of the non-English speaking countries belong to other international language areas based on German, Spanish and Portuguese. Further, the economies of the surveyed countries are different. According to the World Bank country classification based on income, participating countries are characterised by two types of economies. The 13 "high income" countries are characterised by mature economies while the 6 "upper middle income" countries are characterised by emerging economies[5]. Although many other characteristics differentiate participating countries, it is suffice to mention here that also their higher education systems and their national research systems are remarkably different (Cummings, 2008).

The CAP questionnaire addressed several aspects of the academic profession: teaching and research activities, career history and mobility, academics' demographic background, including citizenship and education. It also collected valuable information on international issues including information on periods abroad that respondents spent since the award of their first higher education degree (Huang et al., 2014). More specifically, the CAP survey provides information on events along academics' life course in three spheres of life: family, education and the labour market. All these data refer to a specified point in time and most of them provide information on the country in which they occurred[6].

As the CAP survey collected individual level data on several aspects of respondents' life, we can investigate international academic mobility throughout the entire academics' life course (Teichler, 2011).

Taking as a term of reference data on the country of current employment at the time when the survey was carried out, it is possible to compare the information they provide – on place, time and activity – with other information for which country is specified. As a consequence, it is possible to know whether respondents were born in the country of current employment or not. We consider as migrants those academics who were born in a country different from the country of their current employment and who crossed the borders of that country at different stages of their life and for different purposes. In this way, it is possible to distinguish them from the other respondents.

It is also possible to ascertain whether respondents earned their study degree – 1st and/or 2nd cycle degrees – and their advanced degrees – doctoral and/or postdoctoral degrees – in the country of current employment or not. Three categories of academics can be distinguished combining this information with the previous one.

First, academics who were born abroad but earned their study degrees and/or their advanced degrees in the country of current employment. Second, academics who were born abroad and earned abroad their degrees. Third, academics who, while being born in the country of their current employment, nevertheless earned at least one of their degrees in another country.

Finally, taking into account also information on periods spent abroad, it is possible to identify those academics that although being born and having earned their degrees in the country of their current employment nevertheless spent some time abroad during their career.

TYPES OF INTERNATIONAL ACADEMIC MOBILITY

International academic mobility is not a homogeneous phenomenon. Relying on the CAP data presented above, it is possible to identify six types of academics: five of mobile ones and, besides, one of non-mobile (Rostan & Höhle, 2014).

The first type includes academics who were born in the country of their current employment, earned all their higher education degrees in their native country, and never spent periods abroad during their career. On the basis of available information, we can say that these people never experienced international mobility. This type account for 58% of the CAP international sample.

The second type (16%) includes academics who while being born in the country of current employment, have earned at least one of their higher education degrees abroad. Their experience abroad started early in their life and has had a rather short duration. It was aimed at educational purposes. As this type of mobility entails circulation of academics-to-be across countries' borders, we may refer to it as international educational circulation, and to those involved in it as academics internationally circulating for study.

The third type (10%) includes academics who while being born in the country of current employment and having earned their degrees there, have nevertheless spent short periods abroad during their career. Although CAP data do not tell us how many times they have been abroad, overall they have stayed in another country for no more than two years. Their experience abroad started rather late in their life, has had a short duration and has had professional purposes. This type of mobility entails circulation across the borders of the country of current employment, as well. Consequently, we may refer to it as international short-term professional circulation and to academics involved in it as internationally circulating for work spending short periods abroad.

The fourth type (6%) is similar to the third one, but overall academics included in it have stayed abroad for more than two years. Consequently, we may refer to it as international long-term professional circulation and to academics involved in it as internationally circulating for work spending long periods abroad.

The fifth type (6%) includes academics who were born in a country different from the country of their current employment and have earned all their degrees abroad.

These people entered the country of their current employment being fully qualified for a job in higher education. Their experience abroad started late in their life, and it was still on-going at the time when the survey was carried out. As this type of mobility entails a one-way movement from the country of origin, that is the country of residence at birth, to the country of destination, that is the country of current employment, we may refer to it as international job migration. As mentioned before, we can consider academics involved in it as international late migrants for work.

The sixth type (5%) includes academics who were born in a country different from the country of their current employment and moved to it to earn a degree. These people entered the country where they were working at the time of the survey as student. Later on they found a job in higher education. Their experience abroad started quite early in their life and was still continuing at the time when the CAP survey was carried out. Again, this type of mobility entails a one-way movement from the country of origin to the country of destination. Therefore, we may refer to it as educational early migration and to those involved in it as international early migrant for study.

Table 1. Countries of current employment by the proportion of mobile academics and t ype of mobility

	High	Medium	Low
Early circulation for study	MY, KR, HK	NO, CA, MX, AR, PT, BR	DE, UK, IT, ZA, AU, FI, JP, NL, CN, US
Late short job circulation	IT, JP	BR, KR, FI, NO, DE	US, MY, NL, AU, CA, AR, ZA, UK, PT, CN, MX, HK
Late long job circulation	JP, BR, FI, AU	IT, NO, NL, US, UK	CA, PT, DE, KR, ZA, CN, AR, MX, HK, MY
Early migration for study	AU, CA, US	DE, UK, NO, PT, HK, ZA	NL, FI, BR, MY, JP, MX, AR, IT, KR, CN
Late job migration	HK, CA, AU, NO	UK, NL, FI, US	DE, MY, ZA, MX, PT, IT, BR, AR, JP, KR, CN

Source: CAP Data Set, September 2011.

Notes: Country of current employment is also the country of destination in case of migration. The definition of high, medium and low proportions of mobile academics refers to the average value for each type of mobility; i.e. Low = below average; Medium = between average and one standard deviation above average; High = over one standard deviation above average; average values are provided in the text. Weighted data.

It has to be noted that the countries of origin of the migrant academics who have been interviewed do not necessarily coincide with the countries participating in the CAP survey. The latter must be considered as countries of destination of migrant fluxes while the former are more than 100 countries around the world, excluding the participating ones.

As it is shown in Table 1, the five types of mobile academics are distributed unevenly across the participating countries. International educational circulation is especially frequent in two Asian countries – Malaysia and South Korea – and in the Special Administrative Region of Hong Kong. Academics from Italy and Japan are especially involved in short-term professional circulation while again Japanese academics, and their colleagues from Brazil, Finland and Australia are especially active in long-term professional circulation. Australia, Canada and the United States are the most frequent destinations of early migration while Hong Kong, Canada, Australia and Norway are the most frequent destinations of late migration. On the whole, Australia, Canada and Hong Kong appear to be countries remarkably involved in international academic mobility as they show a high proportion of mobile academics in at least two different types of our classification.

EXPLAINING INTERNATIONAL ACADEMIC MOBILITY

International academic mobility can be influenced by a wide range of factors which can vary according to several dimensions of international academic mobility (Hoffman, 2009). Factors having an impact in the early stages of academics' life course refer likely to family and education while those having an impact in later stages of life likely refer to career and work. On the other hand, factors influencing migration may be different from factors influencing circulation. Moreover, mechanisms which regulate migration and circulation processes are complex and combine different levels of the determinants of individual choices and actions. By using an analytical perspective, we can identify three main groups of determinants. The first one refers to individual ascriptive characteristics, the second relates to the individual career path and to the institutional and organizational settings in which actors are embedded, the third has a macro structural nature and has a strict relationship with contextual characteristics, such as country characteristics. In this chapter, we focus on the influence on academic mobility of factors pertaining to this last level.

For each type of academic mobility presented in the previous paragraph, we have elaborated a multinomial logistic regression including as predictors variables of the three above mentioned levels. In this way, we can use the individual and institutional/ organizational predictors as control dimensions to study the net impact on mobility of macro-context indicators. To respect the logical antecedence between predictors and analysed events, we have included different sets of variables according to the type of mobility analysed in the model. In particular, we have not included any information concerning academic career and work in the models regarding experiences of mobility occurred early in academics' life, either migration or circulation. As shown in the next paragraph, we have included information on both the country of birth and the country of current employment only in the two models referring to migration while in the three models referring to circulation the country of birth and the country of employment coincide.

Before presenting each model of regression and its results, we illustrate the indicators included in the analysis.

PREDICTORS AND CONTROL VARIABLES

As English is increasingly the contemporary *lingua franca* in the academy as it is outside it (Altbach, 2006; Rostan, 2011), the first macro structural dimension included in the models refers to country linguistic tradition. We expect that countries where English is used as the main or the official language, or as one of the official languages, play a different role in influencing migration and mobility patterns than those where English is not the official language or one of the official languages. In studying academic migration, we take into consideration the status of English in both academics' country of birth, that is their country of origin, and country of current employment at the time when the CAP survey was carried out, that is their country of destination. In studying academic circulation, we consider only the country of current employment which is at the same time respondents' country of birth. Countries are divided into three categories: countries where English is the only main or official language, countries where English is one of the official languages, and countries where English is not an official language.

The second interpretative dimension takes into account the size of both the country of birth and the country of academics' employment at the time when the survey was carried out. The indicator has been organised into three classes from the smallest to the largest in terms of population. We have included this indicator to investigate two opposite hypotheses. Compared to small countries, large countries with vast higher education systems can offer to individuals valuable assets such as a broader range of study opportunities, especially at the post-graduate level, better chances to find an academic position, larger scientific communities in all the disciplines, a greater endowment of equipment and devices. According to this consideration, we should expect that respondents being born and working in large countries would be less mobile. On the other hand, large countries may pool more resources to finance the circulation and the internationalization of their students and researchers. Therefore, we should expect that academics living and working in larger countries would be more mobile. In the two models on educational and job migration, we have also included the size of the country of birth to control the hypothesis that people from larger country are less likely to be involved in the migration process because of the greater opportunities they have within their country.

As mobility may vary according not only to country size but also to country wealth, we have included in the explicative models also indicators regarding the economic status of a country. As mentioned, countries participating in the survey, which are also the countries of academics' employment at the time when it was carried out, can be divided into two categories, those characterised by a mature economy and those characterised by an emerging economy according to the World Bank classification of countries based on income. Academics' countries of birth can also be divided into two categories. On the one hand, countries with a mature economy, and, on the other hand, those with emerging and less developed economies, that is countries with a lower income. Thus, we should expect a net impact of the economic status of a country on academic mobility in two directions. First, we can hypothesize that mature economies attract students and researchers from other countries because of the greater supply of job and study opportunities and funds. Second, mature economies may afford much more initiatives for internationalization, enhancing, as a consequence, the mobility of academics.

The last macro structural dimension included in the models refers to countries' cultural, political and organizational tradition. The correspondent indicator discriminates between Asian and non-Asian countries to take into account differences between the two respective macro-regional traditions. Within Asian countries, we also distinguish between China and other countries because of the international role of China and the great number of Chinese respondents included in the international sample.

Moving to individual level indicators we maintain that international academic mobility is influenced by social inequality through ascriptive factors. A wealthy economic condition of the family of origin provides resources to support individual migration projects for purposes of study early in the life course. Moreover, parents' cultural capital could give better cognitive abilities and foster higher social expectations about the usefulness of international experiences, thus influencing the choice of following higher education path, or a part of it, in foreign countries. Sometimes, the acquisition of a higher education qualification abroad represents a convenient credential to enter the elite class in the country of birth. In order to account for this dimension, we include in the analysis an indicator based on parents' education. The indicator assumes value 1 if at least one of the parents has a tertiary education qualification and value 0 if neither father nor mother has a tertiary degree[7].

Others important dimensions of social stratification are represented by gender, age and individual human capital. Both academic recruiting processes and careers are quite different according to them. Women have much more difficulties to gain access to academic positions especially in research contexts while gaining access to teaching contexts is less difficult. Later, their careers are more fragmented and slower than men's ones. Some of the factors explaining gender unbalances in general – such as different styles of socialization, inequalities within organizations (Crompton, 2001; Moss Kanter, 1993), differences in life courses and family responsibilities (maternity, double presence, etc.) – may influence the opportunity to experience international mobility, or impose the choice of short-term mobility rather than long-term or stable experiences. Thus, the crucial role of gender as a control variable is largely accepted. Age is very relevant, as well. We have decided to include in the analyses this indicator in terms of birth cohorts. We aim at controlling two aspects related to age. First, there is the stage of the life course within which individual respondents are placed. Second, there is the historical generation which respondents belong to[8]. Age is divided into four cohorts: born up to 1950, born 1951 – 1960, born 1961-1970, and born in 1971 and after. The last individual indicator included in the analysis refers to respondents' human capital. The indicator assumes value 1 when the subject holds a doctoral or post-doctoral degree and value 0 when he/she does not. This indicator permits to take into account the influence of different levels of qualification on academic mobility. Lastly, we have introduced the linguistic dimension in the analysis relying on an indicator regarding the individual use of English in teaching and research. Respondents are divided into three categories: those primarily using English in teaching and/or research as it is their mother tongue; those primarily using English in teaching and/or research as it is their second language; those who do not primarily use English in teaching and research. English proficiency can increase the probability of international relations and mobility while not being able to use English can represent a barrier hindering mobility. In short, individual competence in using English is deemed essential to determine mobility opportunities.

At the institutional level, we have included in the analysis several indicators. They refer to the type of institution in which individuals practice their profession, academic rank, respondents' academic discipline, the emphasis of their primary research, either basic or applied, or a combination of both, and their preferences for teaching and research. The first indicator concerns the type of institution in which academics are employed distinguishing between universities and other higher education institutions[9]. Academic rank has been included in order to take in account the influence of academic hierarchy on international mobility. Academic rank has been included supposing that rules and practices applying to lower positions inhibit mobility (Musselin, 2004) while higher positions in the academic hierarchy increase the probability of being internationally mobile thanks to wider networks, greater visibility and more resources (Jung et al., 2014; Smeby & Gornitzka, 2008). It is also possible that international research and teaching enhance the chances to enter the professoriate so we can expect a higher proportion of internationally active academics in higher academic positions. The academic rank indicator includes only two positions. The first position includes "senior" academics that are full or associated professors and equivalent ranks. A second position includes "junior" academics and "others" that is lower ranks.

Different disciplinary communities have different levels and practices of international relations (Becher & Trowler, 2001; Braxton & Hargens, 1996; Jöns, 2007). Sharing common paradigms, languages, and research programmes – as it is more frequent within the hard sciences – may foster international collaboration and mobility[10]. In other cases, the international orientation of the objects of study themselves requires a period of mobility, such as in area studies, international politics, historical studies or anthropology. Thus, we have included in the analysis an indicator articulated into five main groups of disciplines. The five groups are (1) Education & humanities, (2) Social sciences, business & law, (3) Science, (4) Engineering, manufacturing, construction & architecture, and (5) Medical sciences, health related sciences & social services. When studying early mobility the discipline of the highest degree is considered while when studying late mobility the discipline of teaching is considered.

Finally, two other parameters for controlling data analysis are provided by indicators on the orientation of individual research – either basic or applied – and on individual preferences in teaching and research activities. In fact, it is supposed that involvement in basic research more frequently implies some international dimensions and consequently different types of geographic mobility than the involvement in applied research. Further, there are differences between the type of mobility required by a research-driven activity and the type required by a teaching-driven activity.

FACTORS SHAPING INTERNATIONAL ACADEMIC MOBILITY

As anticipated, we have estimated a model for each type of academic mobility. Each model tests the probability that an individual has to fall within a specific type of mobility (coded 1) against the probability that she or he has to be included in one of the other types of mobility (coded 2) or the probability of not having experienced any type of mobility during her or his life (coded 0). In this way, from a stochastic point of view, we can evaluate the net impact of predictors on each type of mobility entirely including in each model the surveyed population. Thus, the reliability of the analyses increases controlling possible selection biases.

We first illustrate the two models referring to experiences occurring early in the life course, namely circulating or migrating for study purposes. Second, we present the three models referring to experiences occurring late in the life course, namely short-term and long-term professional circulation and job migration. Tables reporting regression models' estimates are presented in the Appendix[11].

Early in Life: Educational Circulation

The model tests the probability of experiencing educational circulation (Table 2). All the indicators included in the model are significant from a stochastic point of view. The first structural dimension, which is taken into account, is country linguistic tradition. Being born in countries where English is the main or the official language relevantly decreases the probability of early circulation for study. On the contrary, being born in countries where English is just one of the official languages dramatically increases this probability. Country size has the same type of impact of the English language. Regression parameters point out that when the country of birth is small or – to a lesser extent – medium size the net effect on early circulation is positive. This finding highlights the possible existence of a flux of students from smaller to larger countries, thus substantially supporting the view that a wider range of academic opportunities in larger countries acts as a pole of attraction for students from smaller ones.

Further, academics working and being born in a country with a mature economy have a dramatically lower probability to have had an experience of early mobility for study purposes. Finally, compared to academics of the rest of the world, Chinese academics are less likely to have been mobile for study while academics from other Asian countries are more likely to have studied abroad[12].

Summarizing, this model shows that academics who were born and were working at the time when the survey was carried out in countries where English is one official or main language among others or in non-English speaking countries, in small or medium size countries, and in emerging countries are more likely to have been involved in international educational circulation. These findings suggest the existence of a circular movement: people move from smaller countries and emerging economies to larger and mature ones, coming back later on to the former. English-only speaking countries attract academics-to-be for study purposes. Besides, coming from a country where English is one of the widely spoken languages better equip academics-to-be for participating in this movement.

Early in Life: Educational Migration

The second model investigates early migration (Table 3). There are similarities but also important differences in respect to the first model. Compared to academics who were born in non-English speaking countries, both academics who were born in counties where English is the main or the official language and – albeit to a lesser extent – academics who were born in countries where English is one of the official languages are less likely to migrate early in their life. Parameters regarding the status of English in the country of current employment go just in the opposite direction. Working in countries where English is widely used either as main or official language or as one of the official languages, increase tremendously the likelihood of having experienced early migration.

These two predictors are coherent but also independent one from the other. Their estimates can be read together indicating an early "brain drain" phenomenon from non-English speaking countries to English speaking ones. Country size and economic status indicators have an independent effect, as well. Being born in a small or medium size country increases the likelihood of migrating for study purposes. Otherwise, the size of the country of current employment seems to have no stochastic effect.

Finally, parameters regarding the economic status of the country of birth and the country of current employment show tendencies which are very similar to those documented regarding the status of English. Compared to emerging or less developed economies, being born in a country characterised by a mature economy lowers the risk of early migration. On the contrary, working in a mature economy increases the probability of having experienced early migration. Again, we can detect a flux moving academics-to-be from less developed to more developed countries.

It has to be noted that the indicator on the Asian region was not included in the models because, among Chinese academics, those who have experienced early migration are practically absent.

Late in Life: Short-Term & Long-Term Professional Circulation

International circulation for professional purposes is investigated in two separate models. We have distinguished between short-term (Table 4) and long-term (Table 5) experiences.

As expected, the linguistic tradition of the country where academics were employed at the time of the survey has an impact. Working in a country where English is the main or the only official language hinders both short-term and long-term circulation. These findings suggest that academics working in non-English speaking countries are more likely to be involved in international professional circulation than others.

Short-term circulation does not depend on the size of countries. It depends on their economic status and on the divide between China and other countries. Working in mature economies compared to emerging ones enhances short-term circulation while working in China instead of in other countries hinders it. Long-term circulation depends on both country size, country economic status and the divide between China, other Asian countries and non-Asian ones. Working in medium size countries hinders long-term circulation while working in mature economies favours it. Compared to non-Asian countries, working in China hinders long-term circulation while working in other Asian countries favours it.

Late in Life: Job Migration

Job migration is investigated in the last model (Table 6). As it is for educational migration, also for job migration data on the status of the English language in both countries of birth and countries of employment clearly show the direction of the migration fluxes. Academics migrating for employment reasons move from non-English speaking countries to English speaking ones.

Country characteristics have a strong impact on job migration. Academics born in small countries are less likely to be involved in job migration than their colleagues from large countries. On the opposite, parameters show a positive effect of attraction which is played, net of other predictors, especially by smaller, but also by medium-size countries. Finally, migrants clearly move from emerging and less developed economies to mature ones.

CONCLUSIONS

International academic mobility is a quite complex phenomenon to be disentangled. By using a life-course perspective, it has been possible to identify five main types of academic mobility and to analyse the different factors influencing them. The complexity of the phenomenon and the wide range of predictors associated with it have caused the impossibility of calculating one general multinomial regression model including all types of mobility. As a consequence, it was not possible to carry out a direct comparison among them. For these reasons, we have elaborated five models – one for each type – including predictors of different levels of generality, but focusing on the macro-structural one.

We have included at the macro level indicators concerning the status of the English language in the country of birth and in the country of current employment, the size of the country where respondents were born and of the country where they pursue their academic activities, and the economic status of the country of birth and the country of current employment. Finally, an indicator provides information on countries' cultural traditions and other organizational and political features discriminating between Asian or non-Asian country.

A comparative analysis of the models reveals that controlling for individual and organizational dimensions the role of contextual predictors remains relevant in terms of their stochastic impact on each type of academic mobility. This suggests that social and economic macro-structural forces influence individual opportunities and personal strategies of academic mobility.

The five presented types of mobility can be associated with three broad issues, namely brain drain, brain circulation, and the functioning of a global academic labour market. Briefly discussing these issues sheds light on social and economic forces shaping international academic mobility.

Both educational migration and job migration are related to the brain drain phenomenon. In fact, these types of mobility have been identified on the basis of a one-way movement transferring future or actual academics and their human capital from one country to another. According to the CAP data, academic brain drain involves about 10% of the international sample.

The analysis of both educational and job migration shows that people and their human capital move from non-English speaking countries to English-speaking ones, and from emerging or less developed economies to mature ones. These findings confirm the dominant role of the English language within the academy worldwide. Further, they highlight the attractive role of English speaking and wealthier countries which are able to drain academic human resources at the global level. Country size plays a different role in the two types of academic migration. As far as educational migration, academics-to-be move from small and medium size countries to countries of any size. Thus, it seems that country size acts as a push factor but not as a pull one. As far as job migration, academics who were born in small countries are less likely to move compared to those who were born in large countries while small and medium size countries are more likely than large ones to attract academic workers. Finally, it is worth noticing that China as a country of destination seems to be not involved or least involved in the academic brain drain phenomenon as both migrants for study and job migrants are absent in the Chinese sample.

Educational and professional circulation are part of the brain circulation phenomenon. Academics circulating either for study purposes early in life or later on for professional purposes account for 32% of the CAP sample.

The three types of circulation display both differences and similarities as regard as factors shaping them. Academics working in non-English speaking countries are more likely to circulate internationally than others. This does not hold for educational circulation because academics working in countries where English is one of the official or main languages among others are more likely to have studied abroad than academics working in both non-English speaking countries and countries where English is the only official or main language. It might be that the heritage of British colonialism has turned into an advantage for some academics-to-be within an increasingly global higher education. The impact of country economic status is differentiated, as well. Being born and working in a mature economy hinders educational circulation while it favours professional circulation. Thus, it seems that mature economies provide enough opportunities and resources to train at home future academics while providing them enough opportunities and resources to be internationally active once they have entered the profession. While professional circulation is less related to country size – although academics from medium-size countries are less likely to be involved in long-term professional circulation than others – this factor has a strong impact on educational circulation. In fact, academics working in small and medium-size countries are more likely to have studied abroad than their colleagues from large countries. Finally, data analysis highlights a clear divide within Asian countries. Chinese academics are less likely to be internationally circulating either for study or professional purposes than their non-Asian colleagues, but academics working in other Asian countries are more likely to circulate than both their Chinese and Western colleagues. It might be that this "international activism" is part of a broader strategy to "catch up" in a more globalised higher education and research system.

Both long-term professional circulation and job migration provide information on the functioning of the world academic labour market. Academics moving to another country to find a job or because they answered positively to a job offer account for about 12% of the CAP sample. What we know about job migration suggests that while the supply of academic labour force comes from non-English speaking, and emerging or less developed economies, the demand comes from English-speaking countries, and mature economies. Moreover, the demand seems to be stronger in small and medium-size countries than in large ones.

In interpreting findings on long-term professional circulation, it is worth remembering that this type of mobility includes academics who left their native country to work abroad for quite long periods being back home when the survey was carried out. Academics participating in this segment of the world labour market are more likely to be found in non-English speaking countries, mature economies and Asian countries other than China. As we do not know where academics circulating for professional purposes spent long periods abroad, we do not have any information on the demand side of this segment of the labour market. Comparing findings from the analyses of these two types of mobility, we can only speculate that the demand for "long stayers" abroad may come from English speaking countries and mature economies.

To sum up, data collected by the Changing Academic Profession International Survey show that macro-structural factors shape, or continue to shape, international academic mobility. Further, countries' linguistic traditions, size, economic status and regional location do have an impact on international mobility although in different ways according to different types of mobility. Finally, data confirm the existence, or the persistence, of inequalities between English speaking and non-English speaking countries, more developed and less developed countries, smaller and larger countries, and the existence of differences between China, other Asian countries and Western countries.

NOTES

[1] As the CAP questionnaire does not provide information on how many periods abroad respondents have spent, but only on the total length of periods abroad, it has been decided to consider short periods abroad those lasting two years or less and to consider long periods abroad those lasting more than two years.

[2] The reference population of the CAP Survey is composed of professionals in higher education institutions that offer a baccalaureate degree or higher. A minimum "effective" sample size of 800 returned questionnaires with most items answered have been achieved in all countries. Three countries – Canada, South Korea and the U.S – administered the survey on-line; the remaining sixteen administered paper version either through the post or distributed in local academic staff university mailboxes. Average response rates is 28% (St. Dev. 18.4%), with significant variation by country (Huang et al. 2014; Teichler et al., 2013).

[3] Countries with more than 100 million of inhabitants are classified as "large," countries with more than (or equal to) 30 million and less than 100 million inhabitants are considered "medium" size, and countries with less than 30 million inhabitants are classified as "small."

[4] English is not an official language in Malaysia. Nevertheless, historically it was the de facto administrative language, and it remains an active second language especially in education and business. Thus, we consider Malaysia as a country where English is widely used.

[5] See http://data.worldbank.org/about/country-classifications.

[6] These events – and the related individual statuses to which they refer – are the following: 1) birth (year); 2) first degree (year, country); 3) second degree (year, country); 4) doctoral degree (year, country); 5) postdoctoral degree (year, country); 6) first full-time appointment beyond research and teaching assistant in the higher education/research sector (year); 7) first appointment to current institution beyond research and teaching assistant (year); 8) appointment/promotion to current rank at current institution (year); 9) current employment (year, country); 10) current familial status (year); 11) current natural or social parenthood (year); 12), 13), 14) citizenship (at birth, at 1st degree, current; country); 15), 16), 17) residence (at birth, at 1st degree, current; country).

[7] The relationship between the economic, cultural and social conditions of the family is still quite strict (Shavit et al., 2007), so we can assume that parents' educational attainment provides information also on family wealth and social networks.

[8] Following an analytical perspective based on the life course to identify several types of international academic mobility, it is essential to investigate the determinants of each type controlling for age cohorts. Further, age cohorts are, albeit approximately, related to seniority, that is to time spent working in higher education. The role of seniority in determining opportunity and type of mobility could be very significant. Moving to a more global perspective, the historical period when individuals are professionally active could also be relevant. International mobility can be affected by the geo-political characteristics of a period and/or by different phases of expansion of higher education systems. Economic and technological changes are relevant, as well. Progresses in ICT during the last decade have made several opportunities close to hand. A rich flow of information from any part of the world is increasingly available. A conference call with a colleague located very far away is now possible simply using internet and communication devices on a laptop. Besides, low costs of transportation encourage short term visits and meetings. Summarizing, during the last decades of

the XX century and the first of the XXI, technological opportunities have dramatically changed the concept of spatial distance itself (Beck, 1999). We suggest that these aspects could partially be taken into account in the analysis thanks to the age cohort indicator.

⁹   While the latter are considered serving local communities and regional economies, universities have always been more international in scope. More recently, international relations and networks in both research and teaching activities have been considered as an indicator of high quality both at the individual and at the organizational levels. Further, internationalization has been taken into consideration in evaluating universities.

¹⁰   Specific technology labs and facilities, such as in nuclear physics or astronomy, or specific research objects, such as in archaeology, uniquely available in some locations, influences the rate and style of mobility of the individual researchers belonging to a specific community.

¹¹   Tables in the Appendix report only the estimates for the considered type of mobility (code 1). Full tables can be asked to authors (michele.rostan@unipv.it, flavioantonio.ceravolo@unipv.it).

¹²   It has to be noted that, at the time of the survey, only 11.5% of the academics included in the Chinese sample were working at National public universities while most of them (88.5%) were working either at Local public universities or at Local public colleges. This fact, together with the inclusion of both younger and older scholars within the sample, may explain why few Chinese academics have studied abroad.

REFERENCES

Altbach, Ph. G., & U. Teichler (2001). Internationalization and exchanges in a globalized university. *Journal of Studies in International Education, 5*(1), 5–25.

Altbach, Ph. G. (2006). Globalization and the university: Realities in an Unequal World. In J. J. F. Forest, & P. G. Altbach (Eds.), *International Handbook of Higher Education. Part two: Regions and Countries.* Dordrecht: Springer.

Bauder, H. (2012). The international mobility of academics: A labour market perspective. *International Migration* (Article first published online: 21 AUG 2012; DOI: 10.1111/j.1468-2435.2012.00783.x).

Becher, T., & P. R. Trowler (2001). *Academic tribes and territories: Intellectual inquiry and the culture of disciplines.* Milton Keynes, UK: The Society for Research into Higher Education & Open University Press.

Beck U. (1999). *What is globalization?* Cambridge: Polity Press.

Braxton, J. M., & Hargens, L. L. (1996). Variation among academic disciplines: Analytical frameworks and research. In J. C. Smart (Ed.), *Higher education: Handbook of theory and research*, vol. 11. New York: Agathon Press.

Crompton, R. (2001). Gender restructuring, employment, and caring. *Social Politics 8*, 266–291.

Cummings, W. K. (2008). The context for the changing academic profession: A survey of international indicators. *RIHE International Seminar Reports, 12*, 33–56.

El-Khawas, E. (2002). Developing an Academic Career in a Globalising World. In J. Enders, & O. Fulton (Eds.), *Higher Education in a Globalising World. International Trends and Mutual Observations.* Dordrecht: Kluwer Academic Publishers.

Hawthorne, L. (2008). *The growing global demand for students as skilled migrants.* Washington, DC: Migration Policy Institute.

Huang, F., Finkelstein, M., & Rostan, M. (Eds.) (2014). *The Internationalisation of the Academy: Changes, Realities and Prospects.* Dordrecht: Springer.

Hoffman, D. M. (2009). Changing academic mobility patterns and international migration: What will academic mobility mean in the 21st century? *Journal of Studies in International Education, 13*, 347–364.

The Migration of Professionals (2001). Special issue. *International Migration, 39*(5), 3–132.

International Organisation for Migration (2004). *Glossary on Migration.* Geneva: IOM.

Kehm, B. M. (2004). Developing doctoral degrees and qualifications in Europe: Good practice and issues of concern. A Comparative Analysis. In J. Sadlak (Ed.), *Doctoral Studies and Qualifications in Europe and the United States: Status and Prospects.* Bucharest, UNESCO.

Kehm, B. M., & Stensaker, B. (Eds.) (2009). *University rankings. diversity and the landscape of higher education*. Rotterdam and Taipei: Sense Publishers.

Jöns, H. (2007). Transnational mobility and the spaces of knowledge production: A comparison of global patterns, motivations and collaborations in different academic fields. *Social Geography*, 2, 97–114.

Jung, J., Kooij, R., & Teichler, U. (2014). Internationalization and the new generation of academics. In F. Huang, M. Finkelstein, & M. Rostan (Eds.), *The Internationalisation of the Academy: Changes, Realities and Prospects*. Dordrecht: Springer.

Marginson, S., & van der Wende, M. (2009). Europeanisation, international rankings and faculty mobility: Three cases in higher education globalisation. In OECD - centre for educational research and innovation, *Higher Education to 2030*, Vol. 2, Globalisation. Paris: OECD.

Moss Kanter, R. (1993). *Men and women of the corporation*. New York: Basic Books.

Musselin, C. (2004). Towards a European academic labour market? Some lessons drawn from empirical studies on academic mobility. *Higher Education*, 48(1), 55–78.

Musselin, C. (2005), European academic labor markets in transition. *Higher Education*, 49(1/2), 135–154.

Nerad, M. (2010). Globalization and the internationalization of graduate education: A macro and micro view. *Canadian Journal of Higher Education - Revue canadienne d'enseignement supérieur*, 40(1), 1–12.

Rostan, M. (2011). English as "Lingua Franca" and the internationalization of academe. *International Higher Education*, 63, 11–13.

Rostan, M. (2012). Beyond physical mobility: Other ways to internationalise the academic profession. In M. Vukasovic, P. Maassen, B. Stensaker, M. Nerland, R. Pinheiro, & A. Vabø (Eds.), *Effects of Higher Education Reforms: Change Dynamics*. Rotterdam: Sense Publishers.

Rostan, M., & E. Höhle (2014). The International Mobility of Faculty. In F. Huang, M. Finkelstein & M. Rostan (Eds.), *The internationalisation of the academy: Changes, realities and prospects*. Dordrecht: Springer.

Shavit, Y., Arum, R., Gamoran, A., & G. Menahem, (Eds.) (2007). *Stratification in higher education: A comparative study*. Palo Alto: Stanford University Press.

Shin, J. C., Toutkoushian, R. K., & Teichler, U. (Eds.) (2011). *University rankings: Theoretical basis, methodology, and impacts on global higher education*. Dordrecht: Springer.

Smeby, J. C. & Gornitzka, Å. (2008). All cosmopolitans now? The changing international contacts of university researchers. In Å. Gornitzka, & L. Langfeldt (Eds.), *Borderless Knowledge. Understanding the "New" Internationalisation of Research and Higher Education in Norway*. Dordrecht: Springer.

Teichler, U. (2011). Academic Staff Mobility. In U. Teichler, I. Ferencz, & B. Wächter (Eds.), *Mapping mobility in European higher education. Volume I: Overview and trends*. Brussels: European Commission, Directorate General for Education and Culture.

Teichler, U., Arimoto, A., & W. K. Cummings (2013). *The changing academic profession. major findings of a comparative survey*. Dordrecht: Springer.

Welch, A. (2008). Myths and modes of mobility: The changing face of academic mobility in the global Era. In M. Byram, & F. Dervin (Eds.), *Students, staff and academic mobility in higher education*. Newcastle: Cambridge Scholars Publishing.

Wildavsky, B. (2010). *The great brain race: How Global universities are reshaping the world*. Princeton, NJ: Princeton University Press.

AFFILIATIONS

Michele Rostan
Centre for Study and Research on Higher Education System
University of Pavia

Flavio A. Ceravolo
Centre for Study and Research on Higher Education System
University of Pavia

Table 2. Factors explaining Educational Circulation (Multinomial regression's estimates)

		B	E.S.
Intercept			
English	Exclusively English	-.459**	0.085
(country of employment)	English also	.230**	0.075
	No English	0	
Country size	Small	1.307**	0.077
	Medium	.965**	0.069
	Large	0	
Economic status	Mature	-.751**	0.064
(country of employment)	Emerging	0	
Asian country	China	-1.259**	0.116
	Other Asian	1.382**	0.061
	The rest	0	
Gender	Male	.239**	0.05
	Female	0	
Age cohort	Born up to 1950	.692**	0.079
	Born 1951 - 1960	.687**	0.069
	Born 1961-1970	.657**	0.068
	Born 1971 and after	0	
Parents' education	Parents with tertiary education	.276**	0.046
	Parents without tertiary education	0	
Discipline of highest degree	Education & humanities	.282**	0.085
	Social sciences, business & law	.371**	0.084
	Science	.568**	0.083
	Engineering and others	.215**	0.091
	Medical & health sciences	0	

** *P> 0.05*

Table 3. Factors explaining Educational Migration (Multinomial regression's estimates)

		B	E.S.
Intercept			
English (country of birth)	Exclusively English	-2.201**	0.192
	English also	-2.381**	0.207
	No English	0	
English (country of employment)	Exclusively English	3.547**	0.192
	English also	3.782**	0.213
	No English	0	
Size (country of birth)	Small	0.792**	0.202
	Medium	1.113**	0.208
	Large	0	
Size (country of employment)	Small	0.327	0.213
	Medium	-0.254	0.221
	Large	0	
Economic status (country of birth)	Mature	-3.28**	0.189
	Emerging and less developed	0	
Economic status (country of employment)	Mature	3.789**	0.217
	Emerging and less developed	0	
Gender	Male	-0.023	0.092
	Female	0	
Age cohort	Born up to 1950	0.649**	0.142
	Born 1951 - 1960	0.356**	0.128
	Born 1961-1970	0.351**	0.124
	Born 1971 and after	0	
Parents' education	Parents with tertiary education	0.377**	0.089
	Parents without tertiary education	0	
Discipline of highest degree	Education & humanities	0.02	0.152
	Social sciences, business & law	0.05	0.151
	Science	0.071	0.153
	Engineering and others	-0.216	0.188
	Medical & health sciences	0	

** P> 0.05

Table 4. Factors explaining Short-term Professional Circulation
(Multinomial regression's estimates)

		B	E.S.
Intercept		-3.179**	.176
English	Exclusively English	-.570**	.153
(country of employment)	English also	-.485**	.126
	No English	0	
Country size	Small	.093	.107
	Medium	.050	.090
	Large	0	
Economic status	Mature	.474**	.101
(country of employment)	Emerging	0	
Asian country	China	-.710**	.140
	Other Asian	.352**	.098
	The rest	0	
Gender	Male	.066	.066
	Female	0	
Age cohort	Born up to 1950	.530**	.113
	Born 1951 – 1960	.358**	.103
	Born 1961-1970	.439**	.092
	Born 1971 and after	0	
Parents' education	Parents with tertiary education	.213**	.059
	Parents without tertiary education	0	
Doctoral or postdoctoral degree	Yes	.578**	.071
	No	0	
Type of institution	Universities	.413**	.086
	Other institutions	0	
Academic rank	Senior position	.412**	.073
	Junior / other position	0	
Discipline of teaching	Education & humanities	-.046	.103
	Social sciences, business & law	-.067	.099
	Science	-.052	.096
	Engineering and others	-.063	.108
	Medical & health sciences	0	

(*Continued*)

Table 4. Continued

		B	E.S.
Research emphasis: basic vs. applied	Basic	.164**	.069
	Combined	.038	.075
	Applied	0	
Preferences in teaching and research	Primarily in teaching	-.442**	.167
	In both, but leaning towards teaching	-.316**	.099
	In both, but leaning towards research	-.072	.087
	Primarily in research	0	
English as lingua franca in teaching and/or research	Yes, as mother tongue	.218	.157
	Yes, as second tongue	.512	.073
	No	0	

** P> 0.05

Table 5. Factors explaining Long-term Professional Circulation
(Multinomial regression's estimates)

		B	E.S.
Intercept		-3.963**	.222
English (country of employment)	Exclusively English	-.965**	.203
	English also	-1.034**	.192
	No English	0	
Country size	Small	-.005	.130
	Medium	-.578**	.117
	Large	0	
Economic status (country of employment)	Mature	.558**	.139
	Emerging	0	
Asian country	China	-.344**	.167
	Other Asian	.333**	.133
	The rest	0	
Gender	Male	.264**	.084
	Female	0	

(*Continued*)

Table 5. Continued

		B	E.S.
Age cohort	Born up to 1950	.833**	.141
	Born 1951 - 1960	.580**	.130
	Born 1961-1970	.480**	.118
	Born 1971 and after	0	
Parents' education	Parents with tertiary education	.384**	.073
	Parents without tertiary education	0	
Doctoral or postdoctoral degree	Yes	.536**	.089
	No	0	
Type of institution	Universities	.429**	.106
	Other institutions	0	
Academic rank	Senior position	.317**	.091
	Junior / other position	0	
Discipline of teaching	Education & humanities	.096	.124
	Social sciences, business & law	-.179	.125
	Science	.024	.116
	Engineering and others	-.413	.144
	Medical & health sciences	0	
Research emphasis: basic vs. applied	Basic	.450**	.087
	Combined	.170*	.096
	Applied	0	
Preferences in teaching and research	Primarily in teaching	-.580**	.207
	In both, but leaning towards teaching	-.530**	.121
	In both, but leaning towards research	-.181*	.102
	Primarily in research	0	
English as lingua franca in teaching and/or research	Yes, as mother tongue	.992**	.210
	Yes, as second tongue	.719**	.095
	No	0	

** P> 0.05; * P> 0.10

Table 6. Factors explaining Job Migration (Multinomial regression's estimate)

		B	E.S.
Intercept		-6.375**	.328
English (country of birth)	Exclusively English	-1.202**	.303
	English also	-3.361**	.266
	No English	0	
English (country of employment)	Exclusively English	2.487**	.247
	English also	4.760**	.254
	No English	0	
Size (country of birth)	Small	-1.268**	.222
	Medium	.011	.210
	Large	0	
Size (country of employment)	Small	2.674**	.251
	Medium	.787**	.250
	Large	0	
Economic status (country of birth)	Mature	-1.866**	.258
	Emerging and less developed	0	
Economic status (country of employment)	Mature	1.935**	.281
	Emerging and less developed	0	
Gender	Male	.258**	.105
	Female	0	
Age cohort	Born up to 1950	.431**	.182
	Born 1951 - 1960	.290	.160
	Born 1961-1970	.350**	.142
	Born 1971 and after	0	
Parents' education	Parents with tertiary education	.535**	.099
	Parents without tertiary education	0	
Doctoral or postdoctoral degree	Yes	.757**	.141
	No	0	
Type of institution	Universities	.486**	.164
	Other institutions	0	
Academic rank	Senior position	.266**	.119
	Junior / other position	0	

(*Continued*)

Table 6. Continued

		B	*E.S.*
Discipline of teaching	Education & humanities	.213	.168
	Social sciences, business & law	.144	.166
	Science	.208	.167
	Engineering and others	.109	.200
	Medical & health sciences	0	
Research emphasis: basic vs. applied	Basic	.299**	.114
	Combined	-.012	.126
	Applied	0	
Preferences in teaching and research	Primarily in teaching	-.321	.262
	In both, but leaning towards teaching	-.587**	.159
	In both, but leaning towards research	-.067	.130
	Primarily in research	0	
English as lingua franca in teaching and/research	Yes, as mother tongue	.453**	.260
	Yes, as second tongue	.631**	.160
	No	0	

** *P> 0.05; * P> 0.10*

PART 2

RESEARCH TRAINING

ARJA HAAPAKORPI

A CAREER OUTSIDE THE ACADEMY? DOCTORATE HOLDERS IN THE FINNISH PROFESSIONAL LABOUR MARKET

INTRODUCTION

National policies and the strategies of the European Union and the OEDC aiming at innovative technological and economic reforms have highlighted the importance of having a labour force with research and development capacity to contribute to innovation (Kehm, 2006; European Commission, 2008/209; OECD, 2012). According to Kehm (2006), these policies are necessitated by the challenges of global competition. Globalization has altered the landscape of economies through knowledge based production, collaborations between universities and companies and the non-profit sector, development of information and communication technology, and massification of higher education (Brown, Lauder & Ashton, 2011; Rhoades and Sporn 2002; Castells, 2000). It can be assumed that doctorate holders are expected to have employment and career prospects outside the academy, because they have research capacity, which may be applicable to the domains of research and development (R&D) (Gibbons, Limoges, Nowotny, Schwartzman, Scott & Trow, 1994. Doctoral education is expected to supply resources for economic growth (Kehm, 2009).

In the European Union, this positive view of doctoral employment and of the benefits of the innovative capacity of doctoral holders has not been realized as expected. Massification of higher education has multiplied the number of people in the academic labour force and despite the growth of employment in the R&D sector, competition in the professional labour market has tightened (Brown, Lauder & Ashton, 2011). Moreover, the European Commission considers that the quality of research and doctoral education is high, but slow and ineffective in relation to knowledge dissemination (European Commission, 2003). In higher education policy at the national and European Union level, a common subject of concern is how to promote employment of doctorate holders outside the academy, as transition from doctoral programmes to employment is uneven and limited by the discipline and industry (Kehm, 2006). Thus, there is a promise of the demand for the doctoral labour force outside the academy, but it is not met across industries and sectors. This raises a question of the balance of demand and supply of doctoral labour force. The discussion on the over-supply of higher education graduates, including doctorate

J. Branković et al., Global Challenges, Local Responses in Higher Education, 107–125.
© *2014 Sense Publishers. All rights reserved.*

holders, and the mismatch of education and job (Teichler, 2007) continues the debate of the assumed imbalance.

In this article, employment of doctorate holders outside the academy is investigated in two ways. Firstly, job descriptions and positions at work sites are examined, and secondly, competence requirements and reasons for recruiting doctorate holders are studied. The careers of doctoral graduates are explored in relation to those having a lower level degree as the labour market consists of interrelated "territories," which are dominated by groupings of employees with different backgrounds (Abbott, 1988).

The data are based on a survey and an interview study; the latter represents the main data while the former offers complementary data for the analysis.

Despite the country-specific research subject, the findings and analysis can be generalized to some extent as similar tendencies related to higher education and the professional labour market can be detected across nation states, for example problems in the transfer from university to non-academic sectors.

DEMAND FOR AND SUPPLY OF A DOCTORAL LABOUR FORCE IN THE KNOWLEDGE-BASED ECONOMY

Higher education policy, knowledge-driven economy, and the growth of R&D affect the employment opportunities of labour force with higher education. However, massification of higher education increases competition on the labour markets. As there has been a remarkable growth of doctoral labour force, doctorate holders cannot avoid this competition either.

The national policies and the strategies of the European Union have stressed the importance of having a labour force with research and development capacity to contribute to innovation (European Commission, 2003). A flagship initiative is addressed to promote innovation: the need to continue to invest in education, R&D, innovation and ICTs is stressed (European Commission, 2010). Social and economic benefits are expected to be gained with the innovation policy (European Commission, 2010).

However, the national higher education policy in most European nation states and the EU strategies dealing with economic growth, R&D and employment share a common concern about doctoral employment outside the academy and the utilization of the research capacity of doctoral labour force in research & development activities (Kehm, 2006). As academic research institutes are not able to absorb the growing academic labour force, employment possibilities should grow in non-academic sectors (see: Enders, 2004; 2005).

In line with this trend, Gibbons (1994) and Nowotny (2001) with their colleagues claim that the increasing supply of doctorate holders in the labour force generates new employment opportunities. They justify the claim with the following argument: the increase of higher education creates a supply of employees competent in research, and this supply creates demand for specialist knowledge of all kinds (Gibbons, Limoges,

Nowotny, Schwartzman, Scott & Trow, 1994, p. 12). In addition, work organization and patterns are transformed with staff that has research capacity (Gibbons, Limoges, Nowotny, Schwartzman, Scott and Trow, 1994; Novotny, Scott & Gibbons, 2001). With institutionalization of R&D, firms, universities and research institutions tend to converge as universities absorb business-like practices and knowledge-intensive firms adopt "collegial" forms of organisational control resembling academic communities (Kleinman & Vallas, 2001). In addition, academic-mannered work mode is adopted in non-academic work sites (Novotny, Scott & Gibbons, 2001). With this tendency, working patterns and methods and knowledge bodies are also diversified as they are applied in various non-academic sites.

Studies dealing with innovation and R&D claim that the globalised knowledge economy is based on networks of universities with companies and governmental agencies. The networking is carried out with information and communication technology across nation state boundaries (Castells, 2000). Innovation policy is implemented with alliances of universities, research institutions, firms and public agencies and the dominant organizational form of R&D is the network (Etzkowitz, 2003).

The highest academic degree and the membership in the academic community can be assumed to promote a career outside the academy, as the formal degree strengthens the position of doctorate holders on the labour market (see: Abbott, 1988, pp. 60-70). It can be claimed that the institutionalized evidence of the highest academic competence is valued, because it provides its holder with extra credibility in the era of massification of higher education. The value of a doctoral degree is related to academic system, which consists of universities, academic societies and other related organizations with their own practices (Abbott 1988, pp. 65-66, 80-90). The gate keepers of the academic profession regulate the membership in the academic domain, which supplies credential power to doctorate holders (Abbott, 1988).

In spite of the value of the highest academic degree, at work sites, recruitment of doctorate holders is organization-, sector- and industry-specific and related to professional particularities. The niches are negotiated and struggled at work sites with management and employee groupings, clients and stake holders on the basis of requirements, needs and organizational contexts (see: Abbott 1988, pp. 60-70). For example, firms are different as regards to science and innovation strategies, and because of this the requirements for research-specific qualifications vary. Herrmann and Peine illuminate this with the following: firms imitating and diffusing knowledge-based products do not need research capacity, but they need employees with skills connected to markets and expertise in the industry. The need for research competence varies according to the industry, market, products and quality of knowledge (Herrmann & Peine, 2011).

In Finland, the doctorate holders have not been given preference in R&D, although science and innovation policy has been promoted. In Finland, as in Sweden and Denmark, the R&D resources are the highest in the European Union; the intensity was 3.87 of the GDP in 2010 (Eurostat, 2012). R&D personnel from all sectors together also made up more than 2.0 % of the labour force in 2010 (Eurostat, 2012). The high intensity in R&D gives promises on employment opportunities for doctorate holders, but these promises have not been fulfilled as expected. In the business sector and the higher education sector, the number of R&D personnel has increased between 2000 and 2008, although in the business sector, the growth has been minor compared to the substantial growth of the resources (Tohtoritarve 2020-luvulla, 2010). The increase of doctoral labour force in R&D has been relatively slow, taking into account the growth of doctoral labour force. The proportion of those having the highest academic degree was only 14% of the R&D personnel in 2008 (Tohtoritarve 2020-luvulla, 2010). Thus, the employment prospects of doctorate holders on the labour market outside the academy are not extensive and R&D is not an exception in this regard.

A popular discussion related to massification of higher education is the assumed mismatch of education and work. The substantial growth of number of higher education graduates is often considered to be related to inflation of higher education. As a consequence, higher education graduates are claimed to have difficulties to find a job, which match their education. The other tract of this discussion focuses on changing qualifications in work life: in addition to the professional and academic qualifications, "working life skills" are required. (Teichler, 2007) With regard to the doctorate holders, one may assume that the growth of doctoral labour force leads to similar consequences: inflation of degrees, difficulties to find an appropriate job, competition for jobs with those, who have a lower level degree and mismatch of education and job requirements. According to Teichler (2007), the problem of the matching of education and job is multi-layered and it has to be approached from different perspectives.

Doctoral Training and Employment Prospects

The Finnish doctoral education has been shaped by following a national tradition, but following transnational tendencies. The mode of PhD training and academic socialization is influenced by national tradition (Clark 1993). The German mode is based on independency and personal development of doctoral students. The American mode emphasizes systematic training, and instead of the dissertation, coursework is crucial (Bennish-Björkman 1997). In recent years, the American tradition has gained popularity, since it has been considered better for enhancing efficiency of the training an employability of doctorate holders (Kehm 2006). For the purpose of enhancing the employability, a particular program, professional doctorate, has been promoted (Enders 2005; Huisman and Naidoo, 2006), which can also be recognized in Finland (Ministry of Education and Culture, 2013).

In Finland, the aim is to raise the proportion of doctorate holders from 1% (2009) to 1,5% (2020); the corresponding numbers for higher education graduates is 22% and 30% (Ministry of Education and Culture 2013). The systematization of doctoral training has been promoted by regulating the access to doctoral programs, establishing a more intensive pattern of program, "doctorate schools" and developing a more systematized funding model. In addition, a system of tenure track for promoting professional research careers in universities has been created. The purpose of the systematization has been to make the training more efficient (Ministry of Education and Culture, 2013).

Despite of the systematization, a proportion of the training is funded by externally funded research projects. As a consequence, PhD students have a double role in the externally funded projects, as they are independent researchers and PhD students (Hakala, 2009). Although externally funded projects have been argued to be inefficient from the perspective of PhD training (Gumport, 1993), it has also been claimed that they may provide the students with opportunities to develop new types of skills and promote contacts to financiers (Harman, 2002). According to Hakala, the different contexts of carrying out PhD studies deliver new combinations on competence and research patterns on the basis of the academic and non-academic practices (Hakala, 2009).

Study Problem

In this article, the aim is to study employment prospects of doctorate holders outside the academy. First, careers, job descriptions, and positions at work sites are studied. Job descriptions are related to the content of the work and the term 'positions' refers to a hierarchical status in the employer organization. Are there particular tasks for doctorate holders and do they hold special positions in the organizational hierarchy? The position of doctorate holders is compared to those, who have a lower degree.

Second, the reasons to employ doctorate holders and competence requirements are explored to answer the question dealing with the value of doctoral degree. What are the employers' expectations related to the doctoral labour force? What kind of competences do employers value? What do the doctorate holders themselves consider important competences?

METHODOLOGY AND DATA

Methods used in this research are a survey and an interview; the survey was addressed to doctoral degree holders and the interview data dealing with employers' experiences and views were collected from the managers of the employer organisations. The application of both qualitative and quantitative approaches is chosen in order to increase the validity of the study findings.

The aim of the survey was to study the early careers of doctorate holders and the value of the doctoral degree in working life. The data consisted of survey-based material on those who completed the doctoral examination in the academic year 2004-2005 and interview data from their employers. The questionnaire asked doctorate holders about their study motives and funding source of their doctoral studies as well as details on employment and careers. Further queries were made concerning job description, the quality of work and the benefits of doctoral education as preparation for a career. The respondents were also asked to describe what qualifications or competencies were required for the current position held.

The questionnaire was addressed to all those who had completed their examination in the following universities: Helsinki, Jyväskylä, Oulu, Turku and Tampere. The Tampere University of Technology, the Swedish School of Economics and Business Administration, and Åbo Akademi were also among the chosen venues of higher education. The University of Art and Design, Helsinki, which was amalgamated to become Aalto University in 2010, was also included. These universities, in addition to the University of Kuopio and the University of Lapland, had collaborations on studying employment of their doctorate graduates. In Finland, there were 21 universities at the time of the survey and the data was collected from the doctoral graduates of the nine universities. All disciplinary fields except fine arts and theatre were included.

The questionnaire was planned and the data collection was carried out in collaboration with a Finnish network of universities (Aarresaari-network) and funded by the network and the Ministry of Education and Culture. The universities implemented the data collection themselves during 2006 and 2007 and the data from different institutions were integrated. There were 1183 responses to the questionnaire and the response rate was 61% of those who had received the questionnaire and 58% of all those who had completed their degree. The final dataset consisted of 39% respondents from the University of Helsinki and from the universities of Jyväskylä, Oulu, Tampere and Turku each representing 10-13% of the total sample. The doctorate holders from the Swedish School of Economics had the lowest response rate (47%). Women were majority representing 56% of the respondents and the men were in the minority with 44%. In regard to discipline, science (23%) and medicine (21%) were the most common. The doctorate holders in the field of technology had the lowest (44%) response rate and in the field of agriculture and forestry the highest (70%).

Attached to the questionnaire, was a piece of paper on which the respondents were asked to write the name and contact information of their manager for the purpose of conducting an interview. The request was addressed to those respondents, who were employed outside the academy, because the aim was to collect data on non-university employers' views with respect to the doctoral labour force and related industry- and organisation-specific conditions. The aim was to focus on the employers in the private and non-profit private sector. Only 53 respondents wrote their manager's name on the questionnaire and 49 of them were valid as four of these respondents were employed in university institutions.

Twenty-six interviews with employers are included in the data. Most of the organizations were in the private sector (14) while the rest were in some other sector: non-profit, (4); government, (4); municipal, (1), and municipal polytechnics. (3). In the private sector, the lines of business were social and health services, the pharmaceutical industry, media and publishing, consulting services, insurance and telecommunication. The size of the companies were large (6), medium-sized (2), and small (6) measured by the number of employees. A master's degree was the most common requirement for recruitment in these organizations; only in exceptional cases a doctoral degree was required. The analysis was based on the perspectives of employers and management and organizations and their needs and requirements for staff and the institutional environment were studied.

Before the interviews, the R&D activities of the organizations, educational background of the staff and the size of the organization were investigated; the aim was to obtain background information for the interviews. The data were mostly collected from the web pages of these organizations and from authorities funding R&D activities outside the academy. Most (21) of these organizations had R&D or education-related collaborations with universities and research institutes; 15 of them had their own R&D departments. The scale of research activities and collaboration with universities and research institutes varied. Some organizations had a long history of R&D collaboration with universities; some of them purchased research services from universities, while others carried out training programmes with universities. The employers with R&D and training-related collaboration were more positive to the query to be interviewed compared to those employers not actively networked to universities.

The interviews were semi-structured. The interview themes were the following: the purpose, strategy and structure of the organization, staff policy and strategy, positions and tasks of doctorate holders, recruitment and need for a doctoral labour force, benefits of employing doctorate holders, and finally, the future prospects and demand for a doctoral labour force. The interview data, collected during the spring and autumn of 2007, were recorded and written into text files. They were analysed using text analysis methods.

FINDINGS AND ANALYSIS–EXPLORING EMPLOYMENT

Doctoral Employment

The active labour force participation rate was high, which refers to employment opportunities. In addition, the quality of employment was high. The work was usually appropriate to the high level of education. Three per cent of the doctoral degree holders had been unemployed for a while after completing the doctoral thesis. However, 13% of all those who had responded to the questionnaire, had had problems finding employment; most of them held degrees in the disciplines of science (21%), social science (23%) and arts and humanities (16%). The unemployment rate was rather low at the data collection point.

The most obvious problems were the short-term contracts in the labour market, which are common in the European countries (OECD, 2009). One-third of the respondents had short-term employment in 2007. Many worked in universities as scientists and lecturers on short-term contracts. In 2007, the employment situation in Finland was rather favourable and the increasing supply of doctorate holders met the demand for a highly educated labour force. The overall unemployment rate was 6%, as the rate was 8% in 2011 (OECD iLibrary, 2013).

The employment sectors of those doctoral holders who were employed were distributed as follows: universities, 41%; polytechnics, 5%; state and municipal offices, 32%; private sector companies or entrepreneurs, 16%, and private non-profit organizations, 4% Research as a profession was most common (38%) and the other titles held were teacher (21%); manager (8%); medical doctor or veterinarian (15%); coordinator (3%); officer in public administration (2%), and professional in engineering, agriculture and forestry (6%).

The placement was focused on a limited field on the labour market; over half of them were situated in research and education positions in public sector organizations. From the perspective of the current cut-backs in university funding in Finland, it is probable that employment opportunities in the academy will decline. In Finnish higher education policy, the aim is to increase the number of doctorate holders in R&D and outside the academy (Niemi et al., 2011), but the goal has not been achieved to the extent as expected. The labour market has not been able to absorb the flow of doctoral degree holders as in most business fields, doctorate holders are rare in the labour force. However, in the industries, which specialize in R&D, the doctorate holders make up a relatively high proportion of the labour force. In the biotechnology industry, 75% of the professional staff has a doctoral degree, while in the electronics industry, this number is 2-3% (Kestävä ja dynaaminen kumppanuus, 2005). The high proportion of academic labour force correlates with the close relationship to universities. For example, a part of biotechnology industry emerged as spin-off of universities.

No Niche but Opportunities for a Career

In the academic domain, doctoral careers are structured into a four-stage model strengthening the value of doctorate, but in the non-academic domain, there was no special labour market niche for doctoral degree holders. In Finland, doctorate holders compete with master's degree holders on the labour market. Thirty-eight per cent of doctorate holders were researchers and the corresponding number of those holding a master's degree is 11% (Korhonen & Sainio 2006, pp. 14-15). Research careers are not niches for doctoral holders. Recruitment practices are shaped on the basis of organization-, and industry-specific practices and needs. In addition, a doctoral degree does not qualify a person for a management position in non-academic domains. The studies of Enders across nation states supports this finding, as it is common that no added value is related to the doctorate, except in Germany (Enders, 2004).

According to the analysis of the employer interviews, doctoral degree holders did not have higher positions in the organizational hierarchy compared to the other personnel in only a few organizations. In these organizations, doctoral degree holders were managers of R&D departments or education programmes. In addition to R&D, education, marketing, legislative work, management and media, work and tasks related to publishing were carried out by doctorate holders outside the academy. The doctoral degree holders had usually the same kind of job descriptions as the staff members with a master's degree. In general, the research mode was not academic as the aim was to produce knowledge for practical purposes. Thus, doctoral competence was not utilized in an academic way.

> We are required to work fast and carry out applied research as the purpose of our main organization is to influence political decision-making. In our research department, it is clear that our task is to produce knowledge for the purposes of our main organization. Scholars have to take the role of a professional expert. We must have the competence of journalists: write fast and delimit subjects. (Research manager, non-profit private organization)

In many employer organizations, the salaries of doctorate holders did not exceed the average level of professional employees, which describes their position. The size of the salary tends to be related to the valuation of the employee. In the private sector companies, the doctoral degree holders were not better paid, but the employers improved their salary or position, if they considered that the doctoral education had benefits for the company.

However, there were differences between employer organizations as regards to the job descriptions of the doctorate holders. Some of the employers reported that they could not provide sufficient challenges and adequate tasks for doctorate holders and the qualifications of their doctoral staff were slightly under-utilized. These employer organizations did not have extensive R&D activities or the doctoral staff referred to in the interview did not work in R&D tasks.

A majority of employer organizations indicated that they could utilize the doctoral competence of their employees and provide them with special professional challenges. They performed some special tasks or roles, for which the degree provided competence. These special tasks were the following: experts on committees, specialized journalists, leaders of educational programmes, or as marketers in the pharmaceutical industry.

> Sure, when we want *the* most competent experts for committees, parliament and groups preparing new legislation, they are doctorate holders. Their competence is more appropriate for communication, conceptual thinking and writing. (Manager, governmental sector)

The survey data from the doctorate holders did not raise the mismatch of education and job as a substantial problem and the respondents reported rather high rates of matching. On the basis of the survey analysis the jobs were matching as regards to their education, since 76-93% of all respondents considered that the rate was excellent and only small minority reported weak match. However, there was variation by the employment sector. The respondents in the municipal and non-profit private sector organizations reported lower rates compared to the others (table 1). In addition, in the municipal sector organizations, a smaller proportion of the respondents could apply their doctoral training than the other respondents (table 2). In the business and government sector organizations, the mismatch had decreased with time (table 1). The reason for this is probably career promotion.

The question of mismatch is quite complicated as the concept of matching refers to many layers of competence and work (Teichler, 2007). A good example are the doctorate holders in the non-profit private sector organizations 4 years after graduation: they reported rather good opportunities to apply their doctoral education, but considered the matching of education and job lower compared to organizations in the other sectors, the municipal sector excluded. The explanation may be related to profession and organization.

First, in the non-profit private sector organizations, the doctorate holders were often researchers, and the respondents who worked as researchers had better opportunities to apply their education. The proportion of those researchers, who reported "I use my amassed knowledge/ skills all the time" was 82% and the proportion of those researchers, who responded "I can apply what I have learned to some extent" was 15%. The corresponding numbers of the all respondents were 61% and 31%. The proportion of researchers was 51-55% in the government and non-profit private sector organizations, 24% in the private sector organizations, 4% in the municipal sector organizations, 55 % in universities and 14% in polytechnics.

Second, non-profit private sector organizations are usually small-sized, which may be correlated to the lower matching of education and job. The size of the organization can be judged to be related to career opportunities as large organizations have usually better opportunities to provide career prospects. The lower matching of education and job may indicate poorer career prospects despite the opportunities to apply doctoral education. However, a more profound research at work site is needed for validation or re-interpretation of this result. In addition, it should not to be forgotten that the respondents were in the early stages of their careers and their experiences and perspectives were close to doctoral studies. This is supported by the discovery of low importance attributed to the management skills (Table 3).

It can be assumed that doctoral employment opportunities are reinforced in the labour market for two reasons: first, the increase of the doctoral labour force tends to transform working modes at work sites, and second, the specialized tasks and roles tend to be institutionalized. R&D activities and collaboration with universities and other research institutions generated work for which doctorate holders were eligible. In the employer organization, a doctoral degree of the manager or the core professional staff advanced such activities, which favoured doctorate holders in recruitment. Once one doctorate holder had been recruited; more professionals with scholarly competence were employed, which is also recognized by other researchers (Cruz-Castro & Sanz-Menéndez, 2005; Kleinman & Vallas, 2001). The reason was not only a particular human resource policy, but a transformation in working methods

Table 1. Which of the following describes your work most accurately? Matching of education and job/Employment sector

6 month after completing my doctoral degree	Municipal	Non-profit, private	Private	Government	University	Poly technic
My job matched/matches my education well	75%	77%	71%	82%	88%	76%
My job was/is partly less demanding than my level of education	17%	17%	22%	15%	10%	20%
My job was/is clearly less demanding than my level of education	6%	3%	4%	2%	2%	4%
Can't say.	2%	3%	3%	1%	0%	0%
Total %, N	100%189	100%39	100%120	100%138	100%395	100%57
4 years after graduation	Municipal	Non-profit, private	Private	Government	University	Polytechnic
My job matched/matches my education well	76%	78%	89%	93%	89%	93%
My job was/is partly less demanding than my level of education	17%	22%	11%	7%	11%	7%
My job was/is clearly less demanding than my level of education	5%	0%	0%	0%	0%	0%
Can't say.	2%	0%	0%	0%	0%	0%
Total%	100%	100%	100%	100%	100%	100%
N	187	41	123	136	404	55

Table 2. How well you can apply what you have learned during your doctoral studies to your current job? Responds/employment sector

	Municipal	Non-profit, private	Private	Government	University	Poly technic
I use my amassed knowledge/ skills all the time	37%	74%	44%	66%	81%	70%
I can apply what I have learned to some extent	54%	24%	48%	29%	17%	28%
I don´t have much use of my studies	9%	2%	7%	5%	2%	2%
Total%, N	100%191	100%42	100%124	100% 137	100%406	100%57

Table 3. The most important competence according to the employment sector (%)." What proficiency is most important in your current job?" There were no ready-made alternatives for responding the question

Competence	Municipal	Non-profit private	Private	Government	University	Polytechnic
Expertise *	50	36	48	43	11	28
Research	3	33	12	28	43	33
Education	7	2	9	2	10	10
Knowledge acquisition & analysis	10	14	11	7	5	10
Management & coordination	4	2	7	4	3	7
Skills of interaction	5	2	2	1	3	0
No respond	21	11	11	15	25	12
Total %	100	100	100	100	100	100
N	191	42	126	138	406	59

*Industry-specific expertise

and practices. As staff with academic competence was recruited, working methods were re-shaped reinforcing systematic knowledge production and application which followed research designs; There was a tendency in work organizations to reinforce doctoral careers. This tendency was related to networking with universities. There is interplay between collaboration with universities and recruitment of doctorate holders, as collaboration with universities promotes the employment of doctorate degree holders and increasing the number of staff with research-based capacity strengthens contacts with academic institutions.

> In our (consultant) network, we have some professionals who have specialized in research and working with patients. This has made *it* possible to constantly strengthen our competence. The boundaries between the university and our clinic carrying out patient work are much lower now. (A network of consultants, health services industry)

With the tendency to increase special tasks and roles, it is possible that the doctoral work domains in the labour market will be incrementally developed. Although there is not a career niche for doctorate holders, there are career opportunities for professionals with academic competence and status (Borel-Damian, 2009, p. 78). New job descriptions are usually developed when some members of a profession begin to specialize in a particular field. Step by step, their job descriptions will be institutionalized as a separate work domain and with this tendency, the positions in an organizational hierarchy will be re-shaped. However, promoting the higher position and special job descriptions has to be negotiated at work sites, in local conditions, which does not suggest a rapid change in this respect. There has to be strong arguments to legitimise a niche in the labour market for doctorate holders.

Motives to Recruit Doctorate Holders: Knowledge-based Competence, Networking Capacity and Academic Status

According to the employers, the most recognized qualification of doctorate holders was research capacity and doctorate holders were mostly employed for R&D. In addition, the membership in the academic community and the status of the highest academic degree were important for the purpose of developing networks and collaborations with universities.

Knowledge-Based Competence. Employers in both the public and private sector organizations recruited doctoral degree holders to undertake R&D functions as research capacity was mentioned as a special qualification for improving R&D in these organizations. According to the employers, competence on knowledge, acquisition and analysis was also crucial qualifications.

Although research capacity was often mentioned as an employment requirement, the utilization of research capacity varied according to labour division and industry. The R&D based organizations employed doctorate holders for research positions, but in employer organizations without R&D departments, such as the media, research positions were rare. In addition, some R&D-based companies purchased research services by subcontracting rather than hiring full-time staff.

Research capacity was taken for granted, but generic capabilities were examined carefully. Industry- or profession-specific competence was required for research and non-research work.

> Our doctorate holders get the same salary as the others. The level of salary depends on how much experience they have and their competence on our business-specific models. It is more important than a degree. (Research manager, pharmaceutical industry, a large company)

The importance of industry-specific expertise was taken into account in HR practices. Although the employer organizations considered recruitment of young doctorate holders as an easy and time-saving personnel strategy, a good solution was to encourage staff to undertake doctoral studies. Senior professional employees had the necessary industry-specific competence and the many of the interviewed managers considered it reasonable to have experienced doctorate holders. Graswell claims that senior staff is capable to apply their long experience and industry-specific knowledge to their doctoral studies (2007). When the doctoral thesis was regarded as beneficial for R&D purposes, working on the thesis was supported in many ways, particularly in large firms based on R&D activities.

> They are competent to apply the models of our business. In addition, they write scholarly articles and their doctoral thesis when carrying out customer projects. That way we have staff who knows how to work in a private sector company. (Manager, pharmaceutical industry, a small firm)

Employers' support for doctoral studies is confirmed by other researchers (Borel-Damian, 2009, p. 8). However, the crossover of academic research and needs of non-academic domains can be problematic as there are inherent limits of transferability (Graswell, 2007). The senior staff may have better qualifications to cope with the problem, but the crossover may also put extra pressures on their doctoral studies.

The survey findings supported the analysis of the employers' views of the industry–specific expertise. According to the survey study (table 3), the doctoral respondents employed by universities highlighted the importance of research competence, while expertise of the industry or the professional field was most often reported by the respondents working outside the academy, particularly in the municipal and private sectors.

Knowledge-based competence of doctorate holders is appreciated in the academy and outside the academy, but not in similar ways. Research competence is a crucial quality of the doctoral labour force, but outside the academy, generic capabilities are also needed.

Networking Capacity and the Status of the Doctorate. Research capacity and expertise are qualities attached to the doctorate, but the academic cultural and social capital should not be ignored. The degree provides its holders with a membership in the academic, community and the symbolic value of the highest academic degree. For the employer organizations, the reason for employing professionals with the highest academic degree was to strengthen R&D, but also to promote collaboration with universities and research institutions and enhance the professional credibility of the organization.

Most of the employer organizations pursued collaboration with universities and research institutions, as their strategy was to promote partnership-based R&D projects. Doctorate holders advanced collaboration with universities as they benefited from their personal contacts with the academy. Some interviewed managers reported that they had specifically recruited academic staff for that purpose:

> The task of the recently employed doctorate holder is to coordinate the training project which presumes contacts with universities. (Manager, a private, non-profit private organization)

Collaboration with the academic domain was in particular wanted, when the employer organization's R&D was poorly developed or it did not meet academic criteria. In these organizations, collaboration with universities was expected to enhance the quality of research work by promoting higher criteria for R&D. According to studies of R&D, new and inexperienced firms in the R&D market strive for partnerships with universities and employ doctorate holders for this objective (Luo, Koput & Powell, 2009). The convergence of universities and firms promotes academic practices in the private sector (Kleinman & Vallas, 2001), because this convergence is advantageous for firms strengthening their position in knowledge economy.

Membership in an academic community is necessary for creating contacts and partnerships. Research professionals are a community, which crosses boundaries of organizations and sectors and this supplies for employers outside the academy an opportunity to benefit the extensive research capacity based on these communities (Luo, Koput & Powell, 2009). The academic profession unites the members with the particular knowledge body and institutionalized patterns as the members may not know each other.

The employers also recognized the cultural capital, the value of doctoral degree for enhancing the professional credibility of the organization. The highest academic degree was considered beneficial in negotiations and collaborations with academic institutions, because it equalized academic status differences between the partners. According to Luo, Koput and Powell (2009), a doctorate can take three forms in R&D: intellectual capital, network mediation and a signal of academic capital. Academic capital improves the credibility of the firm for partnership in the eyes of funding agencies. Luo, Koput and Powell claim that a staff member with a doctorate signals the following important qualities: it is observable, costly to obtain and correlates to the quality of the organization (2009).

CONCLUSIONS

The research shows that there was no specific niche for doctorate holders outside academy, but the doctorate holders had special tasks or positions, for which the doctoral degree was regarded as appropriate. At work sites outside the academy, the industry-specific competence was considered important, which, however, did not invalidate the value of the highest academic degree. The membership in the academic community was a good reason to employ doctorate holders for the purpose of reinforcing collaboration with universities.

This tendency refers to incremental development of a doctoral career domain, which is judged on the basis of the fact that new professional territories emerge with differentiation and specialisation. The differentiation and specialization was addressed firstly to special tasks demanding doctoral competence and secondly to the membership in the academic community. Thus, the emergence of doctoral domains should be based on various qualities of the doctorate. However, the development of doctoral careers will appears to be uneven and slow, because the professional labour markets are varied and institutionalized employment patterns change slowly. The change will not be overarching but limited by the sector of employment. The national and EU-based science and innovation policy aims at increasing doctoral labour force in R&D outside the academy, but the proportion of doctorate holders has not grown as expected and the growth has been uneven. Relationship (collaboration, spin-off origin of the firm etc.) with university promotes recruitment of doctorate holders. This supports the result of this study: doctorate holders were also recruited for the purpose of reinforcing collaboration with universities or initiating of university cooperation.

Although there was not a niche for doctorate holders outside the academy, the doctorate holders themselves were rather satisfied with their jobs. They considered the matching of their education and jobs as rather high, although not everyone was able to apply what he/she had learnt during the education. The matching of education and job is more or less indirect outside the academy, because academic institutions and non-academic work sites are different. Although similarities and convergence has been recognized in R&D-based work, there are still differences with regard to the purpose of research and related working patterns. Doctoral qualifications have to be translated into industry-specific and organization-based doctoral competence.

The data of the survey and interviews came from the study "Early Careers of Doctorate Holders and the Significance of Education in the Labour Market." It was funded by the network of career service offices of the Finnish universities (Aarresaari-network) and the Finnish ministry of education and culture.

REFERENCES

Abbott, A. (1988). *The system of profession. An essay on the division of expert labour.* The University of Chicago Press.
Auriol, L. (2010). *Careers of doctorate holders: Employment and mobility patterns.* OECD Science,

Technology and Industry Working Papers 2010/4. OECD Publishing. http://www.oecd-ilibrary.org.

Bennich-Björkman, L. (1997). *Organising innovative research. The inner life of university departments.* New York. Pergamon.

Borel-Damian, L. (2009). Collaborative doctoral education. University-Industry Partnership for Enhancing Knowledge Exchange. Doc-carers project. EUA European University Association, Sixth Framework Program, 2009. http://www.eua.be/fileadmin/user_upload/files/Publications/DOC- CAREERS.pdf

Brown, P., Lauder, H., & Ashton, D. (2011). *The global auction. The broken promises of education, jobs and incomes.* Oxford University Press.

Castells, M. 2000. The *Rise of the network society age: Economy society and culture vol. I.* Cambridge, MA; Oxford, UK.

Clark, B. R. (1993). *The research foundations of graduate education. Germany, Britain, France, United States, Japan. Berkeley.* CA: University of California Press.

Graswell, G. (2007). Deconstructing the skills training debate in doctoral education. *Higher Education Research & Development, 26*(4), 377–391.

Cruz-Castro, L. & Sanz-Menéndez, L. (2005). The employment of PhDs in firms: Trajectories, mobility and innovation. *Research Evaluation 14*(1), 57–69.

Enders, J. (2005). Border crossing: Research training, knowledge dissemination and the transformation of academic work. *Higher Education, 49*(1–2), 119–133.

Enders, J. (2004). Research training and careers in transition: A European perspective on the many faces of the Ph.D. *Studies in Continuing Education, 26*(3), 419–429.

Etzkowitz, H. (2003). Innovation in innovation: the triple helix of university-industry-government relation. *Social Science Information, 42*(3), 293–337.

European Commission. Key Figures report 2008/2009. (2009). A more research-intensive and integrated European Research Area. Science, Technology and Competitiveness. European Commission. Directorate-General for Research. Directorate C – European Research Area: Knowledge-based economy. Unit C.3 – Economic Analysis and Monitoring of National Research Policies and the Lisbon Strategy. http://ec.europa.eu/research/.../key-figures-report2008-2009_en.pdf.

European Commission (2010). Europe 2020 Flagship Initiative Innovation Union Communication from the commission to the European parliament, the council, the European economic and social committee and the committee of the regions. Brussels, 6.10.2010. http://eurlex.europa.eu/LexUriServ/ LexUriServ.do?uri=COM:2010:0546:FIN:EN:PDF

European Commission (2003). Third European report on science and technology. Indicators: Towards a knowledge based economy. Brussels: European Commission.

Eurostat. European Commission. (2006). Careers of doctorate holders. Data from pilot CDH collection 2006. http://epp.eurostat.ec.europa.eu/statistics_explained/index.php/ Careers_of_doctorate_ holders#Employment_characteristics_and_work_perception

Eurostat (2012). R & D personnel 2012. http://epp.eurostat.ec.europa.eu/statistics_explained/index.php/ R_%26_D_personnel (accessed October 10, 2012).

Eurostat (2012). R&D Expenditure. http://epp.eurostat.ec.europa.eu/ statis tics_explained/index.php/ R_%26_D_expenditure (accessed October 10, 2012).

Gibbons, M., Limoges, C., Nowotny, H., Schwartzman, S., Scott, P., & Trow, M. (1994). *The new production of knowledge. The dynamics of science and research in contemporary societies.* London. Thousand Oaks. SAGE Publications.

Gumport, P. J. (1993). Graduate education and research imperatives. Views from American campuses. In B. R. Clark (Ed.). *The research foundations of graduate education* (pp. 261–93). Berkeley, CA: University of California Press.

Haapakorpi, A. (2008). Tohtorien varhaiset urat työmarkkinoilla ja tohtorikoulutuksen merkitys työelämässä. (Early Careers of Doctorate Holders and the Significance of Education in the Labour Market). Aarresaari, Hermes, 2008. http://www.aarresaari.net/pdf/TohtoriKirjaKA.pdf.

Hakala, J. (2009). Socialization of junior researchers in new academic research environments: Two case studies from Finland. *Studies in Higher Education 34*(5), 501–516.

Harman, K. (2002) The research training experiences of doctoral students linked to Australian Cooperative Research Centres. *Higher Education, 44*, 469–92.

Herrman, A., &. Peine, A. (2011). When 'national innovation system' meet 'varietes of capitalism' arguments on labour qualifications: On the skill types and scientific knowledge need for radical and incremental product innovations. *Research Policy, 40*, 687–701.

Huisman, J., & Naidoo, R. (2006). The professional doctorate: From Anglo-Saxon to European challenges. *Higher Education Management and Policy, 18*(2), 1–13.

Kehm, B. (2009). New forms of doctoral education and training in the european higher education area. In B. Kehm, J. Huisman, J., & B. Stensaker (Eds.), *The European Higher Education Area: Perspectives on a Moving Target*. Sense Publishers.

Kehm, B. (2006). Doctoral education in Europe and North America: A comparative analysis. In U. Teichler (Ed.), *The Formative Years of Scholars.. Wenner-Gren International Series* Vol 83. London. Portland Press.

Kestävä ja dynaaminen kumppanuus. Yliopistojen, tutkimuslaitosten ja yritysten välinen tutkimusyhteistyö ja tutkijankoulutus. (2005). (Long-term and dynamic partnerships. Research co-operation and researcher training between universities, research institutes and business companies). Suomen Akatemian julkaisuja 3/05 (Publications of the Academy of Finland). Helsinki. Painopörssi Oy.

Kleinman, D. L., & Vallas, S. (2001). Science capitalism, and the rise of the "knowledge worker": The changing structure of knowledge production in the United States. *Theory and Society, 30*, 451–492.

Korhonen, P., & Sainio, J. (2006). Viisi vuotta työelämässä. Monialayliopistoista vuonna 2000 valmistuneiden sijoittuminen työmarkkinoille. (Graduates' Transition to employment from multi-disciplinary universities). Aarresaari. Kirjapaino Hermes Oy 2006 http://www.aarresaari.net/pdf/UraraporttiNetti.pdf.

Luo, X, Koput, K., & Powell, W. (2009). Intellectual capital or signal? The effects of scientists on alliance formation in knowledge-intensive industries. *Research Policy, 38*, 1313–1325.

Ministry of Education and Culture, (2013). Education and Research 2011–2016. A development plan Reports of the Ministry of Education and Culture, Finland 2012:3 http://www.minedu.fi/export/sites/default/OPM/Julkaisut/2012/liitteet/okm03.pdf?lang=en

Neumann, R., & Tan, K. (2011). From PhD to initial employment: The doctorate in a knowledge economy. *Studies in Higher Education, 3*(5), 601–614.

Niemi, H. Aittola, H., Harmaakorpi, V., Lassila, Ol. Svärd, S. Ylikarjula, J., Hiltunen, K., & Talvinen, K. (2011). Tohtorikoulutuksen rakenteet muutoksessa. Tohtorikoulutuksen kansallinen seuranta-arviointi. Korkeakoulujenarviointineuvostonjulkaisuja 15:2011. *http://www.kka.fi/files/1399/KKA_1511.pdf*

Novotny, H., Scott, P., & Gibbons, M. (2001). *Re-thinking science knowledge and the public in an age of uncertainty.* Cambridge: Polity.

OECD. (2008). *Education at a glance. OECD Indicators*, OECD, Paris.

OECD. (2009.) Science, technology and industry scoreboard. Investing in the knowledge economy, Employment of doctorate holders,141-143. http://www.oecd-ilibrary.org.

OECD Factbook. (2010). *Economic, environmental and social statistics. Science and technology. research and development. Gross domestic expenditure on R&D.* http://www.oecd- ilibrary.org/economics/oecd-factbook-2010_factbook-2010-en.

OECD. (2012). *Knowledge networks and markets in the life sciences.* OECD Publishing. doi: 10.1787/9789264168596-en

OECD ILibrary (2013). *Employment and labour markets: Key tables from OECD. Unemployment rate of labour force.* http://www.oecd-ilibrary.org/employment/employment-and-labour-markets-key-tables-from-oecd_20752342.

Rhoades, G., & Sporn, B. (2002). Quality assurance in Europe and the U.S: Professional and political economic framing of higher education policy. *Higher Education, 43*(2), 355–390.

Teichler, U. (2007). Does higher education matter? Lessons from a comparative graduate survey. *European Journal of Education, 42*(1), 111–34..

Tohtoritarve 2020-luvulla (2010). Ennakointia tohtorien työmarkkinoiden ja tutkintotarpeiden pitkän aikavälin kehityksestä (Demand for doctorate holders on labour market 2020) Opetus- ja kulttuuriministe riön julkaisuja 2010:13. http://www.minedu.fi/export/sites/default/OPM/Julkaisut/2010/liitteet/okm13.pdf?lang=fi.

AFFILIATIONS

Arja Haapakorpi
Palmenia Centre for Continuing Education,
University of Helsinki

EMILIA PRIMERI & EMANUELA REALE

EARLY CAREER RESEARCHERS TRAINING: THE CONSTRUCTION AND MAINTENANCE OF ACADEMIC PRESTIGE IN CHANGING ENVIRONMENTS

INTRODUCTION

Several changes are affecting the university system in Europe: the introduction of managerial approaches, the growing internationalization of academic activities, and increasing competition for funding and to gain a higher position in international rankings. In order to improve and maximize excellence positioning and prestige/reputation, universities are developing different strategies which concern, among others, setting up new facilities and labs, merging and enlarging existing structures, driving faculties toward enhanced productivity, modifying the teaching and research balance, and increasing tuition fees for students.

These measures impact on the institutional environments of universities and are supposed to have implications for their organization and activities, while also bringing about major changes in how academics do their work. In this paper, we investigate how the academic institutions' concern for the collective achievement of excellence and good reputation affects the working lives of single individuals, focusing on the selection and training of PhD students and postdoctoral fellows.

PhD students are an important part of the academic workforce (Larivière, 2011) and greatly contribute to the advancement of knowledge. PhD training is affected by changes occurring in academic environments and organizations, as well as in the market place.

The research questions driving our analysis are: how does the prestige of scientific groups shape the training of PhD students and early career researchers? Does the push toward excellence impact on the way in which PhD students and early career researchers are trained? What changes and patterns of PhD transformation can be observed? Do universities still play a role in training the best academics? Two main assumptions underlie this work. Firstly, the methods for the selection and training of PhD candidates and postdoctoral fellows are related to the perception of how academic prestige is constructed and maintained (Kyik & Smeby, 1994; Enders, 2005). Moreover, we argue that the increasing competition for excellence, affecting all academic institutions, also drives changes in the practices for the selection and training of PhD students and early career researchers (Henkel, 2005; Burris, 2004; Shove, 2000).

J. Branković et al., Global Challenges, Local Responses in Higher Education, 127–148.

The empirical basis of this work is represented by two case studies developed within the PRESTENCE project[1] and focusing on a hard science Department (dealing with Chemistry - CD) and a soft science Department (dealing with History - HD), both belonging to a large Italian University. Twenty four interviews with professors, young researchers, and doctoral students were carried out in order to identify key factors shaping excellence and prestige. The analysis is performed at the department level and regards: a) the way in which PhD candidates and early career researchers are selected and trained, b) the relationship between supervisors and students, and c) practices shaping doctoral and postdoctoral research (i.e. collaborations, team vs. individual research, scientific production). Based on what emerges from the interviews, we also try to differentiate between practices mainly related to disciplinary characteristics (size of research teams, type of research, i.e. individual or collaborative, and type of scientific production) and practices perceived as being related to the prestige of the Departments. Changes in these factors, which appear to be driven by greater emphasis on excellence, are discussed for both Departments. The paper is structured as follows: section one introduces the theoretical background. Section two deals with the methodology and the description of the two case studies. Section three illustrates the results of the interviews about the prestige of the two Departments and their role in PhD selection and training, while also pointing out changes driven by increasing attention to and competition for excellence. A discussion of the evidence emerging from the interviews and some final considerations are presented in section four.

CONCEPTUAL AND THEORETICAL BACKGROUND

Since the end of the 1980s, research reputation has become the "strongest academic currency" in higher education institutions (Henkel, 2005). In order to improve reputation and gain a better position in excellence rankings, several strategies are put in place, such as personnel and research evaluation policies and the adoption of strategic management practices. Examples of this are the more and more common practice of hiring star scientists and the push toward increasing publications in highly cited journals (Brewer, 2002; Cyrenne & Granta, 2009). Departments, faculties, and research groups are subject to close scrutiny by the university management for what concerns their productivity rate and research performance.

The institutions' concern for collective achievements, reputation, and resources emerges as an international trend, which has implications for individual working lives and for the institutional structure of national academic institutions (Henkel, 2007). On the one hand, university departments might be reorganized and merge into larger structures which often cross disciplinary boundaries and have new research directions[2]. On the other hand, relationships among academics might also change. For instance, team membership, multiple research profiles, and network connections are increasingly important (Henkel, 2005).

Leisyte and Dee (2012) underline that increasing emphasis on the markets has led many European universities to develop strategies in order to maximize prestige and achieve higher positions in international rankings, so that the declared aim of most academic institutions is to be "world-class universities," "excellent," and "leading institutions." A better position in international rankings also allows academic institutions to increase their funding opportunities (i.e. through grant proposals) and to access new scientific networks or expand those they are embedded in. Hence, the reputation and prestige of academic institutions, made visible through rankings, can be seen as factors facilitating the improvement of universities' social capital (Bordieu, 1986).

Rankings might serve as "fashion arenas" in which institutions compare themselves to one another and hierarchies of universities are created. These hierarchies closely mirror the prestige and reputation attributed by the scientific community to academic institutions but often do not represent fully reliable measures. For instance, Reale and Seeber (2011) point out that, when many people are involved, having one view of reality might reduce bargaining and conflicts, even when the limits of said view are evident. This may be the case for rankings; individual academics have elaborated complex ideas on institutional prestige but these are non-formalized, difficult to communicate, and focused on the discipline in which they work. They will keep referring to their experience in their work, but they have to refer to rankings when communicating with the outside. Thus, rankings make reputational hierarchies public and visible (Federkeil, 2009). However, the concepts of prestige and reputation are quite different from the concept of excellence and based on distinct "ideas" as well as measures and instruments for their assessment (Paradeise & Thoenig, 2013).

The scientific literature (Dill, 2009; Stensaker & Kehm, 2009) argues that positioning in international rankings places emphasis on certain dimensions (e.g. productivity, students-teachers ratio) which do not fully explain the reputation and prestige of academic institutions. Dill, for example, underlines that the academic race for prestige, mirrored by rankings, is based on information which rarely measures real performance and does not consider differences among research units, groups, and faculties within the same academic institution (Dill, 2005; Stensaker & Kehm, 2009). Rather than measurable factors, reputation and prestige should be considered social constructions – symbolic values agreed upon by the scientific community in relation to an institution, group, research unit, or department (Federkeil, 2009). Paradeise and Thoenig (2013) explain that judgments based on excellence and prestige draw upon different ideas: the former mostly rely on analytical measures, the latter usually refer to ideas and representation commonly used in social spheres, often historically or geographically defined. For instance, the reputation of academic institutions is mostly based on mutual acquaintance and recognition of quality and past achievements reproduced and maintained in the present, thus a status attained through time. Hence, reputation mainly refers to the social ascription of some positive characteristics which, in the HE context, are scientific competence, good performance, and excellence (Federkeil, 2009). Reputation often refers to a group of people, a field of science, or a department, even though the perception of the whole institution might be influenced by it (the so-called "halo effect").

Prestige is the recognition of quality achieved by an organization over time and is based on ideas concerning key processes affecting the output produced. In the case of universities, the processes supporting the idea of prestige are, for instance, those related to recruitment selectivity, quality of academic personnel and training, research results, and effective job placement of graduates and PhD students (Sauders & Fine, 2008; Paradeise & Thoenig, 2011).

Although built to some extent upon the prestige and reputation of an academic institution, the notion of excellence mostly refers to measurable and objective quality "standards," which can be assessed using suitable instruments.

These standards are globally recognized as quality judgments aimed, differently from reputation and prestige, at ranking institutions on an ordinal or numerical scale and at providing acontextual judgments (Paradeise & Thoenig, 2013).

Therefore, prestige and excellence refer to two different concepts: the former is an emotive and a contextual category, the latter is an analytical concept, a referential and a-contextual category. Notwithstanding the differences between the concepts of excellence, reputation, and prestige, the increasing competition among academic institutions to be "at the top of the list" (Cremonini et al. 2009) causes these concepts to affect academic institutions at different levels: the institutional level, the level of departments and research groups, and the faculty level.

In this work we consider the meso level of academic institutions, represented by the departments, and we focus on the consequences that the competition to acquire and maintain prestige and reputation might produce on the selection and training of PhD students and postdoctoral fellows.

PhD training and postdoctoral careers represent two important provinces of higher learning and research (Enders, 2005). Doctoral training is the way in which new generations of researchers are educated and become acquainted with academic norms, values, and rules, as well as with the behaviors, attitudes, and know-how of their scientific community (Larivière, 2011; Enders, 2005; Henkel, 2005). Nonetheless, several changes are observed in how PhD students are selected and trained and early career researchers are hired.

Some scholars have detected a shift in the dominant paradigm for PhDs in Europe, away from the so-called Humboldtian model toward a more professional model, in order to boost efficiency, improve employability, and increase knowledge transfer opportunities (Enders, 2005; Kehm, 2007). These changes are driven by several factors: the will to gain greater efficiency in PhD research productivity, to support employability, and to increase innovation gains, represented by the knowledge produced and transferred during and after research training (Enders, 2005).

In this respect, PhD work and doctoral research production are more and more often seen as strategic factors to maximize the reputation and prestige of academic institutions. Indeed, the scientific literature suggests that the reputation and prestige of universities are also influenced by the quality of the students produced (Cyrenne & Granta, 2009; Henkel, 2005). This has led them to implement practices strategically aimed at becoming more attractive to higher quality students, also through more selective application procedures, and at recruiting PhD students from the best universities, instead of preferring "local" applications. Some scholars (Cyrenne & Granta, 2009) highlight that PhD selection and the hiring of early career researchers are often driven by the reputation of the universities in which the students were trained.

Furthermore, the planning of a research activities and priorities, which also includes choosing the topics of PhD theses, and research mentoring (the relationship between supervisors and students) have come to be seen as key factors contributing to collective achievements. Within this framework, the relationship between mentoring and research productivity gains new and emerging importance (Leisyte & Dee, 2012). In particular, "collaborative" mentoring – defined as a mentoring relationship in which the students are asked by their mentors to be the co-authors of papers, conference papers, books, book chapters, or research grant proposals – appears to be significantly associated with research productivity. This means that co-authorship with their advisors/mentors has an influence on the students' publication activities.

Borrowing the categories introduced by Barrier (Barrier, 2011; Leisyte & Dee, 2012), we could distinguish between a patronage model and a partnership model of authority relations between the group leader and the researchers within research units. The former applies mainly to the mentor-student relationship, thus being a hierarchical model, whereas the latter refers to a flatter way of managing group relationships. Furthermore, two different and often contextual kinds of pressure emerge in the way in which research is performed: the first toward increasing individualism in research productivity, and the second toward increasing collaborations in order to take advantage of funding opportunities provided by large, competitive projects. Finally, some authors also underline that changes in PhD training are driven by increasing permeability among research areas and disciplines in universities. Indeed, larger, cross-disciplinary groups are becoming more common than narrow communities clustered around well-defined scientific areas (Enders, 2005).

In this regard, it is worth mentioning that disciplinary fields are an important source of fragmentation within universities. In his seminal book, Whitley (2000) explains that differences in the organization of scientific fields are related to the degree of mutual dependence between scientists (functional and strategic dependence) and of task uncertainty in the sciences (technical uncertainties, because of fragmentation, with ambiguous results and conflicting interpretations, and strategic uncertainties, because of a large number of problems, with limited chances to have dominant paradigms and theoretical orientation). Seeber (2011) discusses the efficacy and limitations of research steering in different disciplines and the need to balance the way in which authority is exerted depending on the features of individual disciplines.

METHODOLOGY AND DESCRIPTION OF CASE STUDIES

This paper investigates two Departments in two different disciplinary fields which are both well established. Indeed, our empirical data refer to two case studies carried out respectively on a hard science Department (Chemistry - CD) and on a soft science Department (History - HD). They belong to one of the largest Universities in Italy, which covers different scientific fields for what concerns both teaching and research and holds a high position in the international ranking[3]. Moreover, the two Departments analyzed are well known nationwide for their teaching and research capabilities.

Desk research concerning the history of the Departments and collection of data about academic staff, PhD students, and postdoctoral fellows constitute the basis of our analysis. Interviews with professors, young researchers, and doctoral students were carried out in the two Departments in order to identify key factors shaping excellence and prestige. In total 24 interviews (15 for History and 9 for Chemistry) were conducted and interviewees included full professors, associate professors, researchers, and PhD students. The information gathered offers different views about the role and importance of PhD, and the main criteria driving selection choices and training practices. Selection and recruitment of PhD students and early career researchers are investigated since they are considered strategic factors in the competition among departments for prestige and excellence.

With regard to doctoral and postdoctoral training, the interviews addressed the ways in which PhD students and early career researchers are involved in the research activities of the Departments and become familiar with them, focusing on their involvement in research projects, research groups, and co-authored publications. With this in mind, this work aims to point out changes in the practices shaping the ways in which PhD students and young researchers are trained. Our study also tries to describe changes related to modifications within the disciplines (team vs. individual research) and those which seem to be driven by the need to improve competitiveness and visibility (i.e. collaborations, scientific productivity). Hence, changes in selection and recruitment practices as well as in training practices are examined, in order to determine whether they are driven by the Departments' need to gain or maintain prestige. This also allows us to focus on new arenas (i.e. internationalization, competition for funding, competition to attract students), which are seen as rather challenging by most academics in both Departments.

The information collected on the two Departments is briefly summarized below.

The CD and the HD are both prestigious institutions, thanks to the reputation built over the years by individual scholars (often eminent scientists), the scientific relevance of their research outputs, their rigorous research methods, the quality of their teaching and research, and the outstanding training of their PhD students.

Today, the CD holds quite a remarkable position in the international ranking, being ranked between 101 and 150[4]. Nevertheless, the reputation of the CD dates back to the early 1900s, when it was established as the Chemistry Institute. Later, in 1982, it became a University Department, due to the merging of four pre-exiting Institutes (Analytical Chemistry, Physical Chemistry, General and Inorganic Chemistry, Organic Chemistry), which were part of the Chemistry Institute. This made it possible for the Department to continue pursuing multiple research lines, which still is one of its main characteristics. In the 1980s, the Doctorate was set up as the highest step in academic education. At the end of the 1990s, the number of students enrolled rose significantly (following the so-called "massification" phenomenon), triggering an increase in academic staff followed by a multiplication of research groups.

The research and teaching focus of the faculty covers 5 areas: Analytical Chemistry, Physical Chemistry, Industrial Chemistry, Organic Chemistry, and Inorganic Chemistry.

The academic staff numbers 118 people, of which 39 full professors, 22 associate professors, and 46 researchers. The number of researchers has grown since 2007, after remaining almost stable from 1999 to 2006, while the number of full and associate professors has slightly decreased since 2007. This could be due to turnover in the positions of full professors, replaced by internal associate professors after retirement, and to the recruitment of new young researchers.

The HD was founded as a School by an eminent scholar at the beginning of 1900s, merging two pre-existing chairs. In the early 1960s, the Institute was created as the first attempt to institutionalize the community. The new Institute improved its facilities and internal organization with the creation of a dedicated library and the assignment of staff to specific tasks, such as administration, library services, and other duties related to the internal division of labor. A director was also elected from among the professors of the Institute. In the 1980s, the Institute was transformed into a Department, following a general reorganization of the University. In August 2010, after another internal reorganization, the number of departments was reduced. As a consequence, the HD became a scientific section within a new, larger Department, which merged different fields (History, Geography, Anthropology, etc.) into a single entity.

The academic staff of the HD, which has always been quite small, included about 20 members in 2010. The number of full and associate professors grew in 2001 and has remained roughly stable since then, with a total of 16 full and associate professors, whereas the number of researchers has decreased considerably (9 researchers in 2000, only 3 researchers in 2010). The Department is now trying to increase the number of its young researchers and has recently recruited two new ones, but limited space and lack of resources are slowing the process down.

The CD awards PhDs in four main study areas and collaborations are in place with other departments, mainly Physics and Biology. The PhD program is a 3-year research program. The PhD of the HD was established in 1985, when doctoral courses were introduced in Italy, and it includes two main fields of study. Calls for applications open every two years; four places are usually available, of which two with a scholarship. Joint agreements with local institutions that are highly specialized in the scientific field used to be the rule. After the merging of the Department into a larger unit, collaborations with other fields (i.e. Anthropology) should have been initiated, but none have been developed yet. Recently and for the first time, an agreement with a French university for a joint PhD has been signed.

There is a great difference in the number of PhD students and early career researchers in the two Departments. In the Chemistry Department, the number of PhD students and postdocs ("assegnisti di ricerca") has remained quite stable over the years, except in 2007 when the number of postdoc positions dropped and that of doctoral students grew. Generally speaking, the data show that the number of PhD students has increased in recent years (60 PhD students in 2005 and 68 in 2010).

The number of PhD students in the History Department has always been quite small and has decreased since 2005 (12 PhD students in 2005 and 5 in 2010). The interviews confirm that increasing the number of PhD students seems to be very difficult, due to limited availability of supervisors and grants for scholarships. Moreover, some changes to PhD rules and regulations, ensuing from the new organization of the Departments, should soon be implemented, but they do not include any strategies to boost the number of PhD students, besides maintaining the two already existing programs.

Table 1. Chemistry Department - PhD Students and Research Assistants

Year	Research associates	Of which PhD students	PhD students, non research associates	With grant
2010	17	0	68	50
2009	15	0	69	44
2008	13	0	61	37
2007	8	1	76	44
2006	10	0	54	29
2005	18	0	60	32

Source: MIUR (Ministry of Education, University, and Research), year 2010

As for early career researchers, an analysis of their CVs provides some information about their degree and PhD studies. Most of them graduated with the same supervisor chosen for their PhD, and their PhD course usually started soon after graduation. Their research career was often conceived as a continuation of their PhD, with roughly the same research group and research lines. In both Chemistry and History, there seems to be a general tendency to prefer local recruitment and linear career paths for academic staff, from graduation to job attainment. Nevertheless, the interviews show that this was the rule in the past, but the shortcomings of this practice are starting to emerge.

Table 2. History Department - PhD Students and Research Assistant

Year	Research associates	Of which PhD students	PhD students, non research associates	With grant
2010	3	0	5	2
2009	0	0	7	4
2008	1	0	8	4
2007	1	0	6	3
2006	1	0	6	3
2005	3	0	12	6

Source: MIUR (Ministry of Education, University, and Research), year 2010

PHD STUDENTS AND EARLY CAREER RESEARCHERS AT A CROSSROADS BETWEEN PRESTIGE AND EXCELLENCE

Three aspects are now investigated using the empirical evidence collected through the interviews, the documentary analysis, and the analysis of the CVs of the interviewees: selection and training of new researchers, mentor-student relationships in doctoral and postdoctoral student training, and doctoral and postdoctoral research practices.

The Importance of Selection And Training of New Researchers to Maintain the Prestige of Departments

In both the CD and the HD, the selection and the training of PhD students and early career researchers emerge as two key factors contributing to reputation and prestige. They ensure the safeguarding of the scientific methods representing the bedrock of the two Departments, the survival of research lines and know-how, and, especially for Chemistry, the maintenance of existing laboratories.

Following a common practice in both Departments, the selection of PhD students already occurs during their degree studies. The professors identify the students who might be able to start an academic career. A PhD is then offered, although a public competition takes place.

> Actually, also Professor..., with whom I had worked, was interested in me and tried to make me stay, so that I could do lab activities. I do the same with students in degree course. I try to figure out who might be interested in continuing with a PhD and I offer it to them, if they are interested – and capable, of course. In the case of some students, for example, all the degree faculties try to make them graduate by the 31st of October, so that they can compete for a PhD. When we see such cases and the students are willing to do a PhD, we do that, although the University does not provide many opportunities. (Interview, Chemistry Researcher)

Responsibility for PhD selection is not shared within the Department. Instead, depending on available resources and places, each professor is essentially free in the choice of PhD students. For instance, at the HD the balance among scientific fields within the Department is the only limit to the freedom the professors enjoy in choosing PhDs students.

> The Department is an abstract entity that does not exist when recruiting choices have to be made. It is the professor who chooses the students and imposes that choice on the Department... Scientific activity and production also have their ways of being transmitted, through a mentor and his school. Surely, if a faculty dictates a methodology, having been trained in that method favors a student over another when a competition takes place. (Interview, Chemistry Full Professor)

> Here we have had great masters, excellent students, and very good researchers, but also mid-level researchers. A non-selective mechanism [for the hiring of researchers] can have terrible effects, because simply splitting the available places among the faculties might replicate mediocrity and might therefore be very risky. (Interview, History Researcher)

PhD courses provide the methodological training to do research, so that continuity between master studies, PhDs, and postdoctoral fellowships can be observed in most cases. Indeed, our investigation shows that, after graduation, many postdoctoral fellows went on to do a PhD with the same professor who had supervised their master degree thesis. After their PhD, they started to do research mostly within the same research group, as is the case for Chemistry, or with the same professor, as is the case for History.

> Integration [between teaching and research] comes later, when the most talented students are proposed for a PhD. (Interview, Chemistry Full Professor)

> I am doing a PhD in Material Sciences and what I studied during my degree course, and for my thesis in particular, was very useful in order to be selected for the PhD. Most of the work is similar to what I studied for my degree and so it is more or less the same. (Interview, Chemistry PhD student)

> I was recruited as a researcher after 12 years spent here as a temporary employee, although I had spent most of my time teaching within this Department. (Interview, History Researcher)

> Yes, I took my degree here and my whole career has been here, at this University. (Interview, History Full Professor)

However, some shortcomings of this practice emerge from the interviews. Several interviewees state that local recruitment and selection, in both Departments, foster the reproduction of existing knowledge, making research mostly self-referential and closed to contributions by peers.

If a School is too "local," the negative aspect might be what we were talking about before: creating clones – that's the danger. (Interview, History Full Professor)

I must say that I am among the few in my generation who spent a major portion of their scientific career abroad. And I think that this has been a positive thing because, in doing so, you are forced to create relationships with other environments. So, the worst thing that might happen is that you become less provincial. (Interview, Chemistry Full Professor)

Excellence in a field can be maintained if mechanisms for personnel recruitment have been put in place, but they have to be effective. These mechanisms stopped 10 years ago. It has been 8 years since we last received resources, and this means that some groups are now obsolete as for cultural input, motivations, personnel. And minor groups have reached higher positions both because they have access to resources and because their average age is lower. (Interview, Chemistry Full Professor)

In the opinion of the CD professors, the selection of PhD students and early career researchers should include meritocratic methods, besides taking affiliation to the Department into account. The most common international criteria for selection (scientific production and internationalization) are often disregarded. Moreover, the ability to attract students from abroad, which represents an important indicator of research quality in international rankings, is too limited because of no fellowship availability, obsolete structures, and almost no opportunities to be recruited as postdoctoral fellows or researchers.

The CD professors and researchers also state that, in order to be competitive, the Department should turn to the market for the best talents, improving the opening of PhD positions to foreign students and promising young researchers, on the basis of internationally agreed criteria (e.g. scientific productivity, studies abroad, participation in research projects). Training as well should be opened to new fields of research, more "attractive" on the market and able to produce new knowledge and valuable research outcomes (i.e. patents, spin-offs).

Our Department has tried to introduce meritocratic selection criteria, evaluating scientific activity and teaching with objective criteria, then splitting resources on this basis. This has been met with strong resistance and the results have actually been very poor. (Interview, Chemistry Full Professor)

I believe that in the last few years our position in international rankings has decreased for what concerns the quality of our work and the ability to attract young scientists, because our investments in research are very limited. (Interview, Chemistry Full Professor)

Some Universities become more competitive and students perceive the differences, they understand who will provide them with more opportunities and where there are several active research groups, especially if they have to do a PhD... By the way, if I want to invite someone, I have no resources for that. This limits our opportunities to recruit from abroad. Moreover, the general tendency is to recruit locally... (Interview Chemistry Researcher)

Differently, in the HD, local selection based on shared methodological approaches to research is preferred, although taking care to avoid the impoverishment of research quality (mentioned in the interviews as the "creation of clones," which represents the main threat to the Department). In line with this approach, opening PhD training to foreign students is considered important and the first joint PhD with a French University has recently been launched. Moreover, increasing attention is paid to PhD training, which should be improved, becoming highly specialized and aimed at preparing promising students for research.

PhD is the real training ground, that's the level in which you achieve your specialization. Scientific specialization is thematic starting from the first two years of specialization. In the PhD a selection of students occurs. (Interview, History Full Professor).

There is a natural need to bring in young people with new ideas and new relationships, willing to work by following other perspectives and not only the mentor-student relationship, continuing a School rather than enlarging it. As far as I am concerned, being the student of someone was not so important in my generation. I feel I owe a debt of gratitude to the professors I studied with, but I have extended my gratitude to all the people I have met around the world and who have taught me something. (Interview, History Researcher)

Finally, the evaluation of the research activities carried out by the University emerges as a common drive for change in PhD and postdoc selection and training in both Departments. PhDs, in fact, are considered a strategic factor in the evaluation of departments and, in this regard, attention should be paid to the ability to attract foreign students and increase joint PhD courses with foreign institutions and the scientific production of PhD students and postdocs.

We are speaking about this, we are still deciding, but the idea is here. Either at the international level or at the national level, with the relationships we have, we should make the PhD something permanent, a permanent research laboratory (Interview, History Associate Professor)

Phd and Postdoc Training: Which Relationship Between Mentors and Students

In the respondents' perception emerging from the interviews, the prestige of the two Departments is also related to the founding and development of the so-called "Schools." Traditionally, the "Schools" were not regulated by formal rules and organizational structures, but rather by informal relationships linking scholars to their leading scientist, so that being the "student" of an eminent academic was often the rule.

In the past, a young researcher who was appreciated by a certain professor was guaranteed to work, even alone. Well, I started working on documents in a different and systematic way, not only on one text after the other, which was almost always the rule, trying to see the development of that method. (Interview, History Full Professor)

Some differences emerge between the CD and the HD for what concerns the relationship between students and supervisors. These differences reflect the different concept of "School" in the two Departments. Whereas in Chemistry the School roughly coincided with the research group in which students shared activities and studies with a supervisor, in History the School was mainly embodied by an eminent scientists and his students, who learned to share a common point of view and to adopt a common scientific approach (or method) to their subject.

Were there great Schools, not PhDs, which enhanced the reputation of the Department? Yes, laboratories, schools for research. But it is no longer the case. Leading groups are almost finished, also because of natural selection: the mentors are retiring and the people around them are dispersing. (Interview, Chemistry Researcher)

The School was a "virtual" structure, there was only one professor. It was very elaborate but virtual. The Institute was already a unit for the coordination of professors, the beginning of the Department as it would become. In the past, this made sense because teaching and research were linked. (Interview, History Associate Professor)

Besides the differences characterizing the concept of School in the two Departments, almost all interviewees underline that the prestige of the CD and the HD was built on, and for many years mainly related to, the reputation of the eminent scientists leading the Schools. This is reported by both young researchers and students, but with different perceptions in relation to the two Departments. As for the CD, the positive aspects of the Schools are emphasized, while their shortcomings are seen, in most cases, as a consequence of shortsighted decisions made by few scientists. At the HD, the young researchers and students' perception is rather different. The School is seen as something belonging to the past, something upon which the reputation of the Department was built, but ultimately unable to reproduce quality and potentially threatening the Department's prestige.

Notwithstanding differences in the opinions expressed by the respondents – young researchers and students – in both Departments PhD training as well as postdoc career opportunities and paths (within the Departments) have traditionally been steered by the supervisors.

In that system losing touch with your mentor was fatal.....Now it is not as it was in the past, and I am not sure that system selected the best talents .... (Interview, Chemistry Associate Professor)

> At the end of my PhD my supervisors retired and so, according to the old logic of the Department, I should not have had a future, my academic career would have been condemned to "death"! (Interview History Researcher)

The different organizations of the disciplines (Whitley, 2006) have strongly influenced the types of relationships established between mentors and students. In Chemistry, PhD students and postdocs are often part of a research group, thus able to keep in touch with a large number of individuals (professors and students). Nevertheless, since the field is highly internationalized, the Department's limited ability to support student training and mobility abroad and scant incentives existing at the national level are perceived as threatening the Department's reputation.

On the contrary, in History the relationships between supervisors and students have usually been closed to external contacts, due to the small number of PhD students and the prevalence of individual activities over collective ones. However, this has produced negative effects, which are acknowledged by most interviewees.

Instead of the scientific and methodological evolution expected as the main result of research training, this practice has led to the creation of "clones," causing an involution of pre-existing scholarly activities. This has also impact on the publishing activities of PhD students and postdocs, with publication efforts concentrated on the Department journal only.

> PhD students were almost imprisoned by the student-professor relationship... Some PhD students understood that the PhD is also a way to open up to new inputs. Yet, others remained linked to the professor they had studied with, for example during their master degree, and they ended up working on the same problem, investigating it further, so that their training was rather limited. (Interview, History Researcher)

> I believe that History has to be studied in its entire evolution; otherwise, it remains limited and not controlled methodologically. The turning point for people recently recruited has been the will to change, for instance, the Department journal. Young people have exerted this authority, and the qualitative leap is evident. An international board of editors was created and publications in English are welcome, so it is obvious that we must create relationships at the international level and that we can provide great, original contributions to that. This means working with foreign institutions, being aware that we can offer innovative proposals with high-level scientific data. (Interview, History Full professor)

Moreover, the traditional hierarchical structure, which characterized the relationships between mentors and students in History, seems to have been replaced by a different organization, in which collaborations and group activities are becoming increasingly important.

> There is a natural need to bring in young people with new ideas and new relationships, willing to work by following other perspectives and not only the

mentor-student relationship, continuing a School rather than enlarging it. As far as I am concerned, being the student of someone was not so important in my generation... (Interview, History Researcher)

Doctoral and Postdoctoral Research Practices

With regard to doctoral and postdoctoral research practices, we have tried to determine whether changes have occurred in collaborations and types of research performed (individual *vs.* team research) and whether a drive toward boosting scientific productivity can be detected. The interviews provide different insights into this matter for the HD and the CD.

As for History, increasing collaborations at the Department level and a push toward strengthening international collaborations are seen as strategic measures to be introduced, although competition in the international arena is not yet perceived as a priority issue.

The merging of the HD into a larger Department is seen as a threat only by very few full professors, mainly those worried about the balance of power among research areas within a larger structure. Conversely, the majority of interviewees – in particular young researchers – consider this change an opportunity for two reasons. Firstly because the "label" of History, which has always been part of the Department's identity, is maintained in the name of the Department, and secondly because being part of a larger entity is supposed to provide more opportunities to develop joint PhDs, which could cross disciplinary boundaries (e.g. joint PhDs with Anthropology and Geography) and foster collaborations among early career researchers.

> We should abandon the label of "History," but it is not a mere label, it is everything to us. Merging into this larger Department might be risky but we have to, for political reasons. Yet, our identity as historians is maintained. (Interview, History Full Professor)

> Today students must have a research project to do a PhD, so they often join courses which are related to their research projects. We also try to provide them with an overview of other PhD courses, so that they can have a broader view. We often try to have many PhD collaborations, international collaborations. Today this is much easier thanks to the funds we have. (Interview, History Associate Professor)

Differently from the past, international collaborations are becoming increasingly important for the HD. This offers new opportunities to develop joint PhDs with foreign academic institutions and to improve participation in joint projects and collaborations.

Therefore, the need to strengthen teamwork and joint activities is gaining greater relevance especially for young researchers, although the type of research performed in History still mirrors a preference for individual work, mainly depending on the type of research and scientific products (i.e. monographs instead of articles). Moreover, in line with tradition, research themes are still considered extremely important.

At the CD, collaborations have always been the rule. Several joint agreements for mobility and joint PhDs have been signed with foreign institutions. International collaborations, joint projects, students and professors' mobility, and co-authorships are seen as evidence of the scientific quality of the Department and as a strategic factor to be improved. The main obstacle hindering the development of international collaborations, especially at the PhD level, is the lack of resources, which limits participation in international conferences, the hosting of foreign students, and does not allow PhD students to spend periods abroad working in foreign institutions.

> It is very difficult to spend periods abroad, the same goes for mobility and exchanges; we do not have resources for that. This limits our chances to open up recruitment to foreign students. (Interview, Chemistry Researcher)

Team research is also a characteristic of the CD. Nevertheless, the past fragmentation of research activities into countless groups is now perceived, especially by young researchers, as a weakness of the Department, since it limits competition for productivity, ranking, and the strengthening of human capital. Traditionally, having their own research group was a way for professors to preserve personal power within the Department. Today, integration among groups is still lacking, but most interviewees, especially young researchers, are aware of the importance of creating a critical mass of researchers in order to compete at both the national and international level.

> There are too many groups, and this is a waste of resources. People do not work together and there are no incentives to do so. I think that resources and efforts should be rationalized by increasing synergies among groups. (Interview, Chemistry Full Professor)

Changes are also driven by the preferences of PhD students, who tend to be attracted by some research groups to the detriment of others. Indeed, PhD students mainly focus on those scientific areas (Analytical Chemistry or Physical Chemistry) that provide better facilities and laboratories, thus ensuring better experimental activities or increased employment opportunities after completion of the PhD. This has caused the marginalization of some groups within the Department, with potential waste of resources and loss of knowledge gathered over time. Hence, a discontinuity with the past emerges within the CD in this respect.

> The group I belong to is dying out. Since the majority of people enrolling choose Analytical, Organic, or Physical Chemistry, there is little left for Inorganic Chemistry. I do not understand why professors go along with it. As for the students, they choose according to employability opportunities after their studies. The students have a clear idea from the very beginning: their choice is made based on employability opportunities and they ask their professors for advice. (Interview, Chemistry PhD student)

The generation gap is also visible for what concerns the publication strategies of both Departments. PhD students, postdocs, and younger professors are very much aware of the importance of publishing in international journals and of producing different types of research products (not only monographs but also articles), as these are two of the main criteria used in the evaluation of research activities. However, increases in research productivity do not emerge as a priority in the History Department (also in the opinion of the PhD students interviewed).

> We are not really interested in quantity. Certainly, there are researchers who feel that they are under publishing pressure, especially to cope with evaluation requirements. (Interview, History Associate Professor)

The interviews highlight that scientific productivity is considered a priority for PhD students in Chemistry. Great attention is paid to increasing the number of publications in high-ranking journals, as this is also considered a key criterion for the selection and recruitment of young researchers.

> It is appreciated if you have at least one publication per year and take part in conferences. I already have 4-5 publications and I have been to conferences. It is not mandatory but the [PhD] commission takes it into consideration because a PhD student must be productive. (Interview, Chemistry PhD student)

Another feature differentiating the CD from the HD is the relevance of the international arena, which is a crucial dimension for knowledge production and communication in the case of the CD, gaining increasing significance for both PhD students and young researchers. On the contrary, the professors and researchers of the HD are more prudent in acknowledging the importance of internationalization, but the generation gap is visible in this case too. Indeed, young professors and researchers show concern about the limited internationalization characterizing the Department in the past (visible, for instance, in some editorial choices), which is perceived as a risk in today's larger and more competitive arena.

> In my opinion, an important indicator of excellence is the level of internationalization, which means professor and student exchanges with those countries that are more advanced scientifically. This is quite common abroad, but Italy is very poor in this regard. When PhD students or postdocs from abroad apply for a fellowship to come and study here, they are often asked why they did not choose another country, and this is a shame for us. Moreover, the number of foreign professors working in our universities is very low. (Interview, Chemistry Full professor)

DISCUSSION AND CONCLUSIONS

This paper focuses on how the perceptions of prestige and excellence affect the training of PhD students and early career researchers. It analyzes two different disciplinary fields, Chemistry and History, represented by two Departments belonging to a large Italian University and with a consolidated reputation for both teaching and research.

The quality of PhD students and research training of new researchers are interpreted as two factors contributing to the prestige of the Departments. On the other way round, the need to maintain and to improve academic prestige impacts on the way in which PhD students and early career researchers are selected and trained.

In both case studies considered, PhD students and early career researchers are mostly selected and recruited locally, based on the decisions of the supervisors and of the leaders of scientific research groups. Furthermore, training is usually shaped by a set of shared practices and habits.

Concerning the way in which PhD candidates and early career researchers are selected and trained and the supervisors-students relationship, three main features emerge. Firstly, there are strong connections between teaching and research within the Departments. Secondly, the selection of PhD students and postdocs has traditionally been managed as a process internal to the Departments and depending on faculty choices. Thirdly, continuity between master degree studies, PhD courses, and research fellowships points to an "investment" in the construction of well-defined career paths for young scientists which takes place at the Department level mainly, so that training emerges to be conceived mostly as a process of nursing brilliant students in order to keep them inside the Department.

The evidence gathered confirms that the prestige of the Departments is related to processes and decisions occurring within them (selection and training), often starting at the master degree level and continuing at the PhD and postdoc level. This is also related to the legacy of the so-called Schools, which characterizes both Departments. In the past, the Schools ensured the handing down of knowledge from one generation of researchers to the next, and shaped the relationships between mentors and students. Whereas the limited number of students in History contributed to a close student-supervisor relationship, the Chemistry School had rather different practices, since it mostly relied on eminent scientists leading large research groups and carrying out innovative research with national and international collaborations.

This different legacy has impacted on the type of relationship between professors and students in the two Departments and produced different effects on the training of PhD students and young researchers. In the case of History, the School mostly evolved within a closed environment, in which the knowledge of the mentors was duplicated with very limited or no innovative effort. In the Chemistry Department, the organization of the School around research group leaders evolved into a fragmentation of groups, which mostly mirrored the faculty members' personal research interests. In the former case, the danger of losing prestige is perceived very clearly, and a new approach to the mentor-student relationship is being introduced. This will allow PhD students and early career researchers to develop new subjects and methodologies in their research activities, crossing disciplinary boundaries and benefiting from new collaborations with other fields (i.e. Anthropology). In the case of Chemistry, the ability of some groups to attract the majority of PhD students and researchers, by providing better laboratories and research facilities, has caused research to concentrate on few specific sub-fields within the Department (mainly Analytical and Physical Chemistry). A generation gap between older and younger scholars also emerges in both Departments. The new generations of researchers and associate professors are more likely to acknowledge the need to modify the concept of "School" and the way in which new researchers ought to be recruited and trained.

Hence, in the discussion about the critical factors affecting the prestige and reputation of the Departments, the selection and the training of PhD students and early career researchers emerge as two key factors. They affect the prestige of the institutions and, in turn, the academics' will to retain and strengthen their influence on them.

As for the impact of excellence judgments on the training of PhD students and early career researchers, no relevant evidence emerges. Excellence appears to be a matter of concern – although limited – in the CD, this being mostly related to the international visibility of the Department. Chemistry also shows a shift, although still limited, toward new and more remunerative research areas, aimed at improving the ability to support scientific productivity and visibility. For History, no impact of excellence judgments on PhD and early career researchers training emerges. Continuing past research is almost the rule in the construction of one's career, although opening up to different research fields is becoming more and more important especially for researchers who have been recently recruited.

Different excellence judgments and classifications mostly seem to affect how research is performed, so that some patterns of PhD transformation have started to emerge.

Collaborations, especially at the international level, are seen as vital to improve research training quality in both Departments. Also, team research is becoming the standard and PhD training must provide students and young researchers with the appropriate tools to collaborate in large research projects with foreign academic institutions. Moreover, most early career researchers, especially the younger ones, are less concerned with having their own research group and research line (which was a priority in the past) and are more interested in creating a critical mass, which allows them to be more competitive and to maximize research collaborations and funding. As for publications, increasing productivity does not seem to be a priority in either Department, thus confirming that this aspect bears little relevance to the prestige of academic institutions. Instead, a push toward improving the type of publications emerges. In Chemistry, PhD students and young researchers feel that prestige and reputation can be improved by publishing in selected high-ranking journals, joining international research teams of high standing. In History, the focus is mostly on improving the peer reviewing processes for national publications, as a source of external accountability and openness of the field, which is supposed to impact on visibility.

In this regard, the importance of international collaborations and publications in highly cited journals plays a crucial role, among other indicators, in the process of evaluation of research performance at the department level.

Turning to the question concerning whether Universities still contribute to training the best academics, evidence gathered in both Departments seems to confirm that the training of young researchers through a PhD does indeed produce the best scientists of the future generation. Nevertheless, there are concerns about the strategies put in place by the University to compete at both the national and international level. Some wonder whether it is advisable to follow the general and globalized trend toward improving excellence, focusing mainly on ranking and performance outputs, instead of investing in the training of young researchers and in the improvement of internal selection and recruitment processes.

Finally, with regard to the disciplinary fields investigated, it is worth underlining that, as the evidence shows, the two disciplinary fields are not affected by the organizational characteristics of the university they belong to, but are marked by interesting differences in their organization as scientific disciplines. Indeed, the field of History is characterized by strong internal cohesion and hierarchy, whereas Chemistry displays greater complexity and fragmentation.

The mentioned characteristics affect, to some extent, the way in which new researchers are selected and trained, the relationships between professors and students, as well as doctoral and postdoctoral research practices. Yet, some common features do emerge. They are related to the peculiarities of the Italian HE system, such as the early training and selection of researchers and the well-known problems of localism and nepotism, which have a negative impact on research performance (Reale & Seeber, 2011). Concerning this matter, our study offers interesting insights into how discipline-specific characteristics and changes should be taken into account when investigating how the reputation and prestige of academic institutions are constructed and maintained and how their excellence is measured.

In brief, the way in which PhD candidates and postdoctoral fellows are selected and trained is related to the perception of how academic prestige is constructed and maintained (Kyik & Smeby, 1994; Enders, 2005). The specific characteristics of the disciplines play an important role in shaping how PhD students and early career researchers are trained, but other factors seem to be relevant: external competition for excellence, evaluation of academic research and performance, size of research groups, and the national features of the HE system.

NOTES

[1] PRESTENCE (From Prestige to Excellence: the fabrication of academic quality) is a project started in 2009 by the ANR within the program "Sciences, technologies et savoirs en sociétés. Enjeux actuels, questions historiques."

[2] In Italy this change took place especially after the approval of University Reform Law 240/2010, which introduced important norms concerning the reorganization of the internal structure of Universities.

[3] Being ranked, as institutions, between 101 and 150 in the Academic Ranking of World Universities (ARWU).

[4] New 2011 QS World University Rankings by Subject - Natural Sciences.

REFERENCES

Barrier, J. (2011). Le science en projets: financements sur projets, autonomie professionelle et transformation du travail des chercheurs academiques. *Sociologie du travail, 53*(4).

Bonaccorsi, A. (2008). Search regimes and the industrial dynamics of science. *Minerva, 46,* 285–315.

Bourdieu, P. (1986). The Forms of Capital. In *Handbook of theory and research for the sociology of education,* edited by John G. Richardson. New York: Greenwood, 241–258.

Brewer, D. J., Gates, S. M., & Goldman, C. A. (2002). *In pursuit of prestige.* New Brunswick (USA) and London (UK): Transaction Publisher.

Burris, V. (2004). The academic caste system: Prestige hierarchies in PhD exchange networks. *American Sociological Review, 69*(2), 239–264.

Cyrenne, P., & Granta, H. (2009). University decision making and prestige: An empirical study. *Economics of Education Review,* 28, 237–248.

Cremonini, L. et al. (2009). Disseminating the right information to the right audience: Cultural determinants in the use and misuse of rankings. In B. Stensaker, B. M. Kehm (Eds.). *University rankings diversity and the new landscape of Higher Education,* Sense publisher.

Dill, D., & Soo, M. (2005). Academic quality, league tables, and public policy: A cross-national analysis of university ranking systems, *Higher Education, 49*(4), 495–533.

Federkeil, G. (2009). Reputation indicators in rankings of higher education institutions. In B. Stensaker, & B. M. Kehm (Eds.). *University rankings diversity and the new landscape of Higher Education.* Rotterdam: Sense Publishers.

Enders, J., (2005). Border crossings: Research training, knowledge dissemination and the transformation of academic work. *Higher Education, 49*(1–2), 119–133.

Enders, J., & De Weert, E., (2004). Science, Training and Career: Changing Modes of Knowledge Production and Labour Markets. *Higher Education Policy, 17,* 135–152.

Hazelkorn, E., & Moynihan, A. (2010). Transforming Academic Practice: Human Resources Challenges. In S. Kyvik & B. Lepori, (Eds.). *The Research Mission of Higher Education Institutes outside the University Sector.* Dordrecht: Springer.

Henkel, M. (2005). Academic identity and autonomy in a changing policy environment. *Higher Education, 49,* 155–176.

Henkel, M. (2007). Shifting boundaries and the academic profession. In M. Kogan, U. Teichler (Eds.), *Key Challenges to the Academic Profession, UNESCO Forum on Higher Education Research and Knowledge,* International Centre for Higher Education Research Kassel INCHER-Kassel.

Kehm, B. (2007). Quo Vadis doctoral Education? New European Approaches in the context of global changes. *European Journal of Education, 42* (3).

Kyik, S., & Smeby, J. C. (1994). Teaching and research. The relationship between the supervision of graduate students and faculty research performance. *Higher Education, 28*(2), 227–239.

Larivière, V. (2011). On the shoulders of students? The contribution of PhD students to the advancement of knowledge. *Scientometrics,* DOI 10.1007/s11192-011-0495-6

Leisyte, L., & Dee, J. R. (2012). Understanding academic work in a changing institutional environment faculty autonomy, productivity, and identity in Europe and the United States. In J. C. Smart, & M. B. Paulsen (Eds.), *Higher Education: Handbook of Theory and Research, Higher Education: Handbook of Theory and Research 27.* Dordrecht: Springer.

Mignot Gérard, S. (2003). Leadership and governance in the analysis of university organizations: Two Concepts in need of deconstruction. *Higher Education Management and Policy, 15*(2), 134–163.

Paradeise, C., & Thoenig, J. C. (2013). Academic institutions in search of quality: Local orders and global standards, *organization studies, 34*(2), 189–218.

Paradeise, C., & Thoenig, J. C. (2011). *The road to world class university. Elites and wannabes,* communication au organization studies workshop, 'Bringing public organizations back in', Les Vaux de Cernay, May 25–27 2011

Primeri E., & Reale E. (2012). How Europe shapes academic research: Insights from departments and research groups' participation in European Union Framework Programmes. *European Journal of Education, Research, Development and Policy 47*(1).

E. PRIMERI & E. REALE

Reale, E., & Poti, B. (2009). Italy: Local Policy Legacy and Moving to an "In-Between" Configuration. In Paradeise, C., Reale, E., Bleiklie, I. & E. Ferli (Eds.). *University Governance: Western European Comparative Perspectives*. Dordrecht: Springer.

Reale, E. (2010). Governance as a policy instrument for shaping the higher education systems balancing between autonomy, accountability and academic freedom, International Conference Tentative Governance in Emerging Science and Technology, University of Twente, The Netherlands, October 28–29.

Reale, E., Seeber, M. (2011). *The transformation of steering and governance in Higher Education: funding and evaluation as policy instruments*, WP1, CERIS-CNR, Turin.

Sauder, M., Fine, G. A. (2008). Arbiters, Entrepreneurs, and the shaping of Business School reputation. *Sociological Forum, 23*(4), 699–723.

Seeber, M. (2011). Efficacy and limitations of research steering in different disciplines. *Studies in Higher Education*, 1–19.

Shove, E. (2000). *Reciprocities and Reputations: New Currencies in Research*. In M. Jacob & T. Hellström (Eds.). The Future of Knowledge Production in the Academy (pp. 63–80). Buckingham: The Society for Research into Higher Education & Open University Press.

Stensaker, B., & Kehm, B. M. (2009). Introduction. In *University rankings diversity and the new landscape of Higher Education*. Rotterdam: Sense Publishers.

Whitley, R. (2000). *The intellectual and social organization of the sciences* (2nd ed.). Oxford: Oxford University Press.

AFFILIATIONS

Emilia Primeri
CERIS-CNR (Research Institute on Firms and Growth)

Emanuela Reale
CERIS-CNR (Research Institute on Firms and Growth)

VIVIANA MESCHITTI & ANTONELLA CARASSA

PARTICIPATION AS A FORM OF SOCIALISATION HOW A RESEARCH TEAM CAN SUPPORT PHD STUDENTS IN THEIR ACADEMIC PATH

INTRODUCTION AND OVERVIEW OF THE LITERATURE

The dynamics related to how PhD students are progressively integrated into their own disciplinary community, and how they learn the academic profession, represent an underexplored topic in the panorama of higher education studies, especially when considering in-depth investigations of specific institutional settings. Learning the academic profession is a complex and long process, and the integration of a researcher into the disciplinary community represents only its last step. The concept of 'socialisation' depicts this path. In this chapter, we will focus on socialisation: we will present a study aimed at showing how socialisation unfolds in the daily life of PhD students belonging to the same research team.

Research on PhD students' socialisation is mainly represented by large surveys or accounts gathered through interviews: in both cases, a focus on what happens in concrete places of interaction is missing, and this makes the comprehension of this phenomenon partial. Our aim is to fill this gap by studying socialisation in a specific context and by relying also on observation and fieldwork.

In this introductory section, we will briefly present some of the best-known studies focused on socialisation of doctoral students; in most of the cases, the studies have been conducted in the US, and they have mainly aimed to understand the conditions in which doctoral students successfully develop and complete their research. For example, Green and Bauer (1995) focused on mentoring and conducted a two-year longitudinal study on more than 200 new PhD students to understand the relationships among the student's potential for mentoring, mentoring functions offered by the supervisor, and student productivity. Golde (1998) focused on first-year doctoral attrition and studied the experiences of more than 50 students in four departments. Boyle and Boice (1998) focused on the detection of best practices for enculturating graduate students. Golde and Dore (2001) presented a large-scale study on the experience of US doctoral students. Austin (2002) conducted a huge longitudinal project on more than 70 doctoral students in two universities to understand how to design an effective and successful socialisation process. Gardner (2010) compared the experiences of 60 PhD students in high- and low-completing departments in the same university.

J. Branković et al., Global Challenges, Local Responses in Higher Education, 149–168.

It is remarkable that all these studies have emphasised the importance of having doctoral programmes that meet students' needs, of offering good mentoring to students, and of providing opportunities for meetings among peers. As we previously highlighted, the data used to draw these conclusions have been based on reporting methods, consequently, PhD students are asked to remember and describe specific events. To study a process that is unfolding over a long period of time, we believe that it can be fruitful to complement such methods with strategies permitting direct observation and in-depth investigation of what is happening in a specific context. Teeuwsen et al. (2012) provide a meaningful example of how qualitative research focused on a unique field brings to rich results for understanding socialization: they investigate the path of part-time doctoral students in a small group at a Canadian university using a reflective approach. This implies a strong attention on individually lived experiences. Our study also privileges an in-depth investigation of a unique field, but it takes a different perspective because we aim to focus on the activities and practices supporting socialization.

Ethnographic methods (O'Reilly, 2005) are well-suited for an in-depth investigation of how socialisation processes develop. Ethnographies of research teams are not without precedent because they were at the core of laboratory studies, which developed especially in the 1980s after publication of Latour and Woolgar's (1979) pioneering research on a microbiology lab. Nevertheless, the doctoral experience is not the main focus of ethnographies of research teams, as it can be also noticed in the review by Doing (2008) about the most recent developments in laboratory studies.

In the area of practice-based studies (Corradi et al., 2010), one can find examples of ethnographies of research teams, inspired especially by ethnomethodology (Mondada, 2005; Jacoby & Gonzales, 1991) and activity theory (Saari, 1999), but often the socialisation of doctoral students is not a core topic. An interesting exception is Ludvigsen and Digernes' (2009) study: they investigated how joint objects are established in two research communities belonging to two university departments. The authors also examined the implications of joint objects for PhD students' learning, but they did not follow the learning trajectory of the PhD students.

It is interesting to note that, from a broader perspective, the study of socialisation of newcomers in organisations, with a focus on the professional and entrepreneurial world, is more developed. In 1982 Moreland and Levine elaborated their well-known model of socialisation in small teams (Moreland & Levine, 2001, 1982), and this inspired considerable work in social psychology (Bauer et al., 1998, provided a review). This topic is of interest to scholars in organisation and management and to scholars in social psychology: both want to understand which phenomena affect socialisation and how newcomers can change team dynamics or creativity (Bauer et al., 2007; Choi & Thompson, 2005; Chen & Klimoski, 2003; Morrison, 2002).

The study of how doctoral students' experience develops in everyday activities will help to build models for understanding socialisation as a complex process, and fieldwork can be strategic to tackle this challenge. From a theoretical point of view, it is fruitful to take inspiration from theories that have been developed outside higher education studies and that have a specific focus on apprenticeship and teamwork. More specifically, we will draw on situated learning theory (Lave & Wenger, 1989), because it highlights the importance of concretely enacting work activities for learning, and the role of colleagues and peers in this process. We will further explain this approach in the next section.

The chapter is structured as follows: the next section is devoted to the theoretical background. Afterwards, we will present the research questions and the methodology. Subsequently, we will provide a comprehensive view of the research team that we investigated. We will focus on its composition, history, organisation, and main activities. This permits a better understanding of how PhD students' socialisation can develop in this environment. Before focusing on the activities that strategically support the socialisation of doctoral students, we will describe the work conditions of PhD students in the team. Then, we will follow the trajectory of a new PhD student on this team. Finally, in our conclusions, we will comment on the results and draw possible lines for future research.

THEORETICAL BACKGROUND

Our aim to investigate how PhD students' socialization unfolds in the daily life of a team brought us to privilege situated learning theory as a background. Its authors, Lave and Wenger, highlight the role of active participation in a specific setting of interaction for learning: the concrete act of taking part in work activities, probably in collaboration with other people (who could also be experts and act as mentors), is strategic for developing new knowledge, and for becoming a practitioner. The place where such processes occur is the 'community of practice,' a group of practitioners regularly sharing the same work routines.

The concept of community of practice (CoP) is widely used in both academic publications and magazine articles. Lave and Wenger strongly emphasised the unique relationship between learning and participating in a practice: a CoP is created through participation in a common activity and through the consolidation of a team of people around that activity. Basically, a CoP is defined and characterised through three coexisting dimensions: mutual engagement, joint enterprise, and shared repertoire. Mutual engagement is considered the base of a CoP. It implies that all the members are committed to work together to achieve shared objectives. Joint enterprise means that the CoP follows a direction and has goals negotiated among its members; it is the engine of a CoP. Shared repertoire indicates that the CoP has developed its own resources that also facilitate the work or are necessary for it: they can be tools or artefacts, but also a specific language or metaphors and stories. Wenger (1998, p. 73) emphasised that:

...the first characteristic of practice as the source and coherence of a community is the mutual engagement of participants. Practice does not exist in the abstract.

It exists because people are engaged in actions whose meanings they negotiate with one another. ... Membership in a community of practice is therefore a matter of mutual engagement. This is what defines the community.

Lave and Wenger (1989) were especially attentive to the process by which a newcomer has the possibility to become an expert and, consequently, a full member of the CoP. They called this process 'legitimate peripheral participation,' and they conceived it as a path from the periphery to the centre of the CoP. At the beginning of the period of apprenticeship, the newcomer is not a full member of the CoP and is positioned at its periphery. On the other hand, the newcomer's active participation in the community is legitimate; he or she is expected to contribute and to build a certain role within the CoP. Lave and Wenger (1989, p. 29) explained legitimate peripheral participation as follows:

Legitimate peripheral participation provides a way to speak about the relations between newcomers and old-timers, and about activities, identities, artefacts, and communities of knowledge and practice. It concerns the process by which newcomers become part of a community of practice.

Socialisation in a CoP is a common topic for scholars in situated learning theory (Bruni & Gherardi, 2002; Boud & Middleton, 2003; Campbell et al., 2009; Cope et al., 2000; Fuller et al., 2005; Hodkinson & Hodkinson, 2004; Schulz, 2005). For this reason, we are convinced that situated learning theory is particularly inspiring for analysing PhD students' socialisation in a research team.

Situated learning theory and its concepts are, at the same time, much used and much criticised. Roberts (2006) effectively explained the criticism, mostly related to scant attention to the dynamics of leadership, power, and gender and to different types of expertise a newcomer can possess. On the other hand, this approach remains one of the most inspiring for analysing teams of professionals and the socialisation of newcomers. Because the concept of legitimate peripheral participation was developed outside the academic field and widely applied, we also refer to Golde (1998), who provided a precise definition of PhD students' socialisation. Following Golde, socialisation unfolds at four parallel levels: the discipline, the role of the PhD student, the profession of academics, and the department. An effective socialisation process must move incrementally through all these levels from the beginning of the doctoral experience, but full socialisation requires a lot of time and probably the entire doctoral process. This definition of doctoral students' socialisation highlights the complexity of the process and helps us to better focus on typical features of the academic profession.

RESEARCH AIMS AND METHODS

The present research, inspired by situated learning theory, seeks to show how the process of doctoral students' socialisation unfolds in practice in the everyday academic routines of a research team. More specifically, it aims to understand:

1. How the trajectory of new PhD students in a specific research team unfolds, and
2. Which team activities affect such trajectory.

Data were gathered in ethnography of an academic research team, as a part of a larger doctoral study on academic collaboration (Meschitti, 2012). The empirical phase lasted for one year, and it was conducted in 2010 by the first author, who was also a PhD student at that time, but in a different department. The team observed belonged to a Swiss department of informatics; it was chosen for its characteristic of trying to maintain a balance among research activities, education of undergraduate students, and education of PhD students whose doctoral works are clearly differentiated, this representing quite a common situation in Switzerland. The methods used were observation of team activities, individual in-depth interviews, and reviews of the team mailing list and the website. Observations were conducted at least once per week, and they were always including team meetings. Interviews were conducted twice, at the beginning and towards the end of the empirical phase. The different steps of the empirical research have been negotiated with the team members before starting the data collection. At that moment, ethical and anonymity issues were also discussed. Before definitely closing the empirical phase, a group discussion was organized to speak about the results, to receive feedback from the team, and to give suggestions on how to improve the team practices. This has been very important to strengthen the validity of our study.

The role of the researcher was near to that of an external observer. Because she was also a PhD student when collecting the data, it is possible that some dynamics of identification occurred, and that this influenced data gathering and interpretations of the results. This was, to a certain extent, unavoidable. Anyway, three strategies have been applied to assure consistency of the findings: interviews and observations always followed the same structure and specific time-lags; interpretations have been regularly and thoroughly discussed with the second author; the first author was particularly careful, when analysing the different types of data, to compare them and to interrogate herself about her role during the data collection.

Data analysis was inspired by the conceptualisation of CoP following Wenger (1998), by the concept of legitimate peripheral participation by Lave and Wenger (1989), and by the four dimensions defining the concept of PhD students' socialisation (Golde, 1998). More precisely, we made an initial mapping of the team and its activities to focus on the trajectories of PhD students, as well as how they participate in team activities and interact with colleagues.

THE FIELD: AN INTERCULTURAL RESEARCH TEAM

The field is represented by an academic research team that was born in 2007 when the professor who is currently leading it was appointed in the department of informatics of a young Swiss university. This department was established in 2004 and, at the time of the research, it included approximately 200 students from all over the world.

English is used as the lingua franca in teaching, research, and administration. In 2010, the academic staff consisted of 24 professors (6 full professors, 10 associate professors, and 8 assistant professors), 10 lecturers, and 99 PhD students. The team analysed for this project does not constitute a research institute, it is a team formed by the lead professor to develop research and grow the PhD students in the information retrieval domain.

When the empirical phase of this research started, 10 people were part of the team: the professor (also the chief of the team and the research advisor), a senior researcher, two post-doc researchers, and six PhD students. The senior researcher, one post-doc researcher, and two PhD students were there from 2007; the others arrived in 2009. The last person to become a member of the team was a PhD student who started in January 2010.

The team is heterogeneous from a cultural point of view, having three Iranians (all PhD students, two women and one man), two Italians (the professor, a man, and the senior researcher, a woman), a Swiss-Italian (PhD student, a man), a Malaysian (PhD student, a man), a Pole (post-doc researcher, a man), and an Australian (post-doc researcher, a man). It is also interesting that the proportion of women is higher than average: in informatics, a strong horizontal segregation persists, and in the department only 14% of the PhD students were women. These data are comparable with Swiss and European data: the Swiss Federal Statistical Office (2011) indicated that in Switzerland only 14% of the PhD students in informatics were women (2010/2011), while in Europe (European Commission, 2009) this proportion was 18% in 2006. The proportion of international students and researchers is also very high in this team, and this reflects the internationality of the department, where 93% of the PhD students and 86% of the professors do not come from Switzerland. This is quite exceptional if we compare these data with the number of foreign PhD students at the Swiss level (49.3%). Consequently, this department of informatics can be considered particularly international: it constitutes a sort of 'multicultural organization,' following Cox (1991). This reflects the internationality and the innovative position of the university where this department is located, features that are explained by Fumasoli and Lepori (2011).

The team is active and involved in 11 research projects. It leads four projects funded by the Swiss National Science Foundation (SNF), the agency that supports both free and oriented research and that, in Switzerland, constitutes the primary source of funding. The team also leads projects funded by other agencies, for example, one funded by the State Secretariat for Education and Research (SER), another funded by a facility in patent retrieval, one funded by a cooperative programme between Switzerland and Russia, and one funded by AT&T Labs. The team is also involved in two COST actions, a European Union funding instrument to foster cooperation and scientific excellence in specific domains of science and to facilitate mobility of researchers. This collaboration offers PhD students the opportunity to spend short-term periods in other research teams in Europe.

The team is well positioned at the European and international level because it has a good network with other teams studying the same topic in other universities, and its members regularly participate in the most prestigious international conferences in their field. Participation in conferences is important for the visibility of the team. In addition, the team is accustomed to hosting guests for brief periods. For example, during the empirical phase, three PhD students from other universities worked in the team for periods of two to three months. These students were integrated into the team; they participated in meetings and collaborated with other team members on specific activities.

As explained by the chief during an interview, the team is especially oriented towards research in the discipline; in fact, this is what appears in the team website and what emerges from observation. At the same time, it is worth highlighting that the team is positioned in an academic department, where all its members have teaching duties and where the education of PhD students is essential. The team is mainly composed of PhD students who need to learn how research should be conducted. Consequently, we can say that the 'official mission,' as depicted by the chief and as presented in the website, must be concealed with the features of the environment in which the team works.

To support its activities and optimise internal and external communication, the team relies on various artefacts, such as the team website, the wiki, and the mailing list: all these artefacts can be considered tools for facilitating team building and participation. Physically, the team members are located on the same floor of the department's building, near the main building of the university. The chief has his own office, the two post docs share an office, and the senior researcher shares her office with other researchers. The PhD students have their own desks in an open space. Team meetings are usually held in the same room on the ground floor or, when only few people attend, in a smaller meeting-kitchen room on the floor where they all work.

Main Group Activities

The most important group activity is the weekly meeting. The team meets regularly, always at the same time (usually 10.30 on Friday morning) for around an hour and a half. This time was selected because all team members were available to meet. The attention to choosing a time that is convenient for all team members is meaningful in understanding how collaborative relationships are cultivated in this team. Meetings also are clearly oriented towards enhancing disciplinary skills, and they originated as reading groups with an important educational aim. As the chief explained,

> Last year we had a course for PhD students about advanced information retrieval. But in fact only our PhD students were coming to the course, apart from one or two from other teams. So, at that point we decided to substitute these lessons with the reading group we have now, where we choose papers that

are interesting to everybody, who is proposing them for sure reads them, and then present them to the others, who try to read them so to have a discussion, even if then somebody cannot read them.

The chief often focuses on the importance of regular meetings, even when he cannot attend. The topic for the next meeting is decided at the end of each meeting and topics can be proposed by any member. Meetings also play a strategic social role because, at the end of each meeting, all team members eat lunch together outside the university campus. However, meetings are not only used as reading groups: during the observation phase, four meeting formats clearly emerged. In addition to the reading group, meetings are used to speak about one's own work, discuss group issues, plan important group activities, and work on these activities. Group meetings are characterised by a participative atmosphere, openness, and informality.

The team also invites speakers from other universities, usually once per month during the academic year. Invited speakers are suggested by team members and then selected together. The group carefully prepares for the arrival of an invited speaker and, very often before or after the lecture, group members have the opportunity to meet individually with the speaker.

Like group activities, personal activities related to individual research projects also play an important role. PhD students and researchers dedicate considerable time to their own research, which has clear-cut borders, and their topics and methods can also differ significantly. This is a precise choice of the chief, reflecting the trend in this academic setting of clearly distinguishing among individual scientific contributions, especially as far as PhD students are concerned. Furthermore, all the group members are involved in teaching or assistantships, and this workload can change from one semester to another.

It is worth noting that group activities (and meetings especially) represent a sort of 'exclusive place' that the group has built for itself. The different impact of the department's institutional framework on the type of activity analysed is evidence of the complexity of universities; as far as research is concerned, universities can be considered 'control-free spaces of work' (Gläser, 2012, p. 1), where the institution itself cannot impose or control the definition of tasks, work flows, and quality. On the other hand, constraints are much higher on teaching activities.

The Situation of PhD Students in the Team

PhD students on this team are all employed part-time by the university (60%-70%), most on projects funded for at least three years. They are hired on yearly contracts that are renewed until the end of their PhD course, and they are expected to finish in three to five years; the maximum time for employment with the university as a PhD student is six years. PhD students are expected to accept assistantships, but there is a high level of flexibility concerning the time spent in the department. These framework conditions are similar to those of other Swiss universities and follow the general guidelines of the Swiss National Science Foundation.

During individual interviews, it emerged that PhD students can dedicate on average half of their week to their own doctorates; depending on their assistantships and the type of course they are assisting. Schedules are flexible, but most of the PhD students are present in the department on a regular basis. However, the chief does not suggest that daily presence is a priority. As a general rule, PhD students meet weekly with their research advisor, who allocates one hour to each of them, but slots often change.

Regarding the different PhD topics, it is important to remember that borders among them are quite clear, as explained earlier. When students work on a funded project, part of their research becomes their PhD project. As one PhD student explained,

For my PhD ... I'm assigned to a Swiss project, that's the main goal to adapt and doing my research and my PhD also.

The trend in the department is to have PhD students work on externally funded projects. This has different advantages, and the ability to attract external funds is also a matter of prestige. On the other hand, the PhD project cannot be exactly the same as the funded research project, and sometimes the work in 'adapting' the project can be quite burdensome.

The department sets clear guidelines regarding the advancement of doctoral studies. After one year, students are required to submit their research prospectus and, after the second year, they must submit their dissertation proposal. The research prospectus is a short document (around four pages) to describe the area in which the student wants to conduct research. It is submitted, and then presented, to a review committee composed of academic and research advisors and two regular or adjunct faculty members appointed by the PhD program director. The committee gives feedback to the student, and every student must pass this review within 18 months of beginning their PhD studies. The dissertation proposal is a longer and more detailed document (20 pages) to present the PhD project, describing in depth the topic, methodology, aims, and time line. The proposal is submitted, and then presented, to a dissertation committee composed of an internal committee (research advisor and two faculty members) and an external committee (at least one research domain expert from outside the department). Every student must pass this review within 36 months of beginning his or her PhD studies. These regulations were established in 2010, and all the PhD students on the team must follow them. PhD students are also expected to attend specific courses offered to them by the department and to gather at least 12 ECTS. The submission of a book-length dissertation and the dissertation defense close the doctoral path; the dissertation committee can also demand changes to the thesis, and this work is compulsory to acquire the degree.

THE TEAM AS A COMMUNITY OF PRACTICE

This team can be considered a CoP where junior researchers are socialised to the academic profession, and thus where a trajectory of learning can occur. In the next paragraphs, we will analyse this CoP following the dimensions indicated by Wenger

(1998): joint enterprise, mutual engagement, and shared repertoire. Then, we will reflect on the dynamics related to hierarchy and leadership, phenomena usually overlooked by situated learning theory but that are constitutive of any team.

Shared enterprise is generally represented by the aim of advancing research in information retrieval, learning, and teaching, but also by the willingness to work together, share knowledge and experiences, and create new knowledge in the field. The fulfilment of such a complex enterprise should permit the construction of an environment in which each member can more effectively accomplish his or her individual objectives (earning the PhD, advancing the individual research project, building a strong curriculum). Team meetings are strategic moments where the joint enterprise is negotiated, and the chief strongly contributes to refine the enterprise with his attitude of promoting team activities and pushing active participation of each member. The chief regularly emphasises the importance of meetings, of exchanging ideas, of giving suggestions to each other, and of participating in conferences and promoting the research conducted in the team. Joint enterprise is also built and reformulated by the other team members. For example, active participation in team activities can be considered a form of adhesion to the enterprise.

Mutual engagement is a core aspect of any CoP. We conceive it as co-orientation of the CoP members, and one can observe it at a very concrete level, especially in daily routines and communicative interactions. Active participation in team activities is clear evidence of the mutual engagement: The willingness to make a personal contribution to team activities, to address doubts and questions of colleagues, and to spontaneously offer help are vital for mutual engagement. Referring to colleagues in case of need and keeping them up-to-date with individual advancements and more general news concerning the department and university are also signs of mutual engagement within the team. In general, interactions oriented towards colleagues and that carry a positive connotation help develop mutual engagement.

The shared repertoire exists and develops at two different levels. First, the specific language of the discipline is characterised by its own concepts and meanings. Then, the language of the team is composed by the team interpretation and knowledge of the discipline, but also by team anecdotes and specific shared meanings. This is directly observable in interactions and in meetings. The knowledge of the language of the discipline permits the CoP to fully participate in the international community. As far as the specific repertoire of the team is concerned, it is worth noting that the repertoire is shaped not only by the discipline, but also by the daily routines of the team and by the meaning that team members give to these routines. For example, the word 'meeting' for this CoP has very specific connotations that shape the actions and expectations of its participants.

This CoP distinguishes itself because of the strong regularity of face-to-face encounters, characterised by an atmosphere of informality that favours exchanges. Moreover, the team members share a high degree of motivation towards the team: Their work at the university is their main occupation and in general it represents the type of activity they would like to invest in for their future.

The formal hierarchy in the team is likely to reproduce the typical hierarchy of the academic career, but the chief favours a participatory structure in the organisation of team activities, such as weekly meetings and invited lectures.

Everyone is asked to bring suggestions for future activities and, during meetings, the chief leaves the floor to other members of the team. It is evident that the chief especially supports the PhD students in being proactive, taking the initiative, talking among themselves, and sharing information and knowledge. Indeed, the chief privileges participative leadership in organising team activities and he has an 'empowering leadership style' (Asmuß & Svennevig, 2009, p. 12). He motivates individual participation and team responsibility, this being reflected in his chairing style.

The participatory structure favoured by the chief makes the team hierarchy fade out, and this leaves space for more symmetric relationships. For example, this happens when, during a meeting, a topic is discussed and nobody has deeper expertise than the others or when a controversial task is debated. In these cases, the confrontation becomes very open, the presence of the chair becomes gradually less intrusive, and different contributions tend to be equally valued. Also, team members other than the chief might initiate exchanges or moderate parts of a meeting. Consequently, leadership is enacted not only by the chief; during meetings, other team members can be positioned higher than their formal role and become leaders at a certain point in the discussion. In this way, expertise becomes more important than formal hierarchy.

Finally, it should be noted that many practices characterising this team have team-building value. The meetings are clearly vital, and the team artefacts (website, wiki, and mailing list) play an essential role in external and internal communication in the display of team identity. In addition, the organisation of get-togethers outside work is an important initiative for strengthening social relationships within the team.

SOCIALISATION ACTIVITIES IN THE TEAM

We explained in the theoretical background that PhD students' socialisation can be considered as encompassing four dimensions: socialisation to the discipline, to the department, to the role of PhD student, and to the academic profession (Golde, 1998). When we mapped the different activities of the team, we could understand how important each activity is for socialising PhD students.

A particularly relevant activity is the team meeting. We said that meetings were born as reading groups and that they regularly take this format. Reading groups are widespread in different disciplines and they are used to improve domain knowledge (Golde, 2007). The possibility to engage in a scientific debate and to critically comment on a paper is essential. The debate on papers permits team members not only to dissipate doubts and questions about specific issues, but also to build new knowledge and to give advice on how to use specific theories, methods, and concepts.

The next excerpt shows how, during a debate on a paper, the discussion is momentarily suspended to focus on a concept that, in the previous part of the discussion, appeared to be unknown to most team members. Mat, a post doc, intervenes to explain a specific method, Lagrange multipliers. At the beginning of the meeting, this is not at the core of the discussion because it is a specific method used in only one of the formulas of the paper, but Mat understands that most team members are not familiar with it but interested in it, so he takes the opportunity to explain. We report here only a few turns, but the part of the meeting dedicated to this topic was longer and characterised by different questions from Mat's colleagues. We noticed that Mat asks the turn to Jan, who is chairing this part of the reading group and had previously commented on the paper. Then Jan, who is already at the blackboard to record the most important formulas of the paper, asks Mat whether he can write down the main points of his reasoning (turn 111), probably to facilitate understanding. Subsequently, Mat also goes to the blackboard, and the all interaction is then shaped by questions from his colleagues.

Excerpt 1

106. MT: Can I explain about Lagrange multipliers?

107. J: Yes.

108. MT: The idea is you have, you have an objective function, right? (indicates blackboard) It maximises M or N, and you have a constraint that all of SI, should be SI, in ECI, right? They have to sum to M, ok? You have to put that information into your constraint, into your loss function, I'm gonna do that, well, if you do, if you write M minus the sum of that SI is gonna be equal 0, right?

109. P: [Ok]
110. G: [Ok]
111. MT: Ok? So if you put, so we add to the loss function (goes to blackboard).
112. J: Can I write?
113. MT: Yes, you can write. Lambda times something that estimates necessarily equal to 0, ok? If it's not equal to 0 we get in trouble, and then we take the derivative of that instead of taking the derivative of the original loss function, it would be better (...) extra information in, ok?
114. S: I didn't understand why we should have that one.

Meetings are really helpful from this point of view because they provide a unique place where new disciplinary knowledge can be built thanks to the contributions of participants with different types of expertise. The meetings where a team member presents his or her own work are also significant from this perspective: presenting one's own work is useful not only for gathering suggestions from more expert colleagues, but also for permitting colleagues to learn new topics or topics about which they do not feel totally confident. Therefore, it is a highly useful moment both for the person who presents and for those who attend the presentation.

Invited lectures are also strategic in fostering disciplinary knowledge, because a researcher coming from another university gives a talk on a specific topic. Thus, this represents an occasion for networking, which supports socialisation to the community. Golde did not explicitly address this point, but it is a necessary step to become an academic. On the other hand, during the invited lectures, the time for open discussion and personal interaction is limited; consequently, there are fewer opportunities to go deeper into specific issues and to build new knowledge.

That PhD students share the same open space, that encounters with peers and colleagues are regular, and that during meetings there is always a slot dedicated to any news to share facilitate a new PhD student in understanding the new role and in becoming better integrated into the department. The sense of isolation is minimised by physical proximity while the possibility of meeting and getting to know other PhD students, researchers, and members of the academic and administrative staff is maximised. The physical proximity augments the possibility for newcomers to take part in relevant exchanges of information, to find available colleagues to obtain information they need, or to help with activities and tasks, while being part of such a CoP enhances opportunities to learn from peers.

Peers hold a strategic position. Actually, more expert PhD students can act as role models for less expert students. Through observation of their colleagues while they debate or they present their own work, newcomers can learn how to behave, approach a scientific text, present a PhD project, and give relevant feedback. New PhD students learn that they can rely on colleagues who are willing to help and that they can pose any question or express any doubt. Being in an atmosphere where mutual engagement is created and reproduced is extremely helpful in learning what it means to start a doctorate. In this case, we can say that peers are important socialisation agents.

The confrontation with role models also helps in becoming socialised to the academic profession. Of course, this is a long process and difficult to isolate in a specific moment. Meetings are strategic in this team; participation in meetings can help PhD students better understand the academic profession for at least four reasons. First, direct contact with role models that hold different positions in the academic hierarchy is provided. Second, topics that are particularly relevant to the academic career are often discussed, as when speaking about publications or about the peer review process. Third, some of the various topics treated during the meetings help PhD students understand how strategic academic activities, such as presentations, research, and readings, should be conducted. Finally, there is also the possibility to concretely enact such activities.

The empowering chairing style of the chief is vital. The general open structure of the meetings, with the presence of reading groups and of moments to discuss one's own work, is also useful. Reading groups are often where scientific debates arise, providing the perfect moment to learn how to critically read scientific research as an experienced academic would. Presenting one's own work also provides a sort of socialisation to the profession because this is a core activity of academia. Thus, meetings offer a breadth of opportunities to be socialised to the academic profession, such as being confronted with role models, developing a better understanding of relevant topics related to the academic career, explicitly speaking about key academic competences including writing, reviewing, and presenting, and also practicing those competences.

Actually, we can interpret each of the four dimensions of PhD students' socialisation, as described by Golde (1998), in terms of a trajectory from the periphery to the centre of four types of communities. For such an operation, we must stretch a bit the concept of CoP, but it is a useful exercise to better reflect on the different targets of each type of socialisation and to understand that a complete socialisation is a highly complex process involving very different actors and requiring very different activities.

When we consider intellectual mastery, the trajectory goes from the periphery to the centre of the disciplinary community. In the case of socialisation to the department, the department itself can be considered the community whose centre must be reached to become a full participant. In the case of socialisation to the role, the trajectory is from the periphery to the centre of the doctoral students' community. In the case of socialisation to the profession, the trajectory is towards the wider community of academics. The last two types of communities appear a bit generic and difficult to delineate without referring to a specific university or a precise scientific domain, but being a PhD student, or being an academic, brings to mind peculiar visions of work, specific approaches to research, and ways of relating to colleagues that differ from other professions and are recognisable as such. Table 1 summarises these arguments, drawing a parallel between Golde's model of PhD students' socialisation and Lave and Wenger's concept of legitimate peripheral participation.

Table 1. Relationships between the Concepts of Golde and of Lave and Wenger.

PhD students' socialisation (Golde, 1998), socialisation in four different domains:	Legitimate peripheral participation (Lave & Wenger, 1989), trajectory from the periphery to the centre of:
discipline	the disciplinary community
role	the PhD students' community
department	the department of informatics
profession	the academic community

If we carefully reflect on the last paragraphs, we can draw two important observations. First, we notice that sometimes a unique activity (e.g., participating in a meeting to present one's own work) can fulfil more socialisation needs (socialisation to the discipline, to the role, to the academic profession), while other activities (e.g., invited lectures) are clearly more strongly linked to one need (socialisation to the discipline). This point can be helpful for highlighting those practices that are particularly relevant to PhD students' socialisation. Second, we note that team meetings offer more opportunities to socialise PhD students, but this would be impossible in the absence of an empowering chairing style. Actually, this leaves space for more comments, ideas, and feedback to emerge; discussion is more vivid, and individual participation is fostered.

Referring to our theoretical background, we know that participation is the key to learning. In this team, PhD students have the possibility, first, to regularly observe role models and interact with them; then, to directly participate, give their ideas, express themselves, and present their own work. These two different types of activities are complementary and essential to empower and socialise new PhD students.

The Journey of a PhD Student into the Team

The beneficial effect of the activities we described above can be observed by carefully looking at the patterns of participation of each PhD student in the activities themselves. The ways in which a PhD student makes a contribution to team activities can reveal a lot about his or her socialisation path. For example, we describe here the trajectory of Paris during our year of empirical observation.

Paris is the youngest PhD student on the team; she started her doctorate in January 2010, just a few weeks before the beginning of our ethnographic observation. We can better understand how Paris accomplished full participation through an analysis of her contributions in the different meetings organised during the year of observation. In her first meetings, she carefully observed, listened, and took notes. During the discussions, she was often positioned as a beginner. For example, the chief addressed her uniquely to ask if she had more questions. She also positioned herself as a beginner; she was mostly silent and spoke only a few times, usually to ask a question about concepts new to her. Sometimes she said explicitly that she did not have a lot of knowledge on some topics or that she was 'just starting to learn'; however, in a few months, she became better acquainted with the team and the discipline, thanks also to support from the chief in getting her involved in team activities and to support from her colleagues.

A remarkable and definitive step in Paris' socialisation to the team can be observed in a meeting in December, where Greg's (another PhD student) work is discussed. At the end of the meeting, she insists that she wants a similar session, and she does not desist even when her propositions seem to become lost in the different suggestions for planning the next meeting. This is important for three reasons. First, it shows Paris' trust in her colleagues and in their suggestions. Second, it shows her feeling about being ready to present her own work. Finally, it shows her knowledge of the functioning of this CoP and her willingness to fully and completely participate. Actually, her ability to push for having a session similar to Greg's signifies that she feels safe, secure, and ready for this important step.

We can see in the next example how Paris clearly states her willingness to have such a meeting. Jan, another PhD student, jokes about the fact that she is too junior (turn 658). This joke seems to point out, even if ironically, that her trajectory to the CoP is not sufficiently advanced. Paris reacts by saying that Mike and Sheila (two other PhD students) provide each other with feedback every day. In this way, she is pointing out that Mike and Sheila conduct an important activity by themselves (this is probably also perceived as a sort of violation of the joint enterprise), and she is claiming her right to have such an opportunity during the meeting. Paris reaffirms her desire at turn 664. At this point, Greg seems to support her arguments, because he states the unwritten rule that the meeting is also for that purpose, but then the discussion fades away and focuses on other topics.

Excerpt 2

657. P: I would be interested to have such a session!
658. J: No, no way, you are too junior (laughs).
659. G: (…) (laughing)
660. P: No, Sheila and Mike are doing it every day, so,
661. S: Just wanted to ask feedback.
662. J: What?
663. G: You want to do this session more frequently?
664. P: No, to have some kind of feedback over my own project.
665. G: Yes, we have the team meeting once a week.
666. P: Yes.

In the next example (excerpt 3), we see that Paris has no problem in coming back to her point. In fact, her colleagues, Sheila and Jan especially, are discussing a paper to be read for the next meeting. When Paris reaffirms her wish, at turn 712, Sheila suggests that she choose a paper related to her work, but Paris argues that there is not a good paper on the topic. Greg seems to propose a compromise (turn 719), and then Paris herself comes up with an idea. It is interesting that Sheila proposes that she choose another paper, but Paris judges it not to be good enough. This moment is relevant because Paris is contradicting one of the most expert PhD students (who also had an important role in socialising her in the months before), and she is doing so by contesting the scientific quality of a paper. Finally, Paris succeeds in having her proposition accepted.

Excerpt 3

712. P: I think this is an opportunity to discuss my own work.
713. S: Pick another paper then!
714. J: Yes.
715. P: But there isn't a good paper (laughs).

716. J: Ok, let's discuss another paper (laughs).
717. P: No no!
718. S: (…)
719. G: You can do it, we can do reading group on that paper and then discuss.
720. P: I can send you a paper from participants in the PROS, the one that has best results, and it's the patent,
721. S: Or you can send us that EGOS, that paper that Jean Lave had.
722. P: That's not good but…

These excerpts show how Paris becomes progressively socialised to the CoP. More specifically, the selected examples mark the most meaningful steps of her path from the periphery to the centre of this CoP. Meetings have a high value in supporting this trajectory because, in these moments, new members are presented and then progressively empowered. They understand how the team functions, they can take part in discussions about team issues, they learn how to moderate a discussion and how to contribute during a debate, and they can propose topics and present their own work. In sum, during meetings, newcomers can start to build their own place in the CoP, get better acquainted with it, and gradually make their individual contribution.

TOWARDS A MODEL OF PHD STUDENTS' SOCIALISATION

This study is based on a unique case, and we are aware that it would be hazardous to generalise the results. However, we can draw important conclusions and provide suggestions. It should be noted that additional factors not discussed here affect the socialisation process during a doctorate.

First, the concrete work conditions are particularly important. In this case, PhD students are paid by the university or by their own projects and the doctorate is their main activity. They share most of their time together at the department, which provides physical space and all the facilities. This is essential for creating solid ground for socialisation to take place.

Second, we focused on a socialisation process unfolding in a team, but this is not the case for all doctoral students because, especially in the humanities, doctoral work is perceived mostly as an individual challenge. This is a very important factor to consider when designing new models able to explain the phenomenon. Thus, in some other cases, PhD students are engaged in a very structured programme, consisting mainly of courses that assure good socialisation to the discipline. All these factors are related to the features and rules of the department, which can be more or less careful in creating opportunities for socialisation.

Third, the relationships with the supervisor and with colleagues sharing the same research interests (and also having the same supervisor) are very important. It is not our aim to explore the features of interpersonal ties, but it is necessary to understand whether such relationships are favoured, as in our case, whether they are regularly cultivated and whether a specific team identity emerges.

Finally, if we consider more strictly a research team, the management and leadership style have a strong impact. In this case, the formal leader is responsible for creating conditions that foster socialisation. Following our results, we can see that some activities, such as invited lectures and meetings, are beneficial. Nevertheless, we do not want to say that these activities always offer the most effective solution. More important is the creation of a space where PhD students can openly discuss and relate with role models. This permits PhD students to participate in their learning trajectory. Such space should not only foster disciplinary knowledge, but also increase awareness of the features of the academic profession and the disciplinary community. Actually, these points, despite their importance, are often not addressed even by formal doctoral programmes, which not only tend to focus solely on disciplinary aspects, but also to privilege traditional methods (e.g., *ex-cathedra* lessons) instead of trying to stimulate debate.

CONCLUSIONS

In this paper, we presented a concrete case of a CoP where PhD students are progressively socialised. Following Golde (1998), we explained that socialisation encompasses four dimensions: socialisation to the discipline, to the role of PhD student, to the department, and to the academic profession. Drawing on situated learning theory, we affirmed that participation in concrete CoP activities is strategic in learning and in being socialised. First, we observed that this team represents a peculiar CoP, with a strong mutual engagement among its members, this being a very good condition to facilitate socialisation. Then, we analysed the team activities and explained how they help in socialisation. We observed that team meetings are particularly important, given the breadth of the topics treated and the open atmosphere, this facilitating free interaction. Invited lectures are also an important activity in fostering disciplinary knowledge.

We emphasised the role of the team chief in enabling the socialisation process. For example, the chairing style that he uses during team meetings motivates individual participation and debate, and this creates solid ground for learning to take place. By observing how PhD students participate in team activities and how they engage in fruitful discussions, as well as their willingness to propose topics for discussion, we proved that such activities are beneficial.

We proposed a model of PhD student socialisation, highlighting the role of the department, the specific work conditions, and the relationships with peers and supervisors, and we argued for the need to create open spaces for discussion to foster socialisation. Future research could employ the multiple case study approach to investigate the impact of specific disciplines and academic environments on the dynamics underlying the socialisation of doctoral students. Researchers could also examine the impact by following students throughout (and also after) their doctoral projects. This would surely help in the challenge of theory building.

REFERENCES/BIBLIOGRAPHY

Asmuß, B., & Svennevig, J. (2009). Meeting talk. *Journal of Business Communication, 46*(1), 3–22.

Austin, A. E. (2002). Preparing the next generation of faculty: Graduate school as socialization to the academic career. *The Journal of Higher Education, 73*(1), 94–122.

Bauer, T. N., Bodner, T., Erdogan, B., Truxillo, D. M., & Tucker, J. S. (2007). Newcomer adjustment during organizational socialization: A meta-analytic review of antecedents, outcomes, and methods. *Journal of Applied Psychology, 92*(3), 707–721.

Bauer, T. N., Morrison, E. W., & Callister, R. R. (1998). Organizational socialization: A review and directions for future research. *Research in Personnel and Human Resources Management, 16*, 149–214.

Boud, D., & Middleton, H. (2003). Learning from others at work: Communities of practice and informal learning. *Journal of Workplace Learning, 15*(5), 194–202.

Boyle, P., & Boice, B. (1998). Best practices for enculturation: Collegiality, mentoring, and structure. In M. S. Anderson (Ed.), *The experience of being in graduate school: An exploration.* San Francisco, CA: Jossey-Bass Publishers.

Bruni, A., & Gherardi, S. (2002). Omega's story: The heterogeneous engineering of a gendered professional self. In M. Dent, & S. Whitehead (Eds.), *Managing professional identities: Knowledge, performativity and the "new" professional* (pp. 174–198). London, UK: Routledge.

Campbell, M., Verenikina, I., & Herrington, A. (2009). Intersection of trajectories: A newcomer in a community of practice. *Journal of Workplace Learning, 21*(8), 647–657.

Chen, G., & Klimoski, R. J. (2003). The impact of expectations on newcomer performance in teams as mediated by work characteristics, social exchanges, and empowerment. *Academy of Management Journal, 46*(5), 591–607.

Choi, H., & Thompson, L. (2005). Old wine in a new bottle: Impact of membership change on group creativity. *Organizational Behavior and Human Decision Processes, 98*(2), 121–132.

Cope, P., Cuthbertson, P., & Stoddart, B. (2000). Situated learning in the practice placement. *Journal of Advanced Nursing 31*(4), 850–856.

Corradi, G., Gherardi, S., & Verzelloni, L. (2010). Through the practice lens: Where is the bandwagon of practice-based studies heading? *Management Learning, 41*(3), 265–283.

Cox Jr, T. (1991). The multicultural organization. *Academy of Management Executive, 5*(2), 34–47.

Doing, P. (2008). Give me a laboratory and I will raise a discipline: The past, present and future politics of laboratory studies in STS. In E. Hackett, O. Amsterdamska, M. Lynch & J. Wajcman (Eds.), *The handbook of science and technology studies* (3rd ed., pp. 279–295). Cambridge, MA: MIT Press.

European Commission. (2009). *She figures 2009. Statistics and indicators for gender equality in science.* Luxembourg: Office for Official Publications of the European Communities.

Fuller, A., Hodkinson, H., Hodkinson, P., & Unwin, L. (2005). Learning as peripheral participation in communities of practice: A reassessment of key concepts in workplace learning. *British Education Research Journal, 31*(1), 49–68.

Fumasoli, T., & Lepori, B. (2011). Patterns of strategies in Swiss higher education institutions. *Higher Education, 61*(2), 157–178.

Gardner, S. K. (2010). Contrasting the socialization experiences of doctoral students in high- and low-completing departments: A qualitative analysis of disciplinary contexts at one institution. *Journal of Higher Education, 81*(1), 61–81.

Gläser, J. (2012). Universities as 'control-free' spaces of research work. *7th Organization Studies Workshop*, Rhodes, Greece.

Golde, C. M. (1998). Beginning graduate school: Explaining first-year doctoral attrition. In M. S. Anderson (Ed.), *The experience of being in graduate school: An exploration* (pp. 55–64). San Francisco, CA: Jossey-Bass Publishers.

Golde, C. M. (2007). Signature pedagogies in doctoral education: Are they adaptable for the preparation of education researchers? *Educational Researcher, 36*(6), 344–351.

Golde, C. M., & Dore, T. M. (2001). *At cross purposes: What the experiences of today's doctoral students reveal about doctoral education.* Philadelphia, PA: Pew Charitable Trusts.

Green, S. G., & Bauer, T. N. (1995). Supervisory mentoring by advisers: Relationships with doctoral student potential, productivity, and commitment. *Personnel Psychology, 48*(3), 537–562.

Hodkinson, H., & Hodkinson, P. (2004). Rethinking the concept of community of practice in relation to schoolteachers' workplace learning. *International Journal of Training and Development, 8*(1), 21–31

Jacoby, S., & Gonzales, P. (1991). The constitution of expert-novice in scientific discourse. *Issues in Applied Linguistics, 2*(2), 149–181.

Latour, B., & Woolgar, S. (1979). *Laboratory life. The construction of scientific facts.* Princeton, NJ: Princeton University Press.

Lave, J., & Wenger, E. (1989). *Situated learning: Legitimate peripheral participation.* Palo Alto, CA: Institute for Research on Learning.

Ludvigsen, S., & Digernes, T. O. (2009). Research leadership: Productive research communities and the integration of research fellows. In A. Sannino, H. Daniels, & K. Gutiérrez (Eds.), *Learning and expanding with activity theory* (pp. 240–256). Cambridge, UK: Cambridge University Press.

Meschitti, V. (2012). *Fostering teamwork and socialization in collaborative working environments. Insights from a situated study on a university research team.* (PhD thesis, Università della Svizzera italiana).

Mondada, L. (2005). *Chercheurs en interaction: Comment émergent les savoirs.* Lausanne, SUI: Presses polytechniques et universitaires romandes.

Moreland, R. L., & Levine, J. M. (1982). Socialization in small groups: Temporal changes in individual-group relations. *Advances in Experimental Social Psychology, 15*, 137–192.

Moreland, R. L., & Levine, J. M. (2001). Socialization in organizations and work groups. In M. E. Turner (Ed.), *Groups at work: Theory and research* (pp. 69–112). Mahwah, NJ: Lawrence Erlbaum Associates.

Morrison, E. W. (2002). Newcomers' relationships: The role of social network ties during socialization. *Academy of Management Journal, 45*(6), 1149–1160.

O'Reilly, K. (2005). *Ethnographic methods.* New York, NY: Routledge.

Roberts, J. (2006). Limits to communities of practice. *Journal of Management Studies, 43*(3), 623–639.

Saari, E. (1999). Dynamics of collaboration: The case of Finnish and American aerosol research groups. *Science Studies, 12*(1), 21–43.

Schulz, K. (2005). Learning in complex organizations as practicing and reflecting: A model development and application from a theory of practice perspective. *Journal of Workplace Learning, 17*(8), 493–507.

Swiss Federal Statistical Office. (2011). *Étudiants des hautes écoles universitaires 2010/11.* Neuchâtel: Office fédéral de la statistique.

Teeuwsen, P., Ratković, S., & Tilley, S. A. (2012). Becoming academics: experiencing legitimate peripheral participation in part-time doctoral studies. *Studies in Higher Education*, DOI:10.1080/03 075079.2012.729030

Wenger, E. (1998). *Communities of practice. Learning, meaning and identity.* Cambridge, UK: Cambridge University Press.

AFFILIATIONS

Viviana Meschitti
Faculty of Communication Sciences
University of Lugano, Switzerland

Antonella Carassa
Faculty of Communication Sciences
University of Lugano, Switzerland

PART 3

INSTITUTIONAL GOVERNANCE

RÓMULO PINHEIRO & BJØRN STENSAKER

STRATEGIC ACTOR-HOOD AND INTERNAL TRANSFORMATION

The Rise of the 'quadruple-helix university'?[1]

INTRODUCTION

In most European countries, the Nordic region included, higher education (HE) has undergone a profound transformation in the last couple of decades. This process is partly a result of substantial changes in society - such as declining birth rates, an ageing population and the rise of a global knowledge-based economy - in tandem with broad policy efforts aimed at modernising the public sector (Peters & Savoie, 1998) as a means of guaranteeing the future sustainability of the (Nordic) welfare state (Christiansen, Petersen, & Haave, 2005). Across Europe, higher education institutions (HEIs) are increasingly expected to respond more efficiently to the needs of society. Amongst other things, this implies taking on board a new set of functions and societal expectations: economic development and innovation (Pinheiro, Benneworth, & Jones, 2012); fostering interdisciplinary collaborations (Nowotny, Scott, & Gibbons, 2001) and carrying out activities in a more efficient (Frølich, Huisman, Slipersæter, Stensaker, & Bótas 2013), professionalised (Gornitzka & Larsen, 2004) and socially-accountable (Stensaker & Harvey, 2011) manner. In order to respond to this rather complex set of external demands, HEIs - within and beyond the Nordic countries - have been adapting their internal goals, strategies and organisational structures (Beerkens, 2008; Pinheiro, 2013a) and strengthening their core competencies, not least in the realm of research (Kyvik & Lepori, 2010; Aksnes et al., 2012). Fiercer competition - for students, staff, funding and prestige (Kehm & Stensaker, 2009) - is leading HEIs to seek the benefits associated with economies of scale, e.g. through formal mergers (Kyvik & Stensaker, 2013; Pinheiro, Aarevaara, & Geschwind, 2013). Some have argued that what we are witnessing is a move from HEIs as loosely-coupled systems (Clark, 1983; Birnbaum, 1988) towards them being more tightly-integrated, strategic, organisational actors (Whitley, 2008; Ramirez, 2010).

These developments raise a number of important questions: How is this so-called transition to a more strategic organisational stance to be understood and interpreted? How is the pressure for 'strategic action' perceived and acted upon by the central steering core (Clark, 1998) of universities? These questions pose both theoretical and conceptual challenges and are pursued in this chapter through the empirical

J. Branković et al., Global Challenges, Local Responses in Higher Education, 171–189.

case of the sweeping internal transformations at one of Denmark's prominent universities, the University of Aarhus. The account provided here both describes and interprets how the combination of external possibilities and strategic initiatives has led to a radical and innovative yet controversial and increasingly challenging internal transformation process. More concretely, we discuss the drivers behind the transformation, the actual process and its outcomes and the core challenges associated with it. Following the introduction, section 2 briefly outlines the recent changes in the national HE landscape. This is followed by a conceptual and operational section. Section four presents the empirical findings and finally section 5 discusses them in the light of ongoing scholarly and policy debates and concludes by reflecting upon the study's implications.

REFORMS AND THE NEW DANISH HIGHER EDUCATION LANDSCAPE

At the end of 2001, shortly before the change of government, a national Research Commission proposed a number of sweeping reforms targeting the HE sector. These encompassed significant changes in the funding system and the internal management of universities, in addition to a reconfiguration of the domestic institutional landscape. The main policy objective was to increase the effectiveness and relevance of national research efforts. Shortly after, when a new empowered Ministry of Science, Technology and Innovation assumed overall responsibility for the national research and innovation agendas, the Commission's proposals were brought to the forefront of the policy-process. Two major reform initiatives came to the fore. The first targeted the research council system with the aim of ensuring an optimal use of public resources, and the second the existing University Act, as a means of simplifying the organisational structure and strengthening the overall management and coordination of the system as a whole. As a consequence, the research funding system was split into two subsystems, with separate councils for independent and strategic research. In addition, a number of new strategic-funding councils were established alongside the traditional research councils. In practical terms this led to a shift: (a) from core funding to funding based on competition; (b) from basic research to strategic research and (c) from smaller to larger grants (Aagaard & Mejlgaard, 2012).

Alongside this process, the internal university governance system also underwent dramatic changes. Central boards, with the majority of members being external, became the superior authority of universities. Senior leaders were no longer elected. Tasks like knowledge exchange, technology transfer and mobility were added as an integral component of universities' missions. The new regulative framework explicitly referred to the key role of central leadership structures in undertaking strategic selections across research and educational areas and in giving these a high long-term priority (through reallocation of funds). The policy aim was to strengthen the institutional profiles of domestic universities on the one hand and to foster strategic collaborations amongst the various actors composing the research and innovation sub-systems on the other.

In 2005 a Danish Globalisation Council, with broad representation from different sections of society, was established. Its main role was to advise the central government on a broader strategy for repositioning Denmark within the context of an increasingly competitive global economy. The final globalisation strategy was officially launched in the spring of 2006. It contained more than 300 specific initiatives, encompassing extensive reforms across key sectors of the economy such as education and research. Its primary aim was to set in motion changes in the framework conditions – institutions, policies, policy-instruments, etc. – to promote growth and innovation in all areas of society.

The most tangible outcome of the globalisation strategy in the realms of HE and research was a rather fast merger process, initiated in 2006, which reduced the number of Danish universities from 12 to 8 with effect from the beginning of 2007. As part of this sweeping reorganisation of the domestic HE and research landscape, the bulk of the standalone public sector research institute sector (12 out of 15 institutes) became part of the remaining public universities. Copenhagen University, the Technical University of Denmark and Aarhus University were the major winners in the mergers, as they became larger (size) and stronger (depth and breadth). Combined, these three "super-universities" account for close to two thirds of all Danish public research. From a policy perspective, these prominent domestic players are expected to be more competitive when applying for external funding (e.g. from the EU) and to aid the recruitment and retention of international scientific talent. In the eyes of the newly established Ministry the so-called "modernised universities" would now be more capable of responding more efficiently to external events and stakeholders' demands *inter alia* by developing new educational offerings and by forming stronger, i.e. tighter, relationships with external partners such as industry.

CONCEPTUAL BACKDROP

The University as a Strategic Actor

The idea that organisations, HEIs included, go to great lengths to adequately respond to changes in their operational environments is not new (Oliver, 1991; Maassen & van Buchem, 1990; Clark, 1998). What is new however, at least as far Continental Europe is concerned, is the impact of external events and stakeholder agendas (Benneworth & Jongbloed, 2010), on the internal fabric of universities (Maassen & Olsen, 2007; Aghion, Dewatripont, Hoxby, Mas-Colelle & Sapir, 2008). The traditional "social pact" between HE and the nation state meant that universities were largely left to their own devices and relatively oblivious to major macro-level events and changing external circumstances (Clark, 1983; Neave, 2002). Amongst other things, this has led to the perception of academic institutions as 'closed systems' (Scott, 2008) largely disconnected from or 'loosely-coupled' (Orton & Weick, 1990) with their surrounding environments, illustrated by traditional perception of universities as 'ivory-towers' (c.f. Höltta, 2000). In Europe, this state-of-affairs started to change in the late 1970s and early 1980s as a result of two distinct, but nonetheless inter-related processes, namely; the exponential growth in student enrollments (Trow & Burrage, 2010) and government led policy-efforts aimed at reforming public sector organisations (Christensen & Lægreid, 2011). In the realm of HE, such "modernising" processes have resulted in profound transformations in the internal governance structures of HEIs (Amaral, Jones, & Karseth, 2002), substantiated around increasing institutional autonomy, mostly of the procedural type (Schmidtlein & Berdahl, 2005), a process known as *self-regulation* (Maassen & Stensaker, 2003). Over time, the sweeping changes affecting the sector have resulted in the "opening-up" of universities to a vast array of external constituencies and stakeholder agendas (Neave, 2002; Jongbloed, Enders, & Salerno, 2008).

One of the ways in which universities went about preparing themselves for the new operational conditions, nationally and internationally, was through strengthening their professional-administrative structures (Gornitzka & Larsen, 2004) and increasing the decision-making powers (centralisation) of leadership structures at both the central and sub-unit levels (Amaral et al., 2003; Clark, 1998). Consequently, such processes have directly contributed to the increasing *rationalisation* of academic structures and activities (Ramirez, 2006), making universities structurally more similar to other types of organisations like firms (Etzkowitz, 2003). This phenomenon is known in the literature as a process in which a stronger *organisational actor-hood* is developed (Krücken & Meier, 2006; Ramirez, 2010; Whitley, 2008), characterised by the prevalence of strategic-planning processes (Rip, 2004; Zechlin, 2010) including, but not limited to, the ability to efficiently respond to unforeseen external events and emerging market demands (Pinheiro & Stensaker, 2013). At the level of the individual university, this means that privileged strategic attention is currently being given to processes of *environmental screening* (Kekäle, 2003) and *sense-making* (Weick, 1995), as a means of fostering a series of structural and cultural adaptations (c.f. Fumasoli, Pinheiro, & Stensaker, 2012), either real or symbolic (Meyer & Rowan, 1991), geared towards decreasing the perceived "gap" between internal academic structures and behavioural postures and external dynamics and demands.

For reasons related to external support for organisational goals, also known as *legitimacy* (Deephouse & Suchman, 2008), as well as *resource dependencies* (Pfeffer & Salancik, 2003), socially-embedded universities that are highly responsive to environmental dictates, as has historically been the case in North America (c.f. Kerr, 2001), have had a general tendency to behave like organisational actors (Ramirez, 2010; see also Slaughter & Rhoades, 2004). It is argued that as organisational actors universities are more likely to be: (a) broadly accessible, i.e. concerned with *equity* issues (Clark, 1982); (b) socially-useful, focusing on social *relevance* across teaching, research and third mission (Pinheiro et al., 2012) and (c) organisationally flexible in the adoption/adaptation of internal structures and procedures in ways that are expected to enhance *responsiveness* to external (market-driven) demands (Beerkens, 2010).

In this chapter we are particularly interested in the latter ramification, pertaining to the notion of rationalised structures and the *de-institutionalisation* of "old" (seemingly outdated) standard operational procedures and, consequently, the *re-institutionalisation* of new, more flexible and efficient ways of organising academic work.[2] In real terms, these processes are manifested *inter alia* in: the widespread adoption – at central and sub-unit levels - of strategic frameworks and operational plans (Zechlin, 2010); the rise of strategic science regimes, particularly within research (Rip, 2004; Aksnes et al., 2012); professionalisation, centralisation and/ or role specification (Clark, 1998; Gornitzka & Larsen, 2004); attempts a reducing dependency on the public purse (Frølich, Kalpazidou, & Rosa, 2010) and orchestrated efforts at developing a distinct institutional profile and/or organisational identity (Fumasoli et al., 2012; Pinheiro, 2012b) that is capable of enhancing universities' competitive standing in an increasingly global market place (Kehm & Stensaker, 2009).

Yet, the processes described above do not occur in a linear fashion and are far from being predictable. Not only are environmental signals, such as shifts in policy logics (Maassen & Stensaker, 2011), rather ambiguous but each individual university is somewhat unique (Clark, 1992, 1998; Krücken, 2003). In spite of the presence of dominant global *ideas*, *blueprints* and/or *archetypes* at the (macro) level of the organisational field of HE (c.f. Beerkens, 2010; Pinheiro, 2012a, b), outcome processes, i.e. local manifestations of structural arrangements and their respective performance effects, differ as a result of the complex interplay between contextual dimensions. These include, but are not limited to: *path and resource dependencies* (Krücken, 2003); core competencies and institutional profiles (Pinheiro, 2012a, b); the degree of institutional *autonomy*, both procedural and substantive (Schmidtlein & Berdahl, 2005); the role played by central leadership structures *or central steering core* (Clark, 1998); *unit-level dynamics and academic aspirations* (Schwartzman, 2008); institutionalised, i.e. taken-for-granted, local norms, traditions and identities (Stensaker, 2004); and national, regional and local imperatives, dynamics and operational conditions (Pinheiro et al., 2012).

Conceptual Model and Operationalisation

The overarching idea surrounding the notion of "actor-hood," as expressed in organisational sociology, is that of *agency* (c.f. DiMaggio, 1988), with a privileged focus on the enabling role of individuals' social positions (in our case central leadership structures) within a particular organisational setting (Battilana, 2006). The general assumption is that, in such circumstances, behaviour, collective and/ or individual, is characterised by a careful calculation of risks, opportunities, and rewards or what March and Olsen (2006) famously refer to as the logic of "outcomes" or "means ends rationality." As far as universities are concerned, there are *three* key areas that are important for the university management to control when fostering local processes of change and adaptation, namely: *culture* (changes in meanings, roles and identities), *structure* (changes in the organisation of people and work) and *resources* (both people and funding). Of these three areas, culture stands out as the area most difficult for university management to control. Although a number of studies suggest a link between strategy and culture within universities (Maassen & van Buchem, 1990; Clark, 1998; Stensaker, 2004; Fumasoli et al., 2012), universities are renowned for institutional persistence or resilience, thus making cultural changes difficult to both initiate and handle (Clark, 1983). In instigating change processes, top-down initiatives are easier to implement with respect to resource allocation and formal structure. Early investigations have pointed to the critical importance of the internal distribution of funding within universities (Hackman, 1985; Covalescki and Dirsmith, 1988) and consequently its critical link to strategic processes initiated from the top-down (Clark, 1998; Pinheiro, 2012a). Hence, in this chapter, we shed light on the processes of strategic initiatives (Rip, 2004; Zechlin, 2010) for stimulating cultural change, especially within the human resource management area, in order to illuminate the ways in which: (a) organisational meanings and local identities are being reconstructed through strategic frameworks; (b) formal roles and responsibilities are being redefined and power/authority and autonomy are being reallocated and (c) scarce resources, mostly funding, are being redistributed across the academic heartland (Clark, 1998), i.e. *who* gets *what, when* and under *what circumstances.*

Figure 1. The study's conceptual model.

Below we provide a brief review of the operational concepts shown in figure 1, as per the adopted conceptual model.

Human Resource Management as a Driver for Culture Change

Strategic decision making in HE is not a new phenomenon (Maassen & van Buchem, 1990), but it has become an increasingly prevalent feature of the inner life of European universities in the last decade and a half (Clark, 1998; Rip, 2004; Zechlin, 2010). Nowadays most universities, regardless of their size and history/

age, are involved with various forms of strategic initiatives. There is currently a growing interest in developing human resource management initiatives that can foster cultural changes within the university (Deem, 1998; Fumasoli et al., 2012). Typically, these take the form of initiatives that intend to vocalise a sense of shared identity (mission) and destiny or ambition (vision); provide training and competence building activities for both academic and administrative staff; improve recruitment; highlight the importance of key constituencies or stakeholders; justify the allocation or concentration of resources, people and funds, across types of activities (core and peripheral) and provide a roadmap for the future development of the institution (scientific and market profile) as a whole.

Organisational Design and Role Redefinition or 'Structure'

Universities, and the various academic communities they host, are increasingly expected to directly contribute to the innovative and competitive capacity of local firms, regions and nations (Schwartzman, 2008; Pinheiro et al., 2012). This means that universities' primary activities and operations are increasingly susceptible to policy shifts and changing external circumstances, including the contradictory demands and expectations of various stakeholder groups (Jongbloed et al., 2008; Benneworth & Jongbloed, 2010). One of the many dilemmas facing contemporary universities in Europe pertains to finding a balance between their global scientific aspirations (*excellence*) and external expectations around the *relevance* of their activities to society and the local economy (Perry & May, 2006). Concurrently, most universities have or are currently in the process of establishing dedicated units such as centres of excellence and or innovation with these goals in mind (Aksnes et al., 2012; Pinheiro, 2012a). Yet, there is growing evidence suggesting that, given their specialised nature and strategic function, structural arrangements aimed at enhancing global excellence and/or local relevance are not necessarily 'tightly-coupled' with core teaching and research activities (Benneworth, 2012; Perry, 2012; Pinheiro, 2012 a, b).

In Europe, shifts in governance arrangements, e.g. enhanced institutional autonomy, accountability, rise of third stream funding etc., have resulted in substantial changes from the way academic activities are organised (c.f. Clark, 1983). Three key aspects are worth referring to. First, the exponential growth of professional administration, both at central and sub-unit levels, which over time has resulted in the *defacto* institutionalisation of a 'dual-structure' within universities (Gornitzka & Larsen, 2004). Second, the reallocation of power and authority as a direct effect of the increasing tendency for the centralisation of decision-making procedures around a smaller number of influential individuals and/or coordinating structures (Clark, 1998; Nguyen, 2012). Lastly, the rise of entrepreneurialism in HE (Clark, 1998; Etzkowitz, 2003; Slaughter & Rhoades, 2004), with academics expected to constantly scan the environment for new strategic opportunities (e.g. funding) and, in the process, contribute to increasing the level of coupling between external dynamics and internal activities (Pinheiro et al., 2012).

Resource Allocation

In many European countries the traditional way in which internal resources were allocated was based on the principle of *equality*, via, for example, the cross-subsidisation of weaker fields by the stronger internal sub-units (Clark, 1983). This situation has started to change in recent years, with a tendency for resources, both people and funding, to be concentrated around a number of strategic areas (Rip, 2004; Zechlin, 2010) expected to have a major impact on universities' institutional profiles and market standings, nationally and globally (Kehm & Stensaker, 2009). Across the Nordic region, efforts by the central steering core of universities aided by changes in national regulative regimes governing HE (Gornitzka, Stensaker, Smeby, de Boer, 2004; Aarrevaara, Dobson, & Elander, 2009), are well underway in order to *de-institutionalise* (Oliver, 1992) a 'culture of equality', where funds are distributed equally between groups, and *re-institutionalise* (Gornitzka, 2007) a 'culture of meritocracy', with resource flows following existing strengths and long-term strategic priorities set from above (Pinheiro, 2012a). This is resulting in the rise of new internal tensions within universities around the search for an adequate balance between: equity vs. excellence (Palfreyman & Tapper, 2008); efficiency vs. effectiveness (Gornitzka et al., 2004); accountability vs. autonomy (Stensaker & Harvey, 2011); and relevance vs. excellence (Perry, 2012).

STRATEGIC TRANSFORMATION AT ARHUS UNIVERSITY

Drivers and Internal Development Process

Until 2005, Aarhus University (AU) was a rather typical or traditional multi-faculty university where, amongst other things, leaders were elected. In the autumn of the same year, a new system based on appointed leaders at all levels of the organisation and a university board composed of a majority of external members were instituted. These changes were part of a larger internal reorganisation, which was a means of strategically responding to a number of key challenges facing the university. On the external front these challenges encompassed: increasing domestic and international competition for research funds and for talented researchers and students; a better understanding of the university's societal role, regionally and nationally; a strengthened focus on strategic research; and, the complexity associated with global challenges such as climate change and the external expectations from policy-makers, civic groups, etc., regarding the role of HEIs in helping to tackle such dilemmas. As for the internal challenges which played a key role in setting in motion internal reform or "modernisation" processes, these included, the need to: increase efficiency; foster multidisciplinary collaborations, as a means of breaking down departmental "silos" and developing collaborations with societal actors across public and private sectors and enhance the scope for strategic leadership.

In 2006, two small universities and two large government research institutions were integrated or amalgamated into the "old" AU, thus initiating the far reaching merger process shown in figure 2. The profile of the newly merged institution changed rather dramatically; from 5 to 9 core academic areas or knowledge domains and a 40% increase in annual turnover. As expected, the merger has also led to a much larger, diverse and geographically spread-out university, with multiple campus across various locations (see Pinheiro, 2013b). *Size*, i.e. the advantages associated with economies of scale and scope (c.f. Horta & Lacy, 2011) within the context of a fiercely competitive environment (Kehm & Stensaker, 2009) seems to have been the key driving factor behind the strategic actions taken by AU's central administration or steering core. This is reflected in the figures. The new AU became responsible for close to a third of the total research efforts across the Danish public-sector, with a study portfolio of more than 200 degree granting programmes, 59% of which are at the postgraduate (master) level.

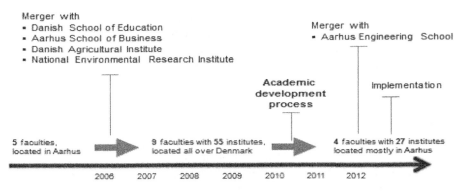

Figure 2: Internal change dynamics 2006-2012
Source: Holm-Nielsen (2012)

Strategic Initiatives for Cultural Change

An important aspect of the internal reorganisation process within AU pertains to the fact that no major structural changes were implemented for the first couple of years after the original merger. As an integral part of the so-called "merger agreements" it was decided that the merged units would continue as independent units ("business as usual") for a limited period of time. The first real step towards structural integration came in 2008, when the university adopted a new five-year strategy which was based around four core functions or activities: research; talent development; knowledge exchange and education (AU, 2008). The new strategic platform stressed the need for sweeping academic reorganisation. From the perspective of the central administration, the merger process had created the ideal conditions for setting in motion a vast array of synergies across the core functions including, but not limited to, the potential for interdisciplinary collaborations.

In March 2010, the Rector initiated the so-called 'academic development process', with the adoption of a new vision statement: "to belong to the elite of universities and to contribute to the development of national and global welfare." (AU, 2008, p.4) By June of the same year, the overall framework for the continuation of the merger/ integration process was determined. During the summer of 2010, each new core academic area undertook a thorough analysis of academic structures and requirements which also encompassed proposals for new departmental structures. Additionally, an assessment of AU's existing administrative structures and requirements was carried out, with the goal of determining how best to organise support functions within the context of the newly established (academic) structure. All in all, the internal reorganisation effort, designed and orchestrated by the central administration, aimed at achieving *five* main goals:

– to further improve quality, impact, and international reach;
– to strengthen performance in terms of academic and financial results;
– to complete the merger process, i.e. create one unified university;
– to tear down internal boundaries and stimulate collaboration across disciplines;
– to ensure a more professional and efficient administration.

Design and Roles

From the autumn of 2011, a new organisational structure (design) was adopted. It was composed of fewer core academic areas (faculties and departments), and a simpler administrative structure. The idea of "one unified university" was intrinsically associated with the strategic aim of tackling internal barriers to collaboration, for example by reducing the number of sub-units. After the original merger in 2006, AU consisted of nine independent faculties and schools and a total of 55 institutes. By the autumn of 2011, with the adoption of the new organisational structure, the number of internal units was reduced to *four* faculties (Arts; Science and Technology; Health; Business and Social Sciences) and a total of 27 departments. As a result, academically-related departments are, to a large degree, now located geographically close to each other in the form of coherent academic environments that cut across the (4) main academic areas. The solution, partly inspired by the most innovative firms within the private sector where horizontal collaboration and vertical integration are key features, was the adoption of a matrix-type organisational structure (see Pinheiro & Stensaker, 2013) as shown below.

An interesting element associated with the new organisational structure lies in the *four* horizontal priorities or core activities (left-hand side), with *talent development* standing out as a novelty. As a consequence of the adoption of the new structure, the central administration has often referred to AU as a 'quadruple helix university',

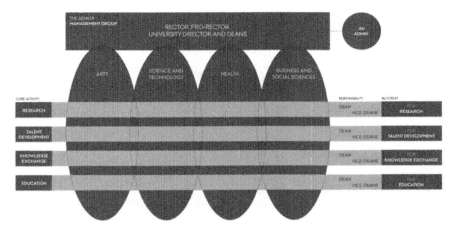

Figure 3. AU's newly adopted (matrix) organisational structure.
Source: Holm-Nielsen (2012)

in contrast with the traditional 'triple-helix'[3] model of teaching, research and third mission widely adopted elsewhere (c.f. Pinheiro et al., 2012). The dynamic relationship between the four core activities is visualised below.

The concept of the 'quadruple helix' university is an interesting one, and it that can be interpreted in different ways. One possible interpretation is that it is a much needed development of the triple helix model. In the traditional triple helix model, much emphasis has traditionally been put on the establishment of structural and systematic administrative links between universities, public authorities and industry (Etzkowitz & Leydesdorff, 2000), without necessarily taking into account what matters (key priorities) to the academic staff, and, in turn, how staff can handle (cope with) all the new expectations directed at them (Benneworth & Jongbloed, 2010), without suffering 'mission overload' (Enders & Boer, 2009). Following this line of thought, 'talent development' can then be seen as a strategic response to the limited scope of the structural linkages associated with the (traditional) triple helix model. Naturally, the specific ways in which this talent development function will take place is an important aspect to take into account in future (follow-up) studies. Hence, whilst an open approach might represent a modern re-interpretation of academic freedom and a broader recognition of the human ('soft') factors that help determine the ultimate success of a university, a more structured-oriented approach might, in turn, represent increased managerial control over academic work, and, as a result, play a role on determining what issues (tasks, goals, functions, etc.) should academics prioritise in the course of their daily activities.

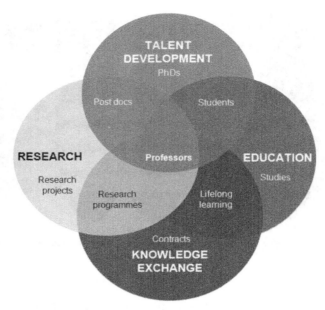

Figure 4. The notion of a 'quadruple-helix university' model.
Source: Holm-Nielsen (2012)

Moving on into role specification (power reallocation), at the level of the central administration or steering core (Clark, 1998), the internal reorganisation process initiated in 2006 has resulted in a shift from a total of no less than ten relatively separate management units towards a unified senior leadership structure (team) with cross-cutting responsibility for strategic management and quality assurance across the entire university. This smaller but much more powerful group of individuals consists of: the Rector, the Pro-Rector, the University Director and the Deans for each of the four core academic areas. The Rector is responsible for the daily management of the university within the framework set out by the University Board. The Deans are responsible for the academic and financial management of their respective academic areas. In addition, and on behalf of the senior management group, each Dean also has responsibility for the oversight of one of AU's core activities, namely: research, talent development, knowledge exchange and education. The remaining members of the senior management group perform their duties and responsibilities in light of the authority given to them by the Rector. The work of the senior management group is aided by three specialised or support units: the senior management group secretariat; the management secretariat and the press office. In addition to the senior management team, AU's executive management is comprised of vice-deans, department heads and study directors, all of whom perform their duties and responsibilities by the authority given to them by the Rector. In order to ensure academic checks and balances, a number of academic councils and internal forums responsible for each of the (4) main academic areas have also been established.

Resource Re-Distribution

In 2010, the University Board decided to establish a strategic financial management fund worth DKK 200 million annually (the equivalent of 3% of AU's annual turnover), totalling DKK 1,150 million in the 5-year period 2011-2016. The aim of this instrument is twofold: to support long-term strategic initiatives across the (4) core academic areas and to launch novel strategic endeavours, such as the establishment of promising interdisciplinary research centres and other initiatives aimed at promoting academic integration across the board. A series of interdisciplinary research centres involving different academic fields and traditions (artic research, i-sequencing, entrepreneurship and innovation, etc.), have been established. According to the central administration, the goal is to leverage the creation of new and groundbreaking scientific areas that are capable of enhancing the university's scientific profile, attracting talented staff and students and consequently leveraging AU's relative position in global research rankings.

DISCUSSION AND CONCLUSION

It is worth starting this section by briefly reflecting on the environmental conditions under which Danish universities currently operate. Developments across Danish university and science policy in the latest decade (Aagaard & Mejlgaard, 2012) have, to a large degree, been inspired or affected by dynamics at the regional/European- (Maassen & Olsen, 2007) and global- (Kehm & Stensaker, 2009) levels. A strong national willingness by policy-makers to pursue pan-European goals (Maassen & Stensaker, 2011) has meant that, as a country/HE system, Denmark has moved faster and more wholeheartedly in the directions set out by the Bologna process and in particular the Lisbon Agenda (c.f. Gornitzka, 2007), when compared to its Nordic neighbours (Gornitzka & Maassen, 2010). Moving our attention from the European arena to the national context, it can be argued that in one way or another all Danish universities have had the same opportunities for pursuing internal change. Yet, anecdotal evidence suggests that they have chosen different strategic responses (Oliver, 1991).

Against this backdrop, the AU case stands out as the Danish HEI that in many respects most pro-actively (and controversially) exploited the opportunities created by significant changes in the institutional (regulation) and technical (competition) environments both domestically and internationally. More specifically, the strategic decision to merge and the on-going internal reorganisation that followed, serve to illuminate the ways in which the privileged social positions, as regards both power and legitimacy, occupied by particular individual (e.g. the Rector) and collective (central steering core) agents at the organisational level play a key role in the process of change and transformation (see Battilana, 2006), even when faced with internal challenges and contestation by members of the academic heartland (Clark, 1998). Stated differently, this case-study serves to illustrate the interplay between external pressures (macro) and strategic opportunities (meso) in the light of framework conditions (field level dynamics) on the one hand and academic aspirations (micro) on the other.

A distinctive characteristic of the transformation process at AU lies in the fact that all major initiatives in the last decade have, in one way or another, been initiated and consequently implemented by the central administration, i.e. top-down. This has resulted in a much more centralised organisation, a distinctive feature of the entrepreneurial turn in HE (Clark, 1998; Slaughter & Rhoades, 2004). In other words this case tentatively suggests that the European university is gradually but steadily moving towards the notion (archetype) of a unified, strategic, organisational actor, that is: capable of pro-actively responding to changing circumstances (Ramirez, 2010; Whitley, 2008); more financially self-reliant (Clark, 1998); increasingly sensitive to the needs and expectations of various stakeholders (Jongbloed et al., 2008; Pinheiro et al., 2012) and more accountable to society (Stensaker & Harvey, 2011).

Turning back to the role played by AU's central administration, it has rather strategically (March & Olsen, 2006) used its strengthened powers to simultaneously address a series of nested tensions and dilemmas, namely: resource dependencies (Pfeffer & Salancik, 2003); legitimacy concerns (Deephouse & Suchman, 2008) and the university's overall competitive outlook (Kehm & Stensaker, 2009). A telling example is the strategic focus on grand societal challenges and interdisciplinary collaborations where attention is paid to scientific (global) excellence and socio-economic (local) relevance (Perry & May, 2006) in an orchestrated attempt to combine somewhat contradictory policy logics (Maassen & Stensaker, 2011). Having said that, it remains to be seen whether the far reaching reforms exercised by AU's central steering core will affect academic postures and activities on the one hand and teaching and research performance at the local level on the other. In this respect we can only assume that, as is often the case when change processes are driven from the 'top-down' (c.f. Clark, 1998), actors across the academic heartland will tend to resist (some of) the new organisational arrangements (c.f. Oliver, 1991), particularly when these are seen as challenging established (taken-for-granted) norms, values, beliefs, roles and identities (Olsen, 2007), as well as the aspirations of particular academic groups across the heartland.

A unique feature of the changes that have taken place at AU is the ambition to promote human resource management (i.e. talent development) as a key strategic area (Zechlin, 2010). In attempts to transform universities into more strategic actors, much focus has traditionally been given to structural and resource-related issues (Krücken & Meier, 2006; Ramirez, 2010; Whitley, 2008). Far fewer initiatives have been taken with respect to human resource management. As such, AU is an interesting case and can be seen as one of the first universities to take the cultural dimension seriously (see Clark, 1992; Dill, 1982; Stensaker, 2004). As indicated earlier, it is somewhat early to assess the implications of this development for the university as an organisation. The strategic ambition of creating the 'quadruple helix' university is a novel concept which, so far, is without real substance. The concept might indicate a more managerial university aiming at creating more flexibility amongst academic staff, and with more strategic control over academic tasks and priorities. Given the many structural and administrative readjustments the university have had to do following the merger, it is not surprising that those in charge of university affairs also need new tools to make the new organization work. Whether the academic staff is willing to engage in its own talent development is yet another issue. For those amongst the academic staff that appreciate higher degrees of autonomy in determining their own affairs, this initiative may be seen as a way to limit (constrain) academic freedom in the realms of research and teaching. In this respect, it is interesting to note that AU has experienced a lot of tensions and conflicts when trying to implement its strategic ambitions. Hence, in the end, whether the ambitions will be realised or not is probably a question of the extent through which internal - steering core and heartland - attempts to instigate cultural change through systematic human resource management will be implemented.

NOTES

[1] An earlier version of this paper was presented at the 25th annual CHER conference in Belgrade, 10–12 September, 2012. We would like to thank Dr. Kaare Aagaard (Aarhus University) for his insightful contribution in an earlier version of the chapter, and to the book editors for their valuable comments. Any remaining errors are our own.

[2] Consult Oliver (1992) and/or Olsen (2010) for a seminal discussion on the inter-related processes of *de-institutionalization* and re-*institutionalization*. For a recent analysis within the organizational field of HE, see Gornitzka (2007) and/or Pinheiro (2012a).

[3] Within the social sciences, the concept of 'triple-helix' was originally introduced (and made popular amongst academic and policy circles alike) in the 1990s by Etzkowitz and Leydesdorff (2000), whilst referring to the importance attribute to university-industry-government relations.

REFERENCES

Aagaard, K., & Mejlgaard, N. (Eds.). (2012). *Dansk forskningspolitik efter årtusindskiftet*. Aarhus: Aarhus Universitetsforlag.

Aarrevaara, T., Dobson, I., & Elander, C. (2009). Brave New World: Higher Education Reform in Finland. *Higher Education Management and Policy, 21*(2), 2–18.

Aghion, P., Dewatripont, M., Hoxby, C., Mas-Colelle, M., & Sapir, A. (2008). *Higher aspirations: An agenda for reforming European universities*. Brussels: Bruegel Blueprint Series.

Aksnes, D., Benner, M., Brorstad Borlaug, S., Hansen, H., Kallerud, E., Kristiansen, E., & Sivertsen, G. (2012). Centres of excellence in the nordic countries: A comparative study of research excellence policy and excellence centre schemes in Denmark, Finland, Norway and Sweden. *Working Paper 4/2012*. Oslo: NIFU.

Amaral, A., Jones, G. A., & Karseth, B. (2002). *Governing higher education: National perspectives on institutional governance*. Dordrecht: Kluwer.

AU. (2008). 'Strategy 2008–2012: Quality and Diversity'. Aarhus: University of Aarhus.

Battilana, J. (2006). Agency and Institutions: The enabling role of individuals' social position. *Organization, 13*(5), 653–676.

Beerkens, E. (2008). University policies for the knowledge society: Global standardization, local reinvention. *Perspectives on Global Development and Technology, 7*(1), 15–36.

Benneworth, P. (2012). The relationship of regional engagement to universities' core purposes: reflections from engagement efforts with socially excluded communities. In R. Pinheiro, P. Benneworth, & G. A. Jones (Eds.), *Universities and Regional Development: A critical assessment of tensions and contradictions*. Milton Park and New York: Routledge.

Benneworth, P., & Jongbloed, B. (2010). Who matters to universities? A stakeholder perspective on humanities, arts and social sciences valorisation. *Higher Education, 59*(5), 567–588.

Birnbaum, R. (1988). *How Colleges Work: The cybernetics of academic organization and leadership*. University of Michigan: Jossey-Bass.

Christensen, T., & Lægreid, P. (2011). *The ashgate research companion to new public management*. Surrey: Ashgate.

Clark, B. R. (1983). *The higher education system: Academic organization in cross-national perspective*. Los Angeles, California: University of California Press.

Clark, B. R. (1992). *The distinctive college*. New Brunswick, N.J.: Transaction Publishers.

Clark, B. R. (1998). *Creating entrepreneurial universities: Organizational pathways of transformation*. New York: Pergamon.

Covaleski, M., & Dirsmith, M. (1988). An Institutional Perspective on the Rise, Social Transformation, and Fall of a University Budget Category. *Administrative Science Quarterly, 33*(4), 562–587.

Deem, R. (1998). "New managerialism' and higher education: The management of performances and cultures in universities in the United Kingdom." *International Studies in Sociology of Education, 8(1)*, 47–7.

Deephouse, D., & Suchman, M. (2008). Legitimacy in organizational institutionalism. In R. Greenwood, C. Oliver, K. Sahlin, & R. Suddaby (Eds.), *The SAGE handbook of organizational institutionalism* (pp. 49–77). London and Thousand Oaks: Sage.

Dill, D. D. (1982). The management of academic culture: Notes on the management of meaning and social integration. *Higher Education, 11*(3), 303–320.

DiMaggio, P. (1988). Interest and agency in institutional theory. In L. G. Zucker (Ed.), *Institutional patterns and organizations: Culture and environment* (pp. 3–21). Cambridge, Massachusets: Ballinger Publishing Company.

Enders, J., & Boer, H. (2009). the mission impossible of the European university: Institutional confusion and institutional diversity. In A. Amaral, G. Neave, C. Musselin, & P. Maassen (Eds.), *European Integration and the Governance of Higher Education and Research* (Vol. 26, pp. 159–178): Springer Netherlands.

Etzkowitz, H. (2003). Research groups as 'quasi-firms': the invention of the entrepreneurial university. *Research Policy, 32*(1), 109–121.

Etzkowitz, H., & Leydesdorff, L. (2000). The dynamics of innovation: from National Systems and "Mode 2" to a Triple Helix of university-industry-government relations. *Research Policy, 29*(2), 109–123.

Frølich, N., Huisman, J., Slipersæter, S., Stensaker, B., & Bótas, P. (2013). A reinterpretation of institutional transformations in European higher education: strategising pluralistic organisations in multiplex environments. *Higher Education, 65*(1), 79–93.

Frølich, N., Kalpazidou Schmid, E., & Rosa, M. J. (2010). Funding systems for higher education and their impacts on institutional strategies and academia: A comparative perspective. *International Journal of Educational Managemen, 24*(1), 7–21.

Fumasoli, T., Pinheiro, R., and Stensaker, B. (2012). "Strategy and identity formation in Norwegian and Swiss universities." Paper presented at the 25th CHER conference, September 10–12 Belgrade.

Gornitzka, Å. (2007). The lisbon process: A supranational policy perspective. In P. Maassen, & J. P. Olsen (Eds.), *University Dynamics and European Integration* (pp. 155–178). Dordrecht: Springer.

Gornitzka, Å., & Larsen, I. M. (2004). Towards professionalisation? Restructuring of administrative work force in universities. *Higher Education, 47*(4), 455–471.

Gornitzka, Å., & Maassen, P. (2011). University governance reforms, global scripts and the "Nordic Model." Accounting for policy change?. In J. Schmid, K. Amos, & A. T. J. Schrader (Eds.), *Welten der Bildung? Vergleichende Analysen von Bildungspolitik und Bildungssystemen* (pp. 149–177). Baden-Baden: Nomos Verlagsgesellschaft.

Gornitzka, Å., Stensaker, B., Smeby, J.-C., & De Boer, H. (2004). Contract arrangements in the Nordic countries: solving the efficiency-effectiveness dilemma? *Higher Education in Europe, 29*, 87–101.

Hackman, J.-D. (1985). Power and centrality in the allocation of resources in colleges and universities. *Administrative Science Quarterly, 30*, 61–77.

Holm-Nielsen, L. B. (2012). Mergers in higher education: University reforms in Denmark–the case of Aarhus university. Presentation at the seminar *"University Mergers: European Experiences,"* Lisbon, March 8.

Horta, H., & Lacy, T. A. (2011). How does size matter for science? Exploring the effects of research unit size on academics' scientific productivity and information exchange behaviors. *Science and Public Policy, 38*(6), 449–460.

Hölttä, S. (2000). From ivory towers to regional networks in finnish higher education. *European Journal of Education, 35*(4), 465–474.

Jongbloed, B., Enders, J., & Salerno, C. (2008). Higher education and its communities: Interconnections, interdependencies and a research agenda. *Higher Education, 56*(3), 303–324.

Kehm, B. M., & Stensaker, B. (2009). *University rankings, diversity, and the new landscape of higher education.* Rotterdam: Sense Publishers.

Kekäle, J. (2003). Academic leaders as thermostats. *Tertiary Education and Management, 9*(4), 281–298.

Kerr, C. (2001). *The uses of the university.* Massachusets: Harvard University Press.

Krücken, G. (2003). Learning the 'New, New Thing': On the role of path dependency in university structures. *Higher Education, 46*(3), 315–339.

Krücken, G., & Meier, F. (2006). Turning the university into an organizational actor. In G. S. Drori, J. W. Meyer, & H. Hwang (Eds.), *Globalization and organization: World society and organizational change* (pp. 241–257). Oxford: Oxford University Press.

Kyvik, S., & Lepori, B. (2010). *Research in the non-university higher education sector in Europe:* Dordrecht: Springer.

Kyvik, S., & Stensaker, B. (2013). Factors affecting the decision to merge: The case of strategic mergers in Norwegian higher education. *Tertiary Education and Management, 19*(4), 323–337.

Maassen, P., & Olsen, J. P. (2007). *University dynamics and European integration.* Dordrecht: Springer.

Maassen, P., & Stensaker, B. (2003). Interpretations of self-regulation: The changing state-higher education relationship in Europe. In R. Begg (Ed.), *The Dialogue between Higher Education Research and Practice* (pp. 85–95). Dordrecht: Springer.

Maassen, P., & Stensaker, B. (2011). The knowledge triangle, European higher education policy logics and policy implications. *Higher Education, 61*(6), 757–769.

Maassen, P. A. M., & van Buchem, M. T. E. (1990). Turning problems into opportunities: The university of twente. *New Directions for Institutional Research, 67*, 55–68.

March, J. G., & Olsen, J. P. (2006). Elaborating the "New Institutionalism." In R. A. Rhodes, S. A. Binder, & R. B.A. (Eds.), *The Oxford handbook of political institutions* (pp. 3–22). Oxford: Oxford University Press.

Meyer, J. W., & Rowan, B. (1991). Institutionalized organizations: Formal structure as myth and ceremony. In W. W. Powell & P. DiMaggio (Eds.), *The New institutionalism in organizational analysis* (pp. 41–62). London: University of Chicago Press.

Neave, G. (2002). The stakeholder perspective historically explored. In J. Enders & O. Fulton (Eds.), *Higher education in a globalising world: international trends and mutual observations: A festschrift in honour of Ulrich Teichler* (pp. 17–37). Dordrecht: Springer.

Nguyen, T. L. H. (2012). Middle-level academic management: A case study on the roles of the Heads of Department at a Vietnamese university. *Tertiary Education and Management, 19*(1), 1–15.

Oliver, C. (1991). Strategic responses to institutional processes. *Academy of management review, 16*(1), 145–179.

Oliver, C. (1992). The antecedents of deinstitutionalization. *Organization Studies, 13*(4), 563–588.

Olsen, J. P. (2007). The institutional dynamics of the European university. In P. Maassen, & J. P. Olsen, (Eds.), *University dynamics and European integration* (pp. 25–54). Dordrecht: Springer.

Olsen, J. P. (2010). *Governing through institution building: Institutional theory and recent European Experiments in Democratic Organization.* Oxford: Oxford University Press.

Orton, J. D., & Weick, K. E. (1990). Loosely coupled systems: A reconceptualization. *The Academy of Management Review, 15*(2), 203–223.

Palfreyman, D., & Tapper, T. (2008). *Structuring mass higher education: The role of elite institutions.* Milton Park & New York: Routledge.

Perry, B. (2012). Excellence, relevance and the construction of regional science policy: Science frictions and fictions in the north west of England. In R. Pinheiro, P. Benneworth, & G. A. Jones (Eds.), *Universities and Regional Development: A critical assessment of tensions and contradictions* (pp. 105–123). Milton Park & New York: Routledge.

Perry, B., & May, T. (2006). Excellence, relevance and the university: The "missing middle" in socio-economic engagement. *Journal of Higher Education in Africa, 4*(3), 69–92.

Pfeffer, J., & Salancik, G. R. (2003). *The external control of organizations: A resource dependence perspective.* Stanford, California: Stanford Business Books.

Pinheiro, R. (2012a). *In the region, for the region? A comparative study of the institutionalisation of the regional mission of universities.* (Ph.D dissertation). Oslo: University of Oslo.

Pinheiro, R. (2012b). University ambiguity and institutionalization: A tale of three regions. In R. Pinheiro, P. Benneworth, & G. A. Jones (Eds.), *Universities and regional development: A critical assessment of tensions and contradictions* (pp. 35–55). Milton Park and New York: Routledge.

Pinheiro, R. (2013a). Bridging the local with the global: Building a new university on the fringes of Europe. *Tertiary Education and Management, 19*(2), 144–160.

Pinheiro, R. (2013b). Designing the merged institution: The multicampus model. Paper presented at the Annual International Conference of the Russian Association of Higher Education Researchers, *'University Traditions: A Resource of a Burden?',* Moscow, September, 26–28.

Pinheiro, R., Aarrevaara, T., & Geschwind, L. (2013). *Mergers across nordic higher education: Stocktaking and future research agenda.* Paper presented at the 35th annual EAIR forum, 28–31 August, Rotterdam.

Pinheiro, R., Benneworth, P., & Jones, G. A. (Eds.). (2012). *Universities and regional development: A critical assessment of tensions and contradictions.* Milton Park and New York: Routledge.

Pinheiro, R., & Stensaker, B. (2013). Designing the entrepreneurial university: The interpretation of a global idea. *Public Organization Review,* (online first) 1–20. DOI 10.1007/s11115-013-0241-z.

Ramirez, F. O. (2006). The rationalization of universities. In M.-L. Djelic & K. Sahlin-Andersson (Eds.), *Transnational governance: Institutional dynamics of regulation* (pp. 225–244). Cambridge: Cambridge University Press.

Ramirez, F. O. (2010). Accounting for excellence: Transforming universities into organizational actors. In V. Rust, L. Portnoi & S. Bagely (Eds.), *Higher education, policy, and the global competition phenomenon* (pp. 43–58). Basingstoke: Palgrave.

Rip, A. (2004). Strategic Research, Post-modern Universities and Research Training. *Higher Education Policy, 17*(2), 153–166.

Schmidtlein, F., & Berdahl, R. (2005). Autonomy and accountability: who controls academe? In P. Altbach, R. Berdahl & P. Gumport (Eds.), *American higher education in the twenty-first century: social, political, and economic challenges* (pp. 71–90). Baltimore: John Hopkins University Pres.

Schwartzman, S. (Ed.). (2008). *University and development in latin america: successful experiences of research centers.* Rotterdam: Sense Publishers.

Scott, W. R. (2008). *Institutions and organizations: ideas and interests.* London: Sage Publications.

Slaughter, S., & Rhoades, G. (2004). *Academic capitalism and the new economy: markets, state, and higher education.* Baltimore, N.J.: Johns Hopkins University Press.

Stensaker, B. (2004). *The transformation of organisational identities: Interpretations of policies the concerning the quality of teaching and learning in Norwegian higher education.* (PhD disertation). Enschede: University of Twente.

Stensaker, B., & Harvey, L. (2011). *Accountability in Higher Education: Global Perspectives on Trust and Power.* New york: Taylor & Francis.

Tirronen, J., & Nokkala, T. (2009). Structural Development of Finnish Universities: Achieving Competitiveness and Academic Excellence. *Higher Education Quarterly, 63*(3), 219–236.

Trow, M., & Burrage, M. (2010). *Twentieth-Century Higher Education: Elite to Mass to Universal.* Baltimore: Johns Hopkins University Press.

Weick, K. E. (1995). *Sensemaking in organizations.* London: Sage Publications.

Whitley, R. (2008). Constructing universities as strategic actors: limitations and variations. In L. Engwall, & D. Weaire (Eds.), *The University in the Market* (Vol. 84). London: Portland Press Ltd.

Zechlin, L. (2010). Strategic planning in higher education. In E. Baker, B. McGaw, & P. Peterson (Eds.), *International Encyclopedia of Education* (Vol. 3rd Edition, pp. 256–263). Amsterdam: Elsevier.

AFFILIATIONS

Rómulo Pinheiro
Department of Political Science and Management,
University of Agder and Agderforskning

Bjørn Stensaker
Department of Education,
University of Oslo

MASSIMILIANO VAIRA

THE PERMANENT LIMINALITY TRANSITION AND LIMINAL CHANGE IN THE ITALIAN UNIVERSITY

A Theoretical framework and early evidences[1]

INTRODUCTION

Literature on organizational change has traditionally focused on processes of different type leading to some kind of changes, more or less manifest and profound, in the structures and operational facets of studied entities (systems, organizations, organizational articulations).

There are different theoretical streams by which organizational change has been studied (e.g.: *strategic approach* [Child, 1972; 1997; Kondra & Hinings, 1998; Oliver, 1991]; *isomorphic change* [Meyer & Rowan, 1977; Powell & DiMaggio, 1991; Tolbert & Zucker, 1983]; *translation theory* [Czarniawska & Joerges, 1995; Czarniawska & Sevón, 1996]). The analysis of change processes and effects has identified at least 3 kinds of changes occurring in organizations:

1. *Adoption*: It is a process by which organizations change their more visible aspects but not their core values and operational practices. It is the ceremonial, or cosmetic, and isomorphic change discussed by new institutional theory (Meyer & Rowan, 1977; Powell & DiMaggio, 1991) for which change assumes a ceremonial and formalistic character or is enacted by institutional pressures of mimetic, normative and coercive kind;
2. *Entrenchment* or *paradigm shift*: This concerns deep organizational change which reshapes structures, values and practice (Simsek and Seashore, 1994; Zeitz et al., 1999), for which change is the manifestation of a state passage close to evolution or revolution;
3. *Adaptation*: It is a change by which organizations try to cope with an unbalance in their task environment to find a new equilibrium, altering some parts of their structures, values and practices (Cameron, 1984).

These are the most common processes which are dealt by organizational analysts. To a large extent change is seen as a linear process. Obviously, in the literature studies on problems arising from a change process are not lacking: for example, analysis on organizational actors' resistance, unintended outcomes, domestication of innovations and the like.

J. Branković et al., Global Challenges, Local Responses in Higher Education, 191–208.

What it is lacking, are studies on a particular stage of change process, namely the *transition phase*[2] which organizations and their members always experience during the changing process. Actually, the word "transition" is widely used in analytical-interpretative approaches to changes, but more as a rhetorical and/or evocative term – mostly to indicate that something is changing – than as particular phase of change processes characterized by its own proprieties, contents, dynamics and possible outcomes to be investigated.

In the transition phase organizations experience a sort of suspended condition which can be labelled as *liminality*. This concept is drawn from the anthropologists van Gennep (1960 [original edition, 1909]) and Victor Turner (1969). Here is used to identify the stage of a change process by which an entity is no more as it was while it is not yet what it will be. Liminality occurring in the transition phase is a critical condition, because it is here that an organization could evolve in certain manner (planned or unplanned) or remain trapped in the transition phase, or liminal state. In this perspective, it is possible to observe in the transition phase a particular change process that I label *liminal change*.

This paper deals with transition and liminality applied to organizational change both in theoretical and empirical perspective. Firstly, I will provide a conceptual definition of transition and liminality. Secondly, I will develop a general theoretical model about transition and liminality and their possible outcomes. Then I will use an empirical case, namely the Italian university, to show how transition phase and liminality – under certain conditions – hinder change and trap organizations into a liminal state.

DEFINING TRANSITION AND LIMINALITY

Change is intrinsically related to concepts of evolution or development of any given entity (physical, biological, social) related to its transformation into something different from it was originally. In such a dynamic the entity does not experience a quantum leap from the original state to the new one, but goes through the more or less long intermediate phase of transition.

Transition denotes a particular state, or stage, in the entity's change process by which it is no more what it was, while it is not what it will be yet: The entity displays some of its original state features and some of the new state ones which stand in an unstable equilibrium.

An entity enters and experiences a transition stage generally as a result of an external factor action – like a change in its environment, or enacted by a purposeful action – which alters its equilibrium state. This is the case of ecological change in biological systems which preludes to an evolution, but also of social systems as when economic, political or cultural changes or revolutions take place. This kind of external shocks is generally *unintentional* and *unexpected*. In social systems shocks take place as an emergent effect of cumulative changes produced in a more or less long time span that in a given point of time reach a threshold beyond which they literally "burst out."

System's shocks can be also produced intentionally, like in scientific experiments or by political willingness. In this latter case, political or powerful actors outside the political arena exert pressures (via policy making, lobbying and collective actions), in order to change system, or parts of it, accordingly to their aspirations, goals, interests and so on.

Less frequently, but as much important, the entity's equilibrium alteration could spring from internal causes, as a process of endogenous development. Differently from biological entities where endogenous change is natural and necessary (e.g. development of animals and human beings), in social system we cannot speak of endogenous factors and processes in this narrow sense when we look to social change dynamics. This is because: 1) every social entity is embedded in more or less wider environment exerting pressures and/or influences on the social entity, conditioning its development; 2) change in any social entity is very often linked to power and thus to someone's purposes and intentionality; 3) social change is affected by a plurality and a heterogeneity of factors, causes and process which cannot be in any way reduced to the sole internal logics and processes.

More generally and in a metaphorical sense, we can speak of endogenous change for social entity when we focus on a single entity, treating it – metaphorically – as an organism with its own "rules" of development (for the use of metaphors in organization analysis see Morgan, 2006).

Given the outlined aspects, a transition stage is intrinsically related to a *crisis* produced by the alteration in an entity's equilibrium. As we will see in the next section, the crisis may lead to diverse processes and outcomes depending on various conditions. What is important here is that any transition process brings a state of crisis in a given entity. We now can formulate a general definition of transition:

> Transition is an intermediate phase, or stage, of any change process, during which a given entity's equilibrium is altered by exogenous or endogenous causes, creating a state of ambiguity and uncertainty leading to a crisis open to different outcomes.

This definition brings us to the concept of liminality, by which we come to a strictly social ground. The word derives from Latin *limen* meaning "threshold" and indicates particular situations characterized by ambiguity, disorientation and uncertainty. This concept has its roots in the anthropological studies of transition rituals inaugurated by Arnold van Gennep and developed by Victor Turner.

Along this line, the concept has been recently renewed and applied to social and political change phenomena by some political anthropologists (see International Political Anthropology Vol. 2 n. 1, 2009 special issue On Liminality). As Horvath, Thomassen and Wydra argue in their introduction to the journal issue (2009), when a social system enter a liminal period, its institutional structure is dissolving, uncertainty arises and grows, the taken-for-granted ideas about the future are no more trustable and become questioned. As Szakolczai (2000, p. 142) argues, 'the very structure of society [is] temporarily suspended'. Further, in this perspective liminality is close to the concept of entropy used by Zucker (1988). In liminal period a social system finds itself in a condition of entropy, for which the old structures are eroded, dismantled, delegitimized, while new structures are on the way to emerge but are still largely undefined, struggling for legitimation and unpredictable.

It is apparent how the concept of liminality is strictly linked to the one of transition, to the point that the two concepts could be used as synonymous. To be more precise, liminality is the condition which characterizes the transition phase occurring in a social context.

Regarding social phenomena, larger than individuals and small groups for which it was originally developed and used, the concept of liminality has been partially redefined, especially in relation to its dynamics and length. In its original formulation and application, liminality refers to a short period, generally socially expected and structured, in which a master of ceremonies – an institutionalized social role – through appropriate institutionalized rituals de-institutes a former status or identity and institutes a new one. In this regard, Szakolczai highlights how during a liminal stage 'the rite must follow a strictly prescribed sequence, where everybody knows what to do and how [and] everything must be done under the authority of a master of ceremonies'. In the same fashion Thomassen (2009, p. 21) underlines that 'members of the society are themselves aware of the liminal state: they know that they will leave it sooner or later, and have "ceremony masters" to guide them through the rituals'. The transitory disorder flows into a new and expected order[3]. In this perspective, liminality is artificially created as a part of the social order, that is, it is an institutionalized social construction (Berger Luckmann, 1966).

In larger social contexts this dynamic rarely occurs. Example of such a dynamic in larger social systems is when a charismatic leader emerges and leads society towards a new configuration (Hitler and Nazism could largely approximate this kind of situation[4]). In larger social contexts a liminality period often emerges in a unexpected way, there is no master of ceremonies, established rituals or other forms of order-building lack, or they are in competition, social groups struggle to impose their different *weltanschauungen*, values, practices, the new order is fuzzy and unpredictable (Thomassen, 2009).

More importantly for the theoretical framework I develop in the next section, liminality could transform itself into a permanent state, where a stable order, for different reasons and circumstances, does not emerge and ever-changing dynamics take place. Actually, Turner (1969) suggested the possibility that liminality may become fixed becoming a permanent feature of the social system concerned. Permanent liminality has been developed by Szakolczai (2000) (see also Thomassen, 2009). Modernity is a good example of permanent liminality and this feature can be traced back to classical sociologists like Marx and Weber up to Bauman's notion of liquid modernity (2000).

Fixed-time liminality and permanent liminality could be seen as two polarity of a continuum and this involves the temporal dimension of liminality. As Thomassen (2009) acknowledges, liminality may be characterized by different time lengths: moments (sudden events), periods (days, weeks, but even months and years) and epochs (decades, generations, or even centuries). It is obvious that the longer a liminal state persists, the easier it become a lasting or permanent feature of the concerned social system. Yet more importantly, this is not a discrete distribution along the temporal axis, but a continuous one: a sudden event, under certain circumstances, may growingly transform itself in a more permanent liminal condition affecting a social system.

Drawing from arguments discussed so far, we can define liminality as it follows:

Liminality is a particular state an individual, a group, a society – or its parts – faces during a transition phase, when the ordinary and taken for granted structures, rules, values and practices followed so far are suspended or dissolve or collapse. Liminal state may has different temporal length depending on circumstances and conditions which may lead to resolve it in a short time span restoring the order or, on the contrary, to make it a kind of permanent feature of the social system which become affected by social entropy.

A THEORETICAL MODEL OF TRANSITION/LIMINALITY DYNAMICS

On the basis of arguments and definitions presented above, now I turn to sketch a theoretical model addressed to analyse dynamics and different outcomes which take place during a transition and liminality stage of change process in an organized social system. Given its purposes, the model cannot be but developed in general and abstract terms. Figure 1 illustrates the model.

Alterations and the unbalance they bring produce displacement, uncertainty and ambiguity which cannot – or only partially can – be faced and managed by usual means and practices. The way reality has been seen, interpreted and acted so far becomes itself fuzzy and ambiguous with few or contradicting each other points of reference. All this produces a certain degree of entropy. Within certain threshold entropy open rooms for exploration, creativity and innovation. It pushes to think and act in unusual way. But if this threshold is passed, entropy grows creating a higher degree of uncertainty and displacement, because there are not reliable and trustable "recipes" (rules, values, cognitive and practical schemes) to face the new conditions, or even there are too many in competition, contradiction and supported by different groups. When there are rival definitions and "recipes," struggles among them and their respective supporting groups arise. Power struggles stake is the definition, construction and legitimation of schemes to re-establish order and stability in the system, as well as in the changed environment. Briefly, it is a struggle for institutionalization. Generally and in ideal typical terms, groups involved in such struggles can be gathered in four broad categories:

1. Innovators: taking advantage of the conditions of erosion of the institutional order, innovators aim at changing deeply the system through innovative institution building taking rid of old institutional order. In other words, they aim at a paradigm shift, using

Simsek & Seashore's concept (1994). Paradigm shift may be produced or reinforced by coercive and normative dynamics enacted by powerful institutions – like the State via policy making, transnational institutions, experts – as both DiMaggio & Powell (1991) and Hall (1990; 1992; 1993) contend;

2. Moderates: although they acknowledge that conditions are changed and the old order is no more appropriate, they aim at a more gradual and prudent change, introducing incremental innovations to adapt the system to changed condition which may be not fully clear yet. It is the case of adaptation following Cameron's terminology (1984), but also and to some extent the case of imitative processes discussed by DiMaggio & Powell (1991);

3. Conservatives: this group struggle to maintain the system's institutional order through deliberate and intentional strategies of resistance or using more subtle strategies like introducing cosmetic changes which are visible but do not change the core values and practices of the system. It is the case of adoption (Zeitz et al., 1999), or ceremonial change (Meyer & Rowan, 1977);

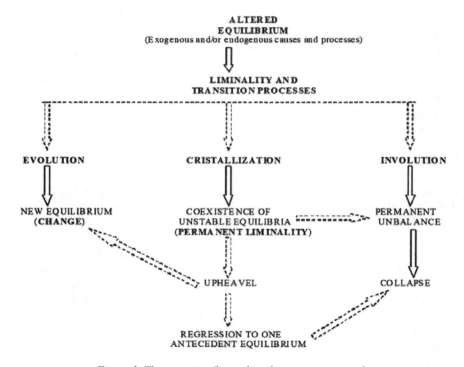

Figure 1. The transition/liminality changing process scheme

Note: The broken-line arrows indicate possible scenarios which may open under certain conditions, while the continue-line ones indicate a state achieved under given conditions.

4. Reactionaries: they are the opposite of innovators acting with same logic: taking advantage of the unstable condition to dismantle the undermined institutional order although not to innovate it, but to restore an "ancient" order, antecedent to the one in crisis, they consider worth.

Now let's focus on what the scheme illustrates and discuss its theoretical implications.

All this complex of factors produces a state of liminality in the concerned social system. How the change process will develop and follow a certain path with certain contents, feature and outcomes depends on: the struggles among those groups; the dialectic among them and between each of them, society and polity; their ability to mobilize resources and alliances supporting each cause. This brings us to consider the possible outcomes of a transition process.

As Figure 1 shows, liminality may resolve in three possible outcomes:

1. *Evolution*: This is the full change outcome; the system is transformed and displays completely, or at least largely, different structural, functional and operational features. The equilibrium with new conditions has been successfully achieved and system is able to operate with the new structures and procedures to pursue new goals, functions and values. Evolution is possible when a coalition of innovators shares a common set of values, ideas, world views, projects, operational "recipes" and they are able to impose them, or to gather allies creating a critical mass – in Gramsci's term, a social block – supporting and legitimating the change project;

2. *Involution*: It is a process by which the system regresses to the previous, or even more antecedent, state. Regression may be produced by: i) a system's inability to find new responses to the new conditions; ii) by the action of conservative groups who oppose and resist to change, aiming at maintaining structural form, functions and values of the system in despite of changed conditions; iii) by reactionary groups aiming to restore a past structural form as a reaction both to the fading present and to the future possible ones. In any case, since the system is pushed to a previous state unfitted with the new current conditions, the unbalance becomes radicalized and system goes towards its collapse;

3. *Permanent liminality*: This is the most interesting condition because it is open to more unpredictable outcomes, as the scheme illustrates. If in a certain point of time transition phase gets frozen, or crystallized, the system enter a stage of liminal changes, displaying at the same time new and old structural features with the coexistence of plural and different equilibria and unbalances. This creates tensions in the system and between it and its environment, given the mix of equilibria and unbalances, producing an entropic state. To some extent this condition is similar to the one described by the concept of punctuated equilibria drawn from evolutionary biology theory and used in economics (see for example Thurow, 1996). Although this state may develop into a full-fledged change or into an involution through upheaval processes, when innovators, or on the contrary,

conservatives/reactionaries win the struggle, it may also become a crystallized feature of the system persisting for a long time. This may occur when: i) none of the struggling groups have enough power to impose their respective world views and order models; ii) it becomes a sort of deliberate and intentional strategy enacted by powerful groups in order to maintain a fuzzy and unstable order; iii) it is an emergent effect of intentional actions to introduce continuous changes and innovations in the system, although not with the explicit aim to produce an unstable order. In any case, if permanent liminality and the entropic state it brings last for a prolonged period and in absence of an upheaval movement aiming at changing, or at least, at stabilizing the liminal changes in more ordered configuration, it may lead to system's permanent unbalance, change process inhibition and possible collapse.

It was previously noted that permanent liminality and entropy could be intentionally produced by powerful actors. Among those actors, political ones could play a crucial role by adopting policies which produce a great amount of instability in a given system, especially when policy making introduce continuous changes. This is important to notice because it casts a different light on what Zucker (1988) argues about entropy, as a state characterizing the micro level which undermines the macro-level order. If we assume that political actors could generate instability, via a policy making dynamic which continuously alters the conditions, it can be said that this is an institutionally produced entropy case. In other word, entropy is produced at the macro level by superordinate institutions and inoculated in the system destabilizing it with continuous changes which generate a permanent liminality state. As I will discuss in the next section this is the case of the Italian university policy-making and change process, characterizing particularly the last decade.

TRAPPED IN TRANSITION: LIMINALITY IN THE ITALIAN UNIVERSITY

The Italian university is a paradigmatic example of liminal change. The main actors responsible of such a dynamic are of political kind, namely the government and the Ministry of University.

After several decades characterized by inertia, since 1989 Italian university and its policy have entered a stage of change. By that time, reforms and changes they aimed at introducing never stopped. In particular, since 2001 university policy-making has been growingly characterized by what I define as hyper-reformism logic. By this term I mean a policy approach which is not based on needs or evidences for innovation but on voluntaristic reform frenzy – both of governments and ministries of universities – aiming at subverting changes introduced by a previous reform process. Since that time Italian university has been hit by several waves of reforms disrupting, partially or more deeply, changes introduced in a former phase.

I will not exam extensively all the reforms of the last twenty years but I focus on three areas of repeated intervention, namely: didactic structure, evaluation infrastructure and academic recruitment system.

Curricular and Didactic Reforms: 1999-2010

In the following years after the first curricular reform in 1991, it became clear that it did not produce the expected outcomes: An active minority of academics started a reflection on the need to change the university curriculum. When in 1996 the centre-left coalition won the general elections, a policy window to introduce changes opened (Kingdon, 1984; Vaira, 2003; 2011a). Between 1996 and 1999 at the Ministry of University special commission of academics worked on the curricular reform design, following the Sorbonne's agreement of 1998 and then the 1999 Bologna Declaration scheme. The reform was meant to meet the changed conditions both at national and international level affecting the higher education field (e.g.: changes on the demand side and students' social composition, push towards a tighter link and collaboration between universities and economic sector, knowledge and disciplinary innovations, knowledge-based economy and competition, harmonization of study programmes at the European level to allow students' and graduates' mobility in the European area). At the end of 1999 the general decree on didactic autonomy and new curricular structure was issued. In 2000 two decrees instituted and regulated the two degree levels (Bachelor and Master). Although the reform was not properly welcome by the majority of academics, reformists' front was enough strong and legitimated by both the new regulations and the Bologna Declaration, so that the large part of universities started to enact the reform framework between 2000 and 2001 (Vaira, 2003; 2011a).

In the spring 2001 general elections was won by centre-right coalition which declared its intentions to reform the reform. In a first time the aim was to abrogate it and to go back to the traditional 4-years structure, but protests and oppositions from the university world (rectors, academics and students) blocked this attempt, although it was supported by a strong minority of academics (especially, but not only, from the Humanities and Law fields). This was only a first defeat: the government in 2002 instituted a special committee with the task to change some parts the reform and one year later a new decree was issued. Although it abrogates the 1999 decree, it didn't change the curricular architecture, but introduced some restrictive criteria for the institution and maintenance of study programmes, called "minimum standard thresholds." These thresholds fixed a minimum number of staffed academics who must be engaged in a study program, the presence of appropriate infrastructural facilities, some general links between a study program and research activities (especially at the Master level) and a minimum number of enrolled students as mandatory requisite for instituting and maintaining a program. This entailed that a certain number of study programmes should have been suppressed; some programs were changed in advance, in order to conform to the reform, while students were already enrolled in such programmes. This created a relevant degree of instability both for universities and students because those changes undermined a structure which was already operating with some positive outcomes.

With the new centre-left government (2006-2008) the reform of the reform was provisionally suspended; universities going on with the previous regulations, albeit with the Damocles' sword that at the end the new framework will have got into force, as actually it did in the spring 2008. Between summer and autumn of 2008, universities worked hard to reform their study programmes. In the winter 2008 the government resigned and new general elections was won by centre-right coalition again.

The new government attacked frontally public university with a dramatic funding cut and part of this attack was to issue a new comprehensive reform. Despite strong and prolonged protests of academics and students, the reform went on, given the moderate support of rectors' association[5]. This created conflict lines among students and academics on one side, the government on the other and Rector's Association in the between.

The first reform step was to make the previous thresholds for study programmes and ministerial control over them even stricter. The result was that universities, which had just changed their study programmes accordingly to the previous reform, had to change them again to meet the new requirements. Between September 2010 and summer 2012 universities reformed their study programmes and a relevant number of them was closed down and other was changed or merged with others. The result is that the current didactic supply of public universities has been markedly reduced in respect of it was previously, while private universities' one has expanded, since for these institutions new regulations were not mandatory.

What is more important, along a decade university has undergone three didactic reforms: one every three years on average. Each post-reform reforming initiative disrupts to a more or less large extent the previous one, introducing new changes which impede the previous ones to stabilize and produce their outcomes and, above all, to allow concerned actors to act in a definite environment with definite rules and operations. Further it produced displacement, confusion tensions and uncertainty both for universities and students, a great amount of work addressed to follow continuous changes and, on the whole, instability in the task environment of universities, academics, institutions governance structures, administrative staff and students. Although these reform waves were justified on innovation, quality, efficiency and effectiveness rhetoric, they have undermined and are undermining one of the core activities of universities (teaching), not to mention the interference they had with other activities. Finally, various changes have settled, one over the other with little organicity if not mutual tensions or contradictions.

The Evaluation Infrastructure Reforms: 1993-2012

The first evaluation agency – the Observatory for the Evaluation University System – was instituted in 1993, but until 1996 it wasn't operative because only in that year all regulations concerning its operational activities were issued. For all the practical purpose, the Observatory's activities were irrelevant in term of effects on the university system and its activities.

In 1998 the Steering Committee for Research Evaluation (CIVR) was instituted and one year later the Observatory was replaced by National Committee for the Evaluation of the University System (CNVSU). The former's task was to evaluate research, while the latter's one was to evaluate the system's performance (teaching, students' performance, finance, recruitment, etc.). In 2003 CIVR launched the first research assessment exercise, started in 2004 and completed in 2007. CNVSU had regularly published its reports on university system since 2001 until 2010. Although the two agencies were fully operative, their reports had very scarce effect on the university system in term of allocation of a part of public funding on evaluation basis, reducing the assessment to a mere formal ceremony (Rostan and Vaira, 2011b; Vaira, 2011b). Actually up to 2010 less than 5% of the total amount of the public funding was allocated on evaluation results and only in 2010 and 2011 this percentage reached 10%. It must be noted that two third of this last percentage has been based on evaluation results of the first research assessment exercise undertaken in 2003. This has created great discontent in several universities: They were funded or not on the basis of research evaluation results of 7 years earlier, regardless whether they have improved their research output and quality and regardless whether other universities which performed well had in the meantime worsened their performance. Further, in these last 7 years evaluation criteria, weights, formulae to calculate block grant percentages to be allocated to each institution have changed several times. As a consequence, criteria used to evaluate institutions and to allocate the funding were not trustworthy and reliable creating a high degree of uncertainty and instability (especially in financial terms) in many universities.

This occurred because of a new reform of the evaluation infrastructure. In 2006 the centre-left government decided to change the university system evaluation infrastructure creating an independent (from both government and universities) and comprehensive evaluation agency. The project entailed that both CIVR and CNVSU should have been suppressed and merged in the new agency called ANVUR (National Agency for the Evaluation of University and Research). Consequently the second research assessment exercise which was in preparation was suspended, waiting for ANVUR institution. As a matter of fact, ANVUR was instituted, but in the meantime the centre-left government had to resign in 2008. ANVUR remained largely on paper until February 2010 when the institution decree was issued; in February 2011 board of governors was nominated by the government and with that ANVUR definitively lost its characterization as an independent agency, becoming a ministerial operational branch, thus highly dependent to the governing political majority. In the spring 2012 the second research assessment exercise for the years 2004-2010 was launched in a suddenly way and with great haste, in parallel to the implementation of the new overall university reform.

ANVUR criteria on which evaluation has been based were largely contested by the academic community. Part of those protests came from more traditional and adverse to evaluation academics, but a relevant part was based on scientific and informed critics to parameters, criteria and metrics which were judged not fully appropriated, untrustworthy and used in a mechanical way to evaluate research products and activities. The reason of those critics was that not only the future funding will depend on evaluations, but also institutions' and departments' ranking will be elaborated through the classification of their research intensity. Such a classification is meant to lead to a rationalization of the university system on the whole. If rationalization is at the stake, it is obvious that it is ought to be pursued by reliable and, above all, largely agreed criteria, which should be elaborated involving the academic community and not imposed as a ministerial diktat.

At the moment (autumn 2013) changes related to system's rationalization processes, if any, are largely unpredictable, since evaluation process has just finished and debates on results are still ongoing.

The Academics' Recruitment Reforms: 1998-2012

In the 1980 a reform changed deeply the structure of professoriate creating two new positions in the career ladder alongside of the Full professor one: Researcher (the first stable position in the academic career) and Associate professor (middle rank position). Until mid '80s the academic recruitment had developed on a quite regular basis, but afterward it started to slow down and by the end of the decade practically stopped. This was due to the highly centralized and bureaucratic recruitment procedures based on a national competitive exam of candidates to Associate and Full professor positions (Researcher recruitment was dealt locally by individual Faculties) which took long time and to the growingly lacking of financial resources. As a consequence throughout the '90s academic staff dynamic was blocked.

In 1998 a new academic recruitment reform was issued: competitive exams were to be called, organized and managed by individual institutions (decentralization) and awarded up to three qualifications for the Associate and Full professor positions. Qualified academics were eligible to be hired by any university. Universities were allowed to open a call for a position only if their costs for personnel do not exceed 90% of their total budget. Recruitment for Researcher position remained local as it was previously. Since 1999 the academic personnel dynamic had started again.

The 1998 reform had three main goals: 1) unlocking the recruitment and career dynamics and making them more regular, 2) allowing institutions to cope directly with their academic personnel needs and in the same time making them responsible of their personnel policy 3) favouring the inter-institutional mobility of academics (Boffo, Moscati, Vaira, 2004; Rostan & Vaira, 2011a). The first goal was fulfilled, the second only partially was and the third was almost a failure. Let's focus on the last point.

Universities largely favoured the academic advancement of local eligibles (90% of newly appointed Full professors came from the ranks of the university which opened the competitive exam for that position and the same was for 75% of newly appointed Associate professors). This phenomenon has been labelled as academic endogamy and it has been interpreted – especially at the political level – as the sign of academic "localism" based on patronage system strengthened by the local competitive exam device. The patronage system is a long lasting feature of the Italian university (Clark, 1977; 1983; Giglioli, 1979). Thus, localism is not a groundless interpretation, but it is partial and used as argument to justify a corrective reform policy and, above all, it masks other basic reasons: a) the public funding of universities since 2001 has been stable or with modest increases in nominal terms, but decreasing in real ones and b) the institutions' budget constraints on personnel expenditure. These economic and financial factors make the local eligibles' advancement more convenient, because their marginal costs are lower than a new full salary to be paid to eligibles not belonging to the institutions' academic staff.

In 2005 a new reform of recruitment/career system had been approved by the centre-right government. With the new reform career advancement was structured in two phases: the first one was constituted by national competitive exams at national level to gain the qualification, by which candidates become eligible to participate at the second phase; this one was a comparative evaluation of eligible candidates carried out at the local institutional level. Thus the new framework was a mix of national and local mechanism. Universities keep to be allowed to hire eligible academics within their financial constraints mentioned above. The Researcher position underwent to a major change: The old stable position was abolished and the new position was to be a fixed term one. Those who entered the position were to be hired with a three years contract renewable for further two years. If within three or five years a researcher hasn't gained the qualification as Associate professor, she/he has to be outplaced in a public administration or in the school sector.

As the 2005 reform was approved, although not fully implemented, years from 2007 to 2010 was characterized by a stop of competitive exams for Full and Associate Professor positions and even recruitment of researchers slowed down markedly. This because, in a first time, the centre-left government stopped the competitive exams waiting for the operative regulations for the new recruitment system to be approved, and then, when the new centre-right government was in charge in 2008, the strong restrictive financial policy – cutting the funding of the university and limiting the personnel turn-over – posed severe restrictions to recruitment and promotion. As a matter of fact since late 2008 no competitive exam for Full and Associate positions have been held.

In December 2010 the new overall university reform had been issued. As far as academics' recruitment/career system reform is concerned, the new reform draws largely on the 2005 previous one, but with a change regarding fixed-term researchers: They can be directly hired by their home institutions – if their financial budgets allow – as Associate professors, once they gained the national qualification.

In other words, the reform introduced something similar to tenure-track system. On the contrary, the "old" researchers have to get the national qualification and then pass through the local evaluation and selection exams to accede to the Associate professor position and thus cannot be directly hired. This created a divide in the lower rank of academic staff and gave rise to a wide protest of "old" researchers who complained the discriminatory effects of the reform.

Incidentally, if these two last reforms aimed at reducing localism, it is quite for sure they will not. The reason is simple: eligibles are recruited through comparative exams held by individual institutions. Thus for each institution will be always much more convenient to hire the local eligible given her/his lower cost; in time of budget reduction this cannot be but the most rational and obvious choice.

Going back to recruitment, two years after the reform, no competitive exam had been held yet. As a matter of fact recruitment and career advancement have been blocked since five years. But in summer 2012 the ministerial machine has started to move, introducing new criteria for academics' career advancement through ANVUR, which has elaborated a complex mechanism. Firstly it has distinguished disciplinary fields into bibliometric (like Sciences, Engineering, and Medicine) and non-bibliometric (like Humanities and Social Sciences). Secondly, a scientific journals ranking has been elaborated in collaboration with the various disciplinary-based associations of academics. Thirdly it has created two different kinds of median (each of them calculated on three partial medians) for bibliometric and non-bibliometric fields: the first one is based on indexed journal and citation index databanks on which the three partial medians were calculated (number of article, number of citations and h-index calculated on the whole citations received by an individual author); non-bibliometric fields' median is a mix of citations (where applicable), kind and number of publications (articles on reviewed journals, chapters in edited book and monographs). Medians are used to filter candidates to national qualification exams for Associate and Full professor position: Only those who exceed at least two out of three medians values are admitted.

This mechanism seems plain, objective and in accordance with the current evaluation practices, but it is not the case. An informal opinion and pressure group, called RoARS (Returns on Academic ReSearch) composed by about one thousand academics belonging to almost all disciplinary fields (with a relative majority from hard sciences fields), has highlighted several flaws, incoherencies, contradictions in the way indicators have been used to build up medians and how they are meant to be used for evaluations.

The current career advancement devices are creating a high degree of uncertainty in the professoriate, especially among researchers who fear that they can be seriously penalized in their career progression chances. Further, uncertainty get sharpened, because rules of the game have been changing both while candidates to qualifications were preparing their applications and during the first stage of evaluation process to award qualifications, currently ongoing (autumn 2013). Finally, whether and how academic recruitment logics and dynamics, and the structure of the Italian professoriate will be affected by ongoing changes is not clear at all, even if not few have serious doubts that it will change for better.

As a matter of fact, given all those conditions created by continuous changes, the professoriate witnessed a decrease equal to 22% (Full Professors -20%, Associate Professors -16%) between 2006 and 2012 given the retirements for age limits not balanced by new recruitment and career advancements. This, obviously, has dramatic implication not only on the professoriate itself, but also on the core activities of university (research, its quality and intensity; study courses supply, since it is linked to the number of staffed academics; quality of teaching), disrupting them.

CONCLUSIONS

In the last twenty years, the Italian university has been hit by four different waves of reform; the three areas selected as cases show, albeit in a synthetic way, the logic underlying each wave and the effects on the system. In these concluding remarks I sketch an interpretative analysis of the cases drawing from the liminality theoretical framework outlined in the first part of the essay.

The first remark concerns the source of liminality affecting the university system which is largely – if not exclusively – political. During the '90s the need to innovate university system after a long period of inertia to be at pace with social and economic developments both at national and international level, was rather felt as crucial by policy makers and a part of the academic estate. The two waves of reforms in these periods (1989-1993 and 1996-2000) were justified and legitimated on this basis. In particular, 1996-2000 reform was necessary to overcome the very limited effects of the previous one caused by passive resistances of the academy itself and after 1999 to align Italian university with the Bologna framework. Things changed in 2001 when university policy entered the stage of hyper-reformism. Both centre-right and centre-left governments and ministries have characterized themselves and their action with such an attitude. Hyper-reformism entailed a disruption – more or less wide and deep – of the previously introduced changes, a relevant degree of instability and uncertainty in the system. Liminal changes started to take place and never stopped so far, creating a permanent liminality with a plurality of unstable equilibria made of old, new and even newer structural features and orders. Those remarks confirm what argued about institutionally-produced entropy, generating a permanent liminality condition.

As a consequence, and this is the second point, continuous changes brought by policy reforms into the system has created and is creating a series of conditions which inhibits change itself. When an organization faces continuous changes in its structures and operational activities, it cannot evolve towards a new ordered configuration, but remain trapped or crystallized in entropic changes. This is a potentially very dangerous condition, in general and for university in particular, because institutions are completely absorbed by continuous changes which distract them from their core tasks. Even if the university system and its institutions are not at a collapse point, such conditions affect very negatively their efficiency and effectiveness, generating a great amount of instability and uncertainty. Actually, continuous change produces disorientation because actors have no stable and sure points of reference on which to structure their goals and activities as well as to make sense of the ever-changing task environment. In a few words, change, meant as evolution, is made very difficult to achieve.

Coming to the third remark, derived from the previous two, the Italian university system and its institutions are currently dwelling a punctuated equilibrium context. The instability brought by the reform waves between 2001 and 2010 has drawn university system and institutions fairly close to a situation of permanent unbalance. Currently the reformist frenzy has calmed down and the system is moving toward a complex liminal state in which latest changes are undergoing their implementation and adaptation to other more or less old structural features. The conditions created by last reform has given rise to a complex power struggle inside institutions among different groups each trying to take profit of the liminal conditions to pursue different and conflictual interests and views

It is not clear yet whether this process will produce an evolution in the system or it will leave in the liminal state of punctuated equilibrium.

NOTES

[1] The article is a revised and updated version of the paper "The Permanent Liminality. How Politics and Reform Policies Inhibit Change in the Italian University" presented at the 25th CHER Annual Conference "Higher Education and Social Dynamics," Belgrade, 9–12 September 2012. The revision made use of comments and remarks of participants at the presentation to whom I'm grateful.

[2] For example in two of the most prominent theoretical streams addressed to analyse organizational change dynamics, namely population ecology (Hannan & Freeman, 1977; 1984; Hannan & Carroll, 1992) and new institutionalism (Czarniawska & Sevón, 1996; Furusten, 2013; Powell & DiMaggio, 1991; Scott, 2008) approaches, transition is a completely neglected analytical topic. Managerial literature deals fairly extensively with the concept of transition. Yet, it does it in normative and prescriptive terms and aims, like in the Change Management approach, where the efforts are devoted to provide structured methods, guidelines and directories to guide, manage and overcome resistances during a transition phase in order to bring an organization from one state to a different desired one (e.g.: Beckhard, 1969; Hiatt, 2004; Jacobs, 1994; Lewin, 1951; Schön, 1983). Again, this is a linear conception of change and transition.

[3] This dynamic is constituted by 3 stages: pre-liminal stage, when the previous status/identity is been dismantling; liminal stage, when the old status/identity does not exist no more and new one hasn't take the previous one place yet; post-liminal stage, when the new status/identity has been created (Turner, 1969; van Gennep, 1960 [1909]).

[4] It must be noted that Szakolczai (2000) consider Hitler, as well as Mussolini, Lenin and Stalin, as "false" charismatic leaders but as *tricksters* (using it not as a moral, but as an analytical and ideal-typical category). During liminality period tricksters are mistaken as charismatic leaders (the "saviour," the "Providence's man"). This is not the place to deepen this distinction; what is important, reasoning in a weberian fashion, is that people during a liminality period see those figures as charismatic leaders, trust and follow them as such, making them masters of ceremonies.

[5] Rectors' consent was won through more a blackmail than an agreement: the Ministry of Economy declared to be ready to attenuate funding cut if rectors didn't oppose to the reform design; rectors accepted and as it was clearly expected to all but the rectors themselves, the "promise" was not fulfilled: all the programmed cuts were completely preserved.

REFERENCES

Antonio, A., Astin, H., & Cress, C. (2000). Community service in higher education: A look at the nation's faculty. *Review of Higher Education, 23*(4), 373–398.

Morison, S. E. (1936). *Harvard College in the seventeenth century*. Cambridge, Massachusetts: Harvard University Press.

Baldwin, R. G. (1996). Faculty career stages and implications for professional development. In D. Finnegan, D. Webster, & Z. F. Gamson (Eds.), *Faculty and faculty issues in colleges and universities* (2nd ed.). Boston, MA: Pearson Custom Publishing.

Bauman, Z. (2000). *Liquid Modernity*. Cambridge/Oxford: Polity Press/Blackwell Publishers.

Beckhard, R. (1969). *Organization development: Strategies and models*. Reading (MA): Addison Wesley.

Berger P. L., & Luckmann, T. (1966). *The social construction of reality*. New York: Dobleday & Co.

Boffo, S., Moscati, R., & Vaira, M. (2004). The international attractiveness of academic workplace in Europe: The case of Italy. In J. Enders, & E. de Wert (Eds.), *The International Attractiveness of the Academic Workplace in Europe*. Frankfurt: GEW.

Cameron, K. S.(1984). Organizational adaptation and higher education. *Journal of Higher Education, 55*(2), 122–144.

Child, J. (1972). Organizational structure, environment and performance. The role of strategic choice. *Sociology, 6*(1), 1–22.

Child, J. (1997). Strategic choice in the analysis of action, structure, organizations and environment: Retrospect and prospect. *Organization Studies, 18*(1), 43–76.

Clark, B. R. (1977). *Academic power in italy*. Chicago: The Chicago University Press.

Clark, B. R. (1983). *The higher education system. Academic organization in cross national perspective*. Berkeley: University of California Press.

Czarniawska, B., & Joerges, B. (1995). Winds of organizational change: How ideas translate in objects and actions. In S. B. Bacharach, P. Gagliardi, & B. Mundell (Eds.), *Studies of Organizations in the European Tradition*. Greenwich (CT): JAI Press.

Czarniawska, B., & Sevón, G. (Eds.) (1996). *Translating organizational change*. Berlin: W. De Gruyter.

DiMaggio, P. J., & Powell, W. W. (1991). The iron cage revisited d: institutional isomorphism and collective rationality in organizational fields. In W. W. Powell, & P. J. Di Maggio (Eds.), *The New Institutionalism in Organizational Analysis*. Chicago: The University of Chicago Press.

Furusten, S. (2013) *Institutional theory and organizational change*. Cheltenham: Edward Elgar Publishing Ltd.

Giglioli, P. P. (1979). *Baroni e burocrati. Il ceto accademico italiano*. Bologna: Il Mulino.

Hall, P. A. (1990). Policy paradigm, experts and the state: The case of macroeconomic policy-making in Britain. In S. Brooks, & A.G. Gagnon (Eds.), *Social Scientists, Policy and the State*. New York: Praeger.

Hall, P. A. (1992). The movement from keynesianism to monetarism. Institutional analysis and British Economic Policy in the 1970's. In S. Steinmo, K. Thelen, & F. Longstreth (Eds.) *Structuring Politics: Historical Institutionalism in Comparative Analysis*. Cambridge: Cambridge University Press.

Hall, P. A. (1993). Policy paradigms, social learning and the state. *Comparative Politics, 25*(2), 275–296.

Hannan, M. T., & Freeman J. (1977). The population ecology of organizations. *American Journal of Sociology, 82*(5), 929–964.

Hannan, M. T., & Freeman J. (1984). Structural inertia and organizational change. *American Sociological Review, 49*(2), 149–164.

Hannan, M. T., & Carroll G. R. (1992). *Dynamics of organizational populations*. Oxford: Oxford University Press.

Hiatt, J. (2006). *ADKAR: A model for change in business, government and the community*. Loveland: Learning Center Publications.

Horvath, A., Thomassen, B., & Wydra, H. (2009). Introduction: Liminality and cultures of change. *International Political Anthropology, 2*(1), 3–4.

Jacobs, R. W. (1994). *Real-time strategic change: How to involve an entire organization in fast and far-reaching change*. San Francisco: Berrett-Koehler.

Kondra, A. Z., & Hinings, C.R. (1998). Organizational diversity and change in institutional theory. *Organization Studies, 19*(5).

Kingdon, J. W. (1984). *Agendas, alternatives and public policies.* Boston: Little Brown.

Lewin, K. (1951). *Field theory in social science.* New York: Harper and Row.

Morgan, G. (1986). *Images of organization.* Thousand Oaks: Sage Publication.

Moscati, R. (1991). Italy. In G. Neave, & F. van Vught (Eds.), *Prometheus bound: The changing relationship between government and higher education in Western Europe.* Oxford: Pergamon Press.

Oliver, C. (1991). Strategic responses to institutional processes. *Academy of Management Review, 16*(1), 145–179.

Powell, W. W., & DiMaggio, P. J. (Eds.) (1991). *The new institutionalism in organizational analysis.* Chicago: University of Chicago.

Rostan, M., & Vaira, M. (2011a). Faltering effects of market-oriented reforms on Italian higher education: Focus on reforms promoting competition. In P. Teixeira, & D. Dill (Eds.) *Public Vices and Private Virtues? Assessing the Effects of Marketization in Higher Education.* Rotterdam: Sense Publishers.

Rostan, M., & Vaira, M. (2011b). Structuring the Field of Excellence. A Comparative View on Policies, Actors, Interests and Conflicts in Four European Countries. In M. Rostan, & M. Vaira (Eds.), *Questioning Excellence in Higher Education. Policies, Experiences and Challenges in National and Comparative Perspective.* Rotterdam: Sense Publisher.

Schön, D. (1984). *The Reflective Practitioner: How Professionals Think in Action.* New York: Basic Books.

Simsek, H. & Seashore Louis, K. (1994). Organizational change as paradigm shift. Analysis of the change process in a large public university. *Journal of Higher Education, 65*(6), 670–695.

Szakolczai, A. (2000). *Reflexive Historical Sociology.* London: Routledge.

Thomassen, B. (2009) The uses and meanings of liminality. *International Political Anthropology, 2*(1), 5–28.

Thurow, L. C. (1996) *The future of capitalism: How today's economic forces shape tomorrow's world.* London: Penguin Books Ltd.

Tolbert, P. S., & Zucker, L. G. (1983). Institutional sources of change in the formal structure of organizations: The diffusion of civil service reform, 1880–1935. *Administrative Science Quarterly, 28*(1), 22–39.

Turner, V. (1969). *The Ritual Process. Structure and Anti-structure.* Chicago: The Aldine Publishing Company.

Vaira, M. (2003). Higher education reform in Italy: An institutional analysis and a first appraisal. 1996–2001. *Higher Education Policy, 16*(2), 179–197.

Vaira, M. (2011a). *La costruzione della riforma universitaria e dell'autonomia didattica. Idee, norme, pratiche, attori.* Milano: LED Edizioni.

Vaira, M. (2011b) Evaluation as Ceremony. In M. Saunders, P. Trowler, & V. Bamber (Eds.), *Reconceptualising Evaluation in Higher Education. The Practice Turn.* Maidenhead: Open University Press.

van Gennep, A. (1960) [or. ed. 1909]: *The Rites of Passage.* Chicago: Chicago University Press.

Zeitz, G., Mittal, V., & McAulay, B. (1999). Distinguish adoption and entrenchment of management practices: A framework for analysis. *Organization Studies, 20*(5), 741–776.

Zucker, L. G. (1988) Where do institutional patterns come from? Organizations as actors in social systems. In L.G. Zucker (Ed.), *Institutional Patterns and Organizations. Culture and Environment.* Cambridge (MA): Ballinger Publishing Company.

AFFILIATIONS

Massimiliano Vaira
Centre for Study and Research on Higher Education Systems (CIRSIS)
University of Pavia

KLEMEN MIKLAVIČ & JANJA KOMLJENOVIČ

BETWEEN WESTERN IDEALS AND POST-CONFLICT RECONSTRUCTION

Meaning and Perceptions of Higher Education in the Western Balkans

INTRODUCTION

Post-socialist Europe followed the considerable expansion of higher education, as witnessed in most of the Western European countries in past decades, with a similar dynamic, but with a considerable delay. It is only recently reaching the steepest parts of the upwards sloping curve in countries of the Western Balkans. This part of Europe is a post-conflict region where tensions and conflicts of various types are still present in its societies. In addition, the region is undergoing a delayed transition from the socialist system to the liberal-democratic institutional arrangement based on a market economy. In such settings, higher education can play a specific role, especially when it comes to reconstructing society, resuscitating civil society, empowering democracy, fostering inter-ethnic reconciliation etc. (Miklavič, 2012, p. 106).

Researching the evolution, role and characteristics of higher education in the post-conflict societies of the Western Balkans unequivocally contributes to a much needed understanding of this little known area of Europe. Scarce research that has been done in the region hints at more regional idiosyncrasies in higher education than the mainstream higher education research in the West of Europe would account for. Besides moving the frontiers of what is known about the societies and institutions, this knowledge is essential for policy makers, development organisations, donors and implementers of projects/policies in the examined region.

In the study presented in this chapter the emphasis was put on understanding what the idiosyncrasies of the region are by letting the local actors express themselves and listening to their stories, priorities, narratives, perceptions and ideas.

DESCRIPTION OF DATA COLLECTION, METHODS AND CONCEPTUALISATION

The data was collected between February and June 2012 as part of a larger project dedicated to higher education reforms in the Western Balkans (CEPS, 2012; Zgaga et al., 2013). The field material consists of 76 interviews conducted with university leaders, government representatives, quality assurance agency officials and national experts from the region. In addition, more than 15 other informants were included in the research through informal talks.

J. Branković et al., Global Challenges, Local Responses in Higher Education, 209–228.
© *2014 Sense Publishers. All rights reserved.*

All eight countries of the region (Albania, Bosnia and Herzegovina, Croatia, Kosovo, Macedonia, Montenegro, Serbia and Slovenia) were included in the research; in each of them we focused on two public universities: (1) the biggest, capital city-based one and (2) a newer one, with the exception of Bosnia and Herzegovina, where the chosen two universities are based in two constituent parts of the country. In addition, we included two small, recently established private institutions - one from Montenegro and one from Slovenia (i.e. three institutions were examined in those countries).

The analytical approach for the interviews is based on grounded theory (Charmaz, 1990; 2006) in an attempt to contribute to the understanding of the discursive meaning and role of higher education in the modern political and social settings of Western Balkans. The fieldwork was prepared and conducted on the basis of general research questions such as *what are the main discourses; what is the political, social, normative framework; what are the underlying ideas and issues in the region; what are the dominant political/economic rationales underpinning the policies and discourses both of this region and in individual identified social and territorial units.*

The analysis was set out from emerging terms turning into concepts – an extended process of constant comparison and iterative questioning whereby we (1) compared the accounts and issues raised by the various interviewees; (2) compared the interview data with the informants and the quantitative questionnaire data; (3) contextualised the issues, discourses and ideas in the local socio-political and historical context; and (4) discussed and compared the findings between the research team colleagues. After the key concepts had been identified and defined, we conducted theoretical sampling consisting of collecting new data to check, fill out and extend conceptual categories.

The parallel checking had been conducted within and between *substantive areas.* For the purpose of further analysis we needed some additional analytical tools and found some elements of the *Critical Discourse Analysis (CDA)* (Fairclough, 2003; Wodak, 2008; Krzyzanowski & Wodak, 2011; Krzyzanowski, 2010) as appropriate for our purpose. The analysis gained context-sensitivity relying on a multilevel definition of context and encompassing the influence of changing socio-political conditions on the dynamics of discursive practices. Besides the interviews and conversations with informants, considerable desk-based research was conducted (especially in historical background, society, higher education system, and related figures) in order to establish the context as thoroughly as possible.

The findings from the interviews were confronted and complemented with the analysis of the quantitative data collected at the higher education institutions chosen as explained above. An electronic questionnaire was sent out to academic staff (i.e. senior and junior professors, lecturers and assistants) with the purpose of collecting their opinions and beliefs regarding their institutions and higher education in their respective country. The total number of respondents was 2,019 and the share is never below 5% of academic staff at major universities (over 1000 academic staff) and below 10% at other universities in the sample. The two small private institutions from Montenegro and Slovenia were excluded from the quantitative part of analysis due to the negligible number of respondents. The quantitative data used for this chapter was statistically analysed checking for *mean* differences between groups based on (i) country of origin (total of 8 groups[1]), (ii) higher education institutions (total of 14 groups[2]), (iii) study fields or disciplines (total of 8 groups[3]).

In order to reveal the mean differences we first used the Leven's test for homogeneity of variance. Based on the result the two standard approaches were used – in case of homogeneity of variance a one way ANOVA and Bonferroni post hoc test and in case of non-homogeneity of variance a Welch test and Games-Howell post hoc test. ANOVA and Welch tests reveal whether there are statistically important differences between groups, but they do not reveal between which groups differences are found. Therefore Bonferroni or Games-Howell post hoc tests were used to see between which groups there are such differences. For all tests the confidence interval was 95%.

ON THE PATH TO CRYSTALLISING CONCEPTUAL CATEGORIES: THE RECURRENT ISSUES DERIVING THE CONCEPT

In the subchapters of the following section some of the most emblematic and representative cases of discursive topics and conceptual categories which emerged from the qualitative analysis are presented. The aim is to sketch the map of dominant ideas, discourses, normative backgrounds, imaginaries and policy trends in the examined region. In most of the cases we confronted the results from the qualitative analysis with the findings from the survey among the academic staff of examined universities.

The "West" as The Referential Model, and Peripheral Identity

In most of the interviews there is a strong explicit (sometimes also implicit) tendency to mention Western institutions, Western systems, Western practice as the reference and direction to move towards. This is understandable, since all of the examined countries relatively recently underwent the transition from centrally planned mono-party systems to a market economy based on liberal democratic arrangements typical of the countries of Western Europe and the USA. The latter are perceived as more developed countries with an advanced organisation of their systems and institutions, including higher education.

The attitudes towards the West are manifold and regularly expressed with the topos of the need to follow the Western example in order to recover from isolation, reconstruct the post-conflict society/economy and make general progress. There is an obvious tendency to copy policy solutions, take over ideas and refer to perceived successful cases. Often the reference comes from a personal experience of study visits to particular universities. These are usually universities from the USA and to smaller extent reputable universities from the UK and Germany.

The relation and attitude towards the European West and the USA implies a certain level of inferiority complex and self-marginalisation, creating a common *peripheral identity* of the region. This phenomenon increases as one moves southwards, where the EU membership is viewed as a distant future. The terms used for conceptualising the peripheral space and regional identity are concentrated in the references to terms such as *these lands of ours* ["ovi nasi prostori"] or *the surrounding countries* ["zemlje u okruzenju"]. In Albania, the peripheral and inferior self-perceptions are linked to the legacy of the decades in which the country was virtually isolated from the rest of the world.

The West is more attractive than the rest of the world also in terms of desired academic cooperation. The quantitative data reveal a substantial inclination of academic staff from the region towards cooperation with academics and institutions from the West in comparison to other world regions. The EU, USA, and Canada are the most preferred group of countries for cooperation by all academics regardless of the analysed country or disciplinary location. Moreover, the preference to cooperate with Western institutions is higher in the south (e.g. academics from Croatia, Serbia and Slovenia evaluate the preferred cooperation with institutions from the EU lower than academics from the rest of the analysed countries).

The concept of *neo-colonialism* was applied to education back in the times when the policies of industrialised nations attempted to maintain their domination over the Third World (Altbach, 1998, pp. 30-31). Today such conceptualisation could be put to good use when analysing the emerging EHEA and, in particular, the Western Balkans on both the material level in terms of the policy course, and in the construction of the social reality with the pertaining normative and value setting. In addition to the normative level, it is possible to observe a more technical/policy level of transfer coupled with the strong ideational background of the economic integration and competitiveness agenda of the EU which is presented in the next two sections.

Europe – The Guideline for Reforms and Transformation

More specific than the concept of the West is the conceptualisation of *Europe*. Europe is seen as something external to the Western Balkans. The discourse contains a frequent reference to the relationship of "us and Europe." From this conceptualisation it is possible to identify a strong peripheral identity. Europe becomes an abstract term which stands more for a destination than a geographical category. To a great extent Europe is a synonym for the EU. The latter appears as the widely accepted and internalised political goal. The Bologna Process is often explained as being part of the necessary adjustment to the EU in the steps of formal accession (especially in Croatia) and as part of the political project of approaching the economic union. The topoi and discursive topics are relatively technical.

The orientation towards the EU is as a common denominator amongst the academic staff of all examined countries and universities also in the responses of the quantitative survey where, for instance, EU member countries are seen as priority cooperation countries. The important differences between groups emerge only when academics express their inclination towards cooperation with higher education institutions from within the Western Balkans. Academics from Croatia and Slovenia are less interested in cooperation within the region compared to academics from the rest of the countries. This might be correlated to the notion of the West in the remaining six countries, since Croatia and Slovenia are already members of the EU (one became a member soon after the survey was carried out) and are therefore the front runners in terms of integration with Europe.

The Impact of the Eu's Dominant Political Rationality of the Knowledge Economy

The influence of the EU and Bologna Process discourses reflects the power of the centre in relation to the periphery and the general normative consensus to follow the path towards the EU. The EU's ideas on the economic role of higher education are disseminated with an elaborated and powerful discourse (see Robertson, 2008; Komljenovič & Miklavič, 2013) and reach down to the micro level of imagining the future models of higher education in the examined region.

The interviews revealed surprisingly little direct reference to the EU's dominant discourse of the knowledge economy and the related EU economic strategies, especially bearing in mind their presence in the written (official) documents. However, when scratching deeper beneath the surface of the discourse one can easily find all necessary components to construct the strong economic relevance attributed to higher education. The most prominent discursive topic is the need to boost the *employability* of graduates. The closely related argumentative device of the *relevance* of higher education to society (and therefore implicitly or sometimes explicitly to the economy) notably carries along an argument that sees the need running in both directions: (1) graduates have to be able to find jobs; and (2) employers need graduate employees to have certain competencies and skills. The interviewees who present this discursive line also stick to the ideas of reforming higher education as favoured by EU institutions, e.g. promoting excellence, increasing cooperation with industry, boost innovation and applied research etc.

Regarding the issue of employability of graduates, the quantitative survey revealed that academics from all of the countries evaluated this focus of their university highly (with the lowest mean being 4.31 on a 5 point scale). However, there are important differences between countries. More precisely, the question asked about the extent to which higher education institutions should emphasise the employability of graduates as its main focus. Academic staff from Albania, Macedonia and Serbia would like to see their university more dedicated to this issue than academics from the rest of the countries.

The resistance to these hegemonic economic discourses and imaginaries is neither considerable among the interviewees nor in the quantitative survey. But we could find an isolated reference to the endangered humanistic role of the university:

> Institution does not need a philosophers and artists, but the society needs them (...) we need to get rid of the invasion of job seekers [people who go to University to find better employment]. (49A; 16/3/12)

This interviewee (a faculty level senior academic from Albania) would strictly separate the labour market preparation institutions from universities. In *part 3* we will return to the discourses and concepts related to equality and egalitarian values where this issue will be dealt with from another prospective.

Engineers' Discourse and Concerns

A very specific economic orientation is present in the discourse of the interviewees in the field of engineering. This area deserves special attention because of exceptionally high level of internal homogeneity and due to its distinction from the interviewees belonging to other disciplines (especially with those from the field of humanities and arts).

The engineers are particularly keen on *cooperation with industry*, especially on *innovation*. They perceive their subject areas as a basic, productive and tangible sector which is most important for economic growth or in some cases reviving a stagnating post-war economy:

> In this need of society which is completely normal – to increase the number of educated people - it is pushed to the extreme in the sense that often the necessity for these higher education graduates [engineering graduates] is forgotten. The necessity is not forgotten in the sense of not producing this human resource [orig. "kadar"] but it is forgotten in a sense that there is not enough investment in human resources which are primarily essential for society. This is the view from the point of view of a technical scholar [engineer]. We [higher education of today] create consumers, but what will we consume if we do not produce... (68A; 27/3/12)

This reasoning is often grounded in the concern for the lack of engineering graduates in comparison to those flocking to the social sciences, business and economics.

The distinctive disciplinary perceptions and preferences emerged also in quantitative data. Academics coming from the fields of engineering and science feel that their university is currently putting higher effort on innovation and cooperation with industry than academics from the fields of education, humanities and social sciences[4] (see Figure 1). This may also be the case as academics from technical and natural science faculties in fact have more cooperation with industry which is not seen or noticed by academics from the fields of social science and humanities.

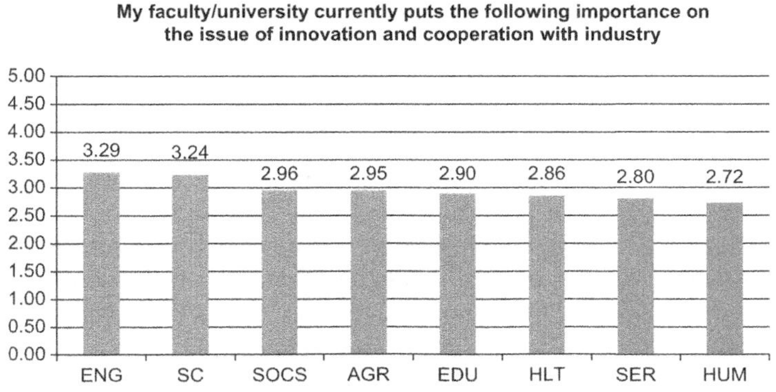

My faculty/university currently puts the following importance on the issue of innovation and cooperation with industry

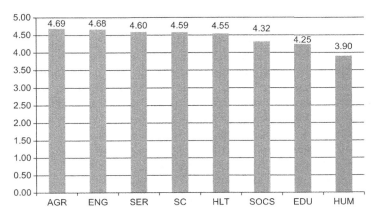

Figure 1. Means of groups of disciplines on the question of higher education institutions' actual focus on innovation and cooperation with industry (N=1.606).

We found a similar, but not identical situation when we asked academics how much they think their university should focus on innovation and cooperation with industry. Academics from the humanities and arts importantly differ statistically to academics from all of the other disciplines except from services (see Figure 2). Interestingly they differ also to academics from the fields of education and social sciences. It is, however, possible to form two groups of disciplines that are different to each other. Thus academics from the disciplines of agriculture, engineering and science value this focus of their university more highly than academics from education, humanities and social sciences.

In my opinion, my faculty/university should put the following importance on the issue of innovation and cooperation with industry

Figure 2. Means of groups of disciplines on the question of higher education institutions' desired focus on innovation and cooperation with industry (N=1.606).

The discourse of the engineering field distinguishes itself also in some other aspects of higher education. For example, it is predominantly input-oriented and teacher-centred. There is a strong resistance and reaction to the Bologna cycles by advocating the return to long cycles or opting for 4+1. This is strengthened by their establishing a common-sense situation with the topos of *it is*

impossible to produce a good engineer in 3 years. There is little consideration of an utterly changed higher education as a consequence of massification. The discourse and conceptualisation of bad and good students is very present in the case of engineering interviewees from all across the region, to which we will return later (in part 3). In the countries of former Yugoslavia, engineering interviewees tend to understand autonomy as the decentralised organisation of the university with faculties as separate legal entities managing funds independently from each other and the rectorate. At those faculties of engineering where the institution underwent an integration (centralisation) process with the university, there was a strong discursive inclination to complain about the detrimental effect of the central governance on flexibility, financial autonomy (especially in managing the funds earned through cooperation with industry) and the *administrative efficiency* of the faculty.

Moreover, the engineers' discourse is noticed in academics' attitude to the range of roles of the university (Figures 3 to 7). When asking about how academics see the current importance of preparing young people for active citizenship at their institution (Figure 3) statistical tests reveal several important differences between groups. Academics from the fields of education, humanities and social sciences in comparison to the academics from engineering and agriculture disciplines stated that their university better serves this role. Interestingly, the academics from across the spectrum of disciplines believe that their institution is not particularly dedicated to preparing youth for active citizenship (see Figure 3). Moreover, when asking about the preferred focus of their institution on these issues, academics from the fields of engineering and science importantly evaluated them lower (see Figure 4). It is thus both — the engineers' opinions on the current situation as well as their idea on how their university should act — that distinguishes them from the rest of the academics.

The distinction of engineering (and to a great extent also natural science) academic staff can partly be associated with the takeover by the dominant economic rationality pertaining to the knowledge economy imaginary, but partly also to the role of the engineering faculties in the industrialisation and modernisation process during the socialist period in both Albania and former Yugoslavia. Perhaps there is a good match between the modernisation discourse and the knowledge economy imaginary where so-called productive knowledge is valued more highly than, for example, in the humanities (Skulasson 2008). Despite the considerable distinction found in the case of engineering and science and in the perception of the meaning and role of higher education in modern society, there are no differences between them regarding the role in individual's personal development and the competitiveness (within the country and internationally).

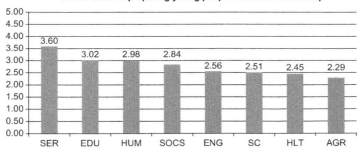

Figure 3. Means of the groups of disciplines on the question of higher education institutions' actual focus on preparing young people for active citizenship (N=1.606).

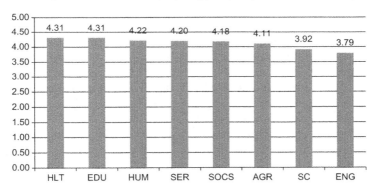

Figure 4. Means of the groups of disciplines on the question of higher education institutions' desired focus on preparing young people for active citizenship (N=1.606).

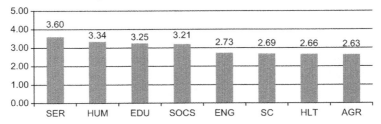

Figure 5. Means of the groups of disciplines on the question of higher education institutions' actual focus on being a venue for free thinking and a critical voice in society (N=1.606).

**In my opinion, my faculty/ university should put the following
importance on being a venue for free thinking and a critical voice in society**

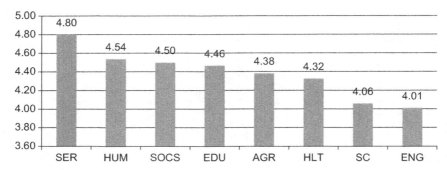

*Figure 6. Means of the groups of disciplines on the question of higher education institutions'
desired priority of being a venue for free thinking and critical voice in society (N=1.606).*

State-, Nation- and Economy-Building: The Grand Projects

One of the region's outstanding specific features is the understanding of the role of
higher education in the *reconstruction of a post-conflict and transitional society/
economy*. There are a few discursive lines indicating a constitutive role of higher
education in *state-building* or *nation-building*. Such discursive elements are not
surprising in a region which recently went through an escalation of tensions in
society culminating in several armed inter-ethnic conflicts.

Even though the above outlined categories are present throughout the region, the
discourse varies between the countries. For example, in Kosovo there are both the
argumentative device of national emancipation and the one on statehood-building,
whereas in Croatia there is a stronger presence of the argumentative device of nation-
building and the economic competitiveness of the country. There is variation also
within countries. For example, in Republika Srpska (BA) there is a strong view of
higher education as the constitutive element of a fully functioning state, whereas in
the Federation of BA and on the state level they view HE more as the nation-building
and economy-resuscitating role of universities. The usual nation-/state-building
discursive topic views the capital city university as the frontrunner and the institution
which should be developed into the knowledge flagship of the nation, whereas the
other universities should diversify into regional or field-specific institutions. This is
also well in line with the ideational background model preferred by the European
Commission for organising universities in a vertical hierarchy with only a few
excellent, world-class research universities (Komljenovič & Miklavič 2013).

The survey among academic staff also included some questions that can be
associated to the category of state and nation building. For example in comparison
with the academics from other countries, the academics from Albania and Kosovo
attribute higher priority to preparing people (students) for active citizenship (see

Figure 7). It is difficult to claim a direct correlation, but at least this result represents a good indicator in the direction of civic and social concerns of the academic staff in the young and unstable institutional settings.

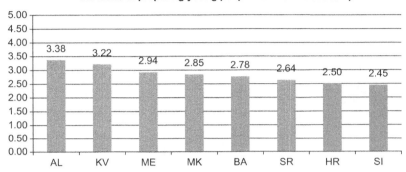

Figure 7. Means of the groups of countries on the question of higher education institutions' actual concern for active citizenship (N=1.678).

On the contrary in the more stable North-Western part of the region the preoccupation with citizenship is lower. Academics from Croatia and Slovenia are importantly less inclined towards the idea that their institution should prepare people for active citizenship (see Figure 8). This could be explained by the fact that the new system/state building project is phasing out and the new challenges and ideas are now flowing into the political space, especially in the context of joining the Euro-Atlantic integrations.

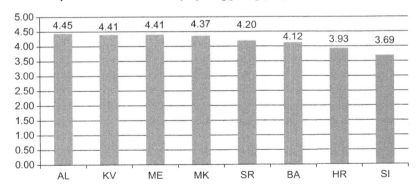

Figure 8. Means of the groups of countries on the question of higher education institutions' desired dedication to encouraging active citizenship (N=1.678).

219

Academics from Albania, Kosovo and Macedonia wish for their university to be a venue for free thinking and a critical voice in society more than academics from Croatia and Slovenia (see Figure 9). This can be correlated with the unstable structures and internal processes in the societies, where university represents a certain safe space for the opposition to the politics of newly forming political elites, not always in line with the opinion of the social groups that are most represented among the academic staff.

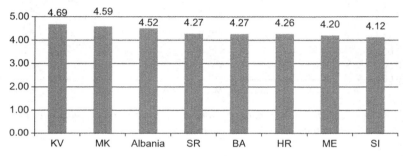

Figure 9. Means of the groups regarding countries on the question of higher education institutions' desired focus on being a venue for free thinking (N=1.678).

There is another ideation of the role of the university, included in the quantitative survey that can be correlated to the category of nation building - the conceptualisation of the *national university*. Its origins can be found in the grand narratives/ideas of 19th and 20th centuries related to the European national project, with the university as one of the constitutive institutions of the nation state. The examined countries have a relatively short statehood and national sovereignty tradition (in the modern era). The universities played a tremendously important role in the process of forming the nation and in the changes and transformations of the 1990s. The university as a national institution was most present in the discourses of academics from Albania, Kosovo and Macedonia. Albania stands out, differing to all countries but Kosovo (Welch=0.000) with the highest mean on a 5 point scale. In Bosnia and Herzegovina academics least feel that their university is fulfilling this purpose and this group is statistically importantly lower than Albania, Macedonia, Serbia and Slovenia.

When asking academics about how much importance their institution should give to being a national university, we found that most academics from Albania, Kosovo and Macedonia feel that their university should play this role. On the other hand, academics from Bosnia and Herzegovina, Croatia and Slovenia gave the lowest preference in relation to this.

My faculty/university currently puts the following importance on the issue of being a national university (educating for national needs)

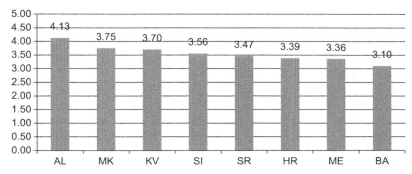

Figure 10. Means of the groups of countries on the question of higher education institutions' actual focus on representing a national university (N=1.678).

In my opinion, my faculty/university should put the following importance on the issue of being a national university (educating for national needs)

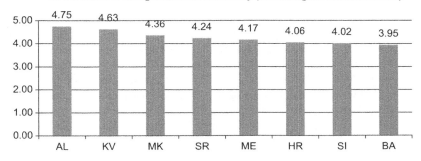

Figure 11. Means of the groups regarding countries on the question of higher education institutions' desired importance of being a national university (N=1.678).

The low importance of the national role of the university in Bosnia and Herzegovina can be explained by the ill-functioning state and absence of a unitary national identity. On the other hand, academic staff from Croatia and Slovenia appear least concerned with these issues as the countries with the most stable state institutions and the EU membership which pushes the nation building project lower on the political and public agendas.

Fragmentation of the Universities and Dominance of the Capital City University

The discussion on the *integration of the university* is indeed the common denominator among the interviewees from the area of former Yugoslavia. The idea of integration is external to the region. It can be considered one of the strongest and in the same time highly controversial external policy guidelines that made their way to the agendas of policymakers, academics, experts and sometimes also the general public. The idea to integrate (centralise) the university belongs to the larger model of the institutional management proposed by the EU and some other European actors. According to this model the competences of governance should be concentrated in a relatively *autonomous managerial leadership*. In turn, this is expected to increase the agility of the management, accelerate the decision making process, and enable the development of an overall institutional strategy. Thereby the universities would improve their comparative advantages and consequently better *compete* with the growing number of higher education institutions in the world (Robertson, 2008; Komljenovič & Miklavič, 2013). Where proposed, this model encountered strong resistance, which is not surprising given the institutional practices and tradition in the region. Namely the formerly *loosely bound faculties*, with their own legal entity status, have tremendous difficulties giving up their autonomy in administrative and financial issues in favour of a centrally administered and strategically run university. One of the main arguments against integration is the feared inefficiency and bureaucratisation of central administration which slows down the *agility of the faculties*.

However, the opposition to integration of the university is far from unanimous. It is possible to detect two blocs in the issue of integration. The interviewees from the ministries, the experts and the state administrative workers tended to follow the European trends in institutional governance. Sometimes the members of the university leadership took the idea over as well. On the other side (resistance to integration) it was possible to find Faculty Deans or interlocutors from the teaching staff (particularly from the engineering fields). The cleavage was visible also between the old teaching staff and the young ambitious scholars. The preference for the integration of the university was especially openly expressed by latter.

The Flagship University in the Capital City

The fragmentation is also connected to the non-formal categorisation of public universities in the region where the classical national configuration consists of the oldest, capital city university and other universities. The exception is Bosnia and Herzegovina, where the political reasoning and ethnic identity might influence the definition of the capital city. The capital city university is also the biggest in all cases, therefore covering the largest range of disciplines and thus subject to a higher degree of fragmentation.

The role of universities in the capitals emerged in the quantitative survey e.g. when academics evaluated the tendency for national competition (see Figure 12). Typically the academics from the 'second' university in the country do not view their university pursuing the status of the first university in the country. The analysis of statistical differences between universities reveals that there are important differences between universities within in Croatia and Slovenia. In both cases universities from the capitals attribute more importance to being the "first in the country" than the other universities in the country. This is not surprising since the question refers to the role of being the best in the country and universities of Zagreb and Ljubljana perhaps undisputedly hold this position. Interestingly, it is not so in other countries including in Serbia with similar configuration of universities.

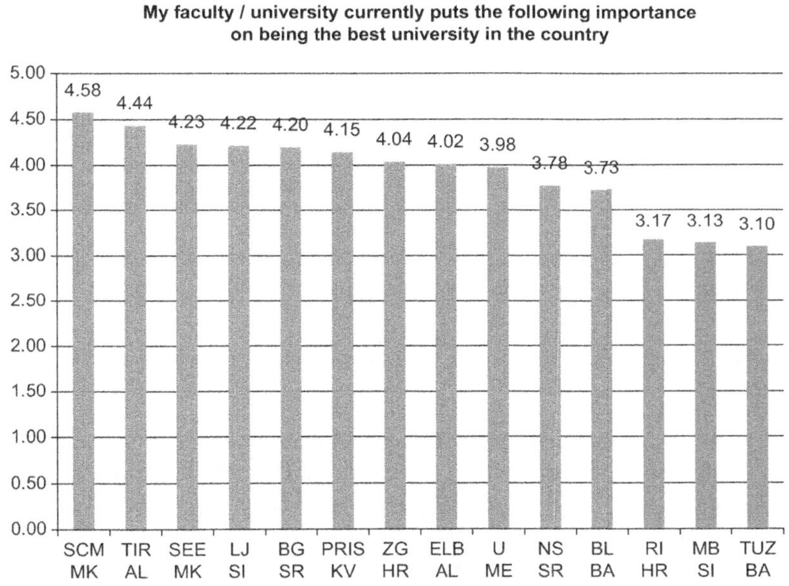

My faculty / university currently puts the following importance on being the best university in the country

Figure 12. Means of the groups of higher education institutions on the question of higher education institutions' focus on national competitiveness (N=1.653).

Academic staff from all of the examined countries evaluated the necessity of their university to compete on the national scale highly (see Figure 13). Moreover, it is possible to conclude with statistical relevance that academics from Croatia and Slovenia are importantly less interested in their university becoming the best university in the country in comparison to academics from elsewhere, which adds to the hypothesis of the higher EU influence and its ideation of global competition as opposed to national one.

The examination of differences between higher education institutions shows a trend of the second university in the country not aspiring to this role as highly as the first university in the country. Interestingly the University of Ljubljana and the University of Zagreb (both flagship universities in the country) are positioned rather low.

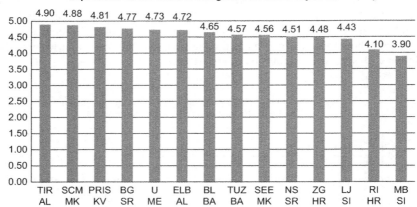

Figure 13. Means of the groups of higher education institutions on the question of higher education institutions' desired focus on national competitiveness (N=1.653).

Egalitarian Values Subdued to Quality And Excellence – The Role of Prestigious Institutions

Eventually we tackle equality – a highly normative category, that can be considered transversal, at least in Europe, but yet it resonates differently in various regional and national settings. In the Western Balkans the issue of equality reflects the normative setting and some social characteristics of the previous political system as well as recent turbulent transitions. Below are exposed some elements that emerged from the grounded approach.

Probably the most outstanding construct found region-wide is the conceptualisation of good (the best) and bad students. Based on this presumption the academic staff strongly believes in meritocracy and is consequently convinced in the necessity for performance-based selection. Well elaborated criteria for the examination are supposed to ensure social justice and academic quality at the same time. The presence of this rationale in the interviews and the discourses analysed is so strong that it is possible to talk about a sort of *meritocratic elitism.*

The reference to equality was present through the interviews despite this meritocratic elitism, even if only on declarative level. For example, on the question of whether there are downsides to entrance selections, an interviewee showed his consideration of equality in the context of selection at the entrance to the university:

Rural regions have a lower level of knowledge, even if they have the same programmes – but the quality of the students is lower. It maybe seems to be an injustice for such categories of students, but we are working on quality (58A 23/3/12).

Thus, some interviewees were aware of the exclusion caused by entrance exams, but subdued the issue of justice (equality) to quality. The discursive use of the *excellence* and reference to *good and bad students* is notably stronger in Albania and Kosovo and was present throughout the region, especially in the field of engineering.

Particularly in Kosovo, the interviewees connected the meritocratic exclusion to the state- and nation-building process (see also above). In their view Kosovar society needs an educated elite in order for the social structure to take shape and in order to develop institutions in the process of building a "European state." University becomes the core institution in this process since it is conceptualised as a generator of the nations' elite. The discourse of constructing the state and reconstructing the economy (as part of state building) is very powerful and overshadows the concern for egalitarian values – '*there is elitism but we get high quality in return*' (63E; 21/3/12).

Even though the hidden social selection and reproduction of social classes through the meritocratic selection mechanisms is a well known phenomenon in sociology scholarship, this issue does not figure as relevant in the discourses in the Western Balkans. Particularly among the senior academic staff the concern for equality gave way to other values and priorities.

Within the same rationale (the necessity for quality and elite building), tolerance to economic exclusivity also emerged. Improving quality and outcomes justifies high (exclusive) tuition fees. An illustrative case is the role of the expensive and highly reputable private (trans-national) institutions in Kosovo, notably the American University of Kosovo (AUK) – a private institution, run under a contract with the Rochester Institute of Technology from the USA. According to the interviewees and informants the graduates of this university (unlike the other private institutions) are well accepted by the labour market and stand a good chance of vertical progression in society. The entrance filter is primarily represented by the relatively high tuition fee[5]. Consequently the enrolment is to a great extent contingent to one's economic background (confirmed by the informants, including members of the AUK's teaching staff).

One interviewee was very outspoken on this matter. He viewed tuition fees as a guarantee for quality. Accordingly, limiting tuition fees would in his view surely lead to decreasing quality and reducing the AUK to mediocrity like the other private HEIs. The discourse of normality provides an apologetic argument for the *elitist* role of the institution:

> Usually in every country we have the richest people, that's it. The richest people go to the best institutions to study (...) Like in your country [referring to the interviewers homeland] (63E; 21/3/12).

In this case, it is possible to observe a defensive attitude and at least two types of discourse: (1) the class-specific apology that being rich is not in any way bad and that it is logical that rich people will school their children in the *best institutions* and (2) the argument of Kosovo being the same as the other countries, of course referring to the Western liberal democratic capitalist countries.

To conclude on egalitarian values, the concerns for equality were residual or absent in the accounts of interviewees regardless the country or institution. Instead, the concern for access is more present in the governments' discourses and policies in Macedonia and Kosovo where higher education assumed an outstanding role in the reconstruction of post-conflict society and in emancipation of the remote rural areas. The policymakers in such settings are faced with increasing interest for studying. This is resulting in the process of rapid expansion of enrolments without adequate parallel increase in funding and is causing degrading of otherwise highly regarded university education.

CONCLUSION

In many aspects the region of the Western Balkans reflects the main thoughts, ideas and perceptions of the rest of Europe. However, the seemingly faithful West-following countries in the outskirts of the Old Continent reveal a different reality when one scratches the surface of the mere written and declared policies and programs.

On the discursive level the West is idealised as the advanced part of the world. In the accounts of the academics, policymakers and experts, the reference to the West, Europe and the EU typically stands for the developed liberal democracies of Europe and northern America. The hegemonic Western ideas and imaginaries are substantially present in the local discourse. The ideations of Europe and EU are forming an external entity - the *centre*, thereby implying the peripheral status of the Balkans. Europe represents a political goal and a normative model for these countries. The self-imagined *peripheral identity* stimulates the process of emulation, at least on the discursive level. This process is not necessarily induced by transfer of models from Western countries; it is more likely reflecting the ideas originating from the regional and international platforms (e.g. EU, Bologna Process).

On the other hand, the observed region is characterised by strong idiosyncrasies and controversies stemming from long isolation, conflicts, political instability, tensions between social/ethnic groups and not least the post-conflict condition that most of the region is still facing today. Higher education is not immune to these circumstances. Its role and meaning relates closely to the region-specific processes and conditions and therefore differ substantially from what the researchers usually find in the stable liberal democracies. For the very same reasons the "western" ideas, policy recipes and discourses encounter *resistance* and infertile ground for the *Europeanization* reforms.

Especially in the countries that suffered most from the armed conflicts and internal restructuring of societies (Kosovo, Bosnia and Herzegovina) and Albania (which started the transition after a several decades-long isolation) higher education plays a significant role in the imagined state or nation construction. Both, political and academic communities subscribe to this narrative.

The differences between the discipline faculties and their perception of higher education might in many ways resemble those in other European countries. However due to the distinctive nature of social processes and because higher education is often one of the most stable and therefore crucial social institutions, the disciplinary distinctions have deeper reaching repercussions. To a large extent the disciplinary division and the outstanding institutional fragmentation (in the countries of former Yugoslavia) are mutually constructed. The latter represents a strong academic and institutional identity and as such acts as the major force of resistance to the idea of an integrated university much promoted by the EU and other European organisations. The comparison of the findings from the qualitative enquiry with the quantitative survey proved especially beneficial in these matters.

The inductive approach was found beneficial for exploring and understanding this relatively poorly known region of Europe, especially in terms of processes, norms, values of the local socio-political environment and overall characteristics of higher education and its role in the local societies. This was for example very obvious in the case of the attitude towards egalitarian issues and equity. The reconstruction of society, formation of intellectual elites and nation building are often given priority over the issues dear to the stable Western settings. These have often too little in common with the region examined in this research.

NOTES

[1]   Albania (AL), Bosnia and Herzegovina (BA), Croatia (HR), Kosovo (KV), Macedonia (MK), Montenegro (ME), Serbia (SR) and Slovenia (SI)

[2]   University of Tirana, Albania (TIR AL),University of Elbasan, Albania (ELB AL), University of Tuzla, Bosnia and Herzegovina (TUZ BA), University of Banja Luka, Bosnia and Herzegovina (BL BA), University of Zagreb, Croatia (ZG HR), University of Rijeka, Croatia (RI HR), University of Pristina, Kosovo (PRIS KV), The Ss. Cyril and Methodius University in Skopje, Macedonia (SCM MK), SEE University, Macedonia (SEE MK), University of Montenegro (U ME), University of Belgrade, Serbia (BG SR), University of Novi Sad, Serbia (NS SR), University of Ljubljana, Slovenia (LJ SI), University of Maribor, Slovenia (MB SI)

[3]   Agriculture and veterinary (AGR), Education / teacher education (EDU), Engineering, manufacturing and construction (ENG), The humanities and arts (HUM), Science, mathematics and computing (SC), Services (SER), Social sciences, business and law (SOCS), Health and welfare (HLT)

[4]   The statistically important difference to mention (W=0.000) is between the groups of engineering and science on one side and humanities, social sciences and education on the other. (Engineering and education (G.H.=0.004), engineering and humanities (G.H.=0.000), engineering and social sciences (G.H.=0.008), science and education (G. H.=0.023), science and humanities (G.H.=0.000), science and social sciences (G.H.=0.048)).

[5]   During the field research it was not possible to ascertain the sum, but the interlocutors whose children study there reported a tuition fee of several thousand Euros.

REFERENCES

Altbach, P. (1998). *Comparative Higher Education Knowledge, the University and Development*. Westport: Ablex publishing corporation.

CEPS (2012). *Differentiation, equity, productivity: The social and economic consequences of expanded and differentiated higher education systems – internationalisation aspects* (DEP-08-EuroHESC-OP-016). The Western Balkans Survey (January 2012 – June 2012). Internal materials. Ljubljana: August 2012.

Charmaz, K. (1990). Discovering chronic illness: Using grounded theory. *Social Science & Medicine,* *30*(11), 1161–1172.
Charmaz, K. (2006). *Constructing grounded theory.* London: Sage Publishers.
Fairclough, N. (2003). *Analysing discourse: Textual analysis for social research.* Milton Park: Routledge.
Komljenovič, J., & Miklavič, K. (2013). Imagining higher education in European knowledge economy: Discourse and ideas in the communications of the EU. In P. Zgaga, U. Teichler J. Brennan (Eds.). *The globalisation challenge for European Higher Education. Convergence and diversity, centres and peripheries.* Frankfurt am Main: Peter Lang.
Krzyzanowski, M. (2010). Discourses and concepts: Interfaces and synergies between Begriffsgeschichte and the discourse historical approach in CDA. In R. D. Cillia et al. (Eds.) *Diskurs-Politik-Identität / Discourse -Politics -Identity.* Tübingen: Stauffenburg Publishers.
Krzyzanowski, M., & Wodak, R. (2011). Political strategies and language policies; the European Union Lisbon strategy and its implications for the EU's language and multilingualism policy. *Lang Policy, 10,* 115–136.
Miklavič, K. (2012). Europeanisation in action: The (re)construction and role of higher education in post-conflict settings. *Journal of the European Higher Education Area, 2,* 93–108.
Robertson, S. L. (2008). Embracing the global: Crisis and the creation of a new semiotic order to secure Europe's knowledge-based economy. In B. Jessop, N. Fairclough., & R. Wodak (Eds.), *Education and the knowledge based economy in Europe.* Rotterdam: Sense.
Skulasson, P. (2008). *Autonomy and Governance in European Universities. Autonomy, Governance and Management in Higher Education in Asia and Europe.* Lecture conducted from EU Asia Education Platform, Hanoi.
Wodak, R. (2008). Introduction: Discourse Studies – Important Concepts and Terms. In R. Wodak,, & M. Krzyzanowski, (Eds.) *Qualitative Discourse Analysis in the Social Sciences.* New York: Palgrave Macmillan.
Zgaga, P., Klemencič, M., Komljenovič, J., Miklavič, K., Repac, I., & Jakacic, V. (2013). *Higher Education Reforms in the Western Balkans: Key findings from field research.* Ljubljana: CEPS.

AFFILIATIONS

Klemen Miklavič
Center for Education Policy Studies,
University of Ljubljana

Janja Komljenovič
Graduate School of Education,
University of Bristol

ORLANDA TAVARES, SÓNIA CARDOSO & CRISTINA SIN

MAPPING PORTUGUESE INSTITUTIONAL POLICIES ON ACCESS AGAINST THE EUROPEAN STANDARDS AND GUIDELINES

INTRODUCTION

One major achievement of the Bologna process regarding the quality assurance agenda is constituted by the Standards and Guidelines for Quality Assurance in the European Higher Education Area (ESG) (Kohoutek, 2009; MAP-ESG steering group, 2011). ESG can be defined 'as a supranational (...) policy programme that includes three sets of standards accompanied by the corresponding guidelines to be taken account of and implemented into the quality practices of the quality assurance agencies and higher education institutions of the Bologna-signatory countries' (Kohoutek, 2009, p. 17).

ESG Part 1 is specifically directed at higher education institutions (HEIs). The underlying global aim is to promote HEIs' commitment and the implementation both of a quality culture and of a strategy, policy and procedures for the continuous assurance and enhancement of quality at study programme level (ENQA, 2009). Although access is not specifically mentioned in the ESG, it is one of the several dimensions likely to impact on quality, therefore deserving the attention of HEIs. Among the ESG, two of these apply, even if indirectly, to access issues: the definition of institutional policies and specific quality assurance strategies and procedures (ESG 1.1) and the development of information systems ensuring the collection, systematisation and use of information for the effective management of programmes (ESG 1.6).

Since access seems to constitute 'a poorly-defined term in the context of European higher education systems and subject to considerable variation in the way it is articulated through national legislation and institutional policy and practice' (Land et al., 2011, p. 2), one can assume that, at this level, HEIs might be adopting different strategies and even experiencing different difficulties in implementing what is recommended by ESG. This may be valid not only for institutions among different European countries, but also for institutions in the same country.

This study analyses the initiatives which Portuguese HEIs develop on student access and the extent to which these align with the ESG. This is particularly relevant since access to higher education in Portugal occurs mainly through a nationally centralised and regulated system of *numeri clausi* (Magalhães, Amaral, & Tavares, 2009; Tavares, Tavares, Justino, & Amaral, 2008). Specifically, the study addresses

J. Branković et al., Global Challenges, Local Responses in Higher Education, 229–243.
© *2014 Sense Publishers. All rights reserved.*

two research questions: 1) What is the Portuguese HEIs' policy on access? and 2) What is the link between access and quality assurance processes? This analysis was undertaken in the context of a European research project (IBAR) on the implementation of the ESG for quality assurance in European higher education institutions.

In order to answer the two above-mentioned questions, we will focus on three main issues: (1) the collection and disaggregation by HEIs of data on their vacancies/enrolments/non-completion/graduation rates, according to different student cohorts; (2) the existing institutional mechanisms to support the admission and progression of distinct cohorts of students (lower socio-economic groups; ethnic minorities; non-native language speakers; mature students; students with disabilities) and the variation of such mechanisms by academic programme; (3) the changes occurred in the last decade in HEIs' pattern of enrolments as well as the main drivers of these changes. Furthermore, we also intend to identify the problematic issues surrounding access and the extent to which these are linked with the institutional approach to quality assurance. Finally, the analysis also considers the existing barriers to effective policies and procedures for access.

THE PORTUGUESE ACCESS SYSTEM

Portugal has a binary system comprising almost one hundred and sixty HEIs, both universities and polytechnics, public and private. While universities are oriented towards research and knowledge production to ensure a solid scientific and cultural preparation (offering first, second and third study cycles), polytechnics are vocational and oriented towards applied research to assure theoretical and practical knowledge and its application for the pursuit of professional activities (offering first and second study cycles).

Following the 1974 democratic revolution the Portuguese higher education system expanded at a very fast rate, moving from what was an elite system, with a low participation rate, to a massified system, with a gross enrolment rate above 50%, in the early years of the present century (Tavares et al., 2008; Tavares, 2011). The governments in power after 1974 have assumed the need to widen access and expand higher education both for social justice and for economic reasons. Nevertheless, the governments' efforts were confronted with a number of managing paradoxes deriving from contradictions between socialist egalitarian ideals and factors such as the economic context, lack of resources, pressures from the World Bank and the International Monetary Fund, etc. (Magalhães, Amaral, & Tavares, 2009). Presently, after a great increase in student enrolments, there is a declining trend which has created competition for students and new management challenges, including the need to attract students, to establish quality standards and to define institutional identities (Ibidem).

Access has been one major area of state regulation of the higher education system due to the significant consequences higher education has for national economic and social development. Regulations have addressed: the size and composition of enrolments, participation opportunities for all, social equity and redress, the costs of the system and the contribution to economic competitiveness. Successive governments have consistently used access to higher education as a way to regulate the system and parts of its subsectors, centrally overseen by the Ministry responsible for higher education. Regarding access policies, Portugal is now moving from a quantity to a quality paradigm, to a more clear definition of the binary divide, to a more diversified offer of programmes and to a more diverse public (Magalhães, Amaral, & Tavares, 2009).

Access to the public higher education system occurs through a nationally centralised and regulated system of *numeri clausi*, which were previously used to control the number of vacancies for every study programme. At present, institutions have some autonomy since they can manage and distribute vacancies for each of the offered study programmes within limits previously defined by the Ministry for different areas. Therefore, instead of defining the vacancies for every programme the Ministry defines more aggregated numbers that HEIs are allowed to allocate to individual programmes. In the case of the private higher education sector, the Ministry defines the numbers for the vacancies of individual programmes but applications are managed by the respective institutions, without using the centralised placement system used for the public sector.

There are three main ways to access public higher education:

1. National competition, which includes a general track (students hold the secondary education diploma or equivalent and do the national exams) and a special track for students from the Portuguese islands (Azores and Madeira), Portuguese emigrants, students with disabilities and militaries. This national competition takes place in two phases. However, if the available vacancies are not filled during the second phase, a third one can be opened locally by the HEI.
2. Special competition, for mature students, which includes students older than 23 years (students prove their ability to attend the study programme through specific tests carried out by HEIs) and students with other appropriate post-secondary qualifications, for instance a technological specialisation course (Curso de Especialização Tecnológica – CET).
3. Special regimes, which are directed at specific or special groups of students as, for instance, high performance athletes, or students who come from the Portuguese former colonies (as Angola or Mozambique) and do not require national exams.

Therefore, access to higher education is available to all students who have completed secondary education (or equivalent) or fulfil the requirements of the special access routes, such as the regime for candidates older than 23 years. The majority of students enter public higher education by means of the national competition and the centralised placement system, which takes into account students' preferences and their grades both in secondary education and national exams. After an education route lasting 12 years (9 years of basic education and 3 years of upper secondary education), the condition for becoming eligible to enter a higher education programme combines the student's performance in upper secondary education, their performance in national exams (with a 95 minimum score out of 200) in the disciplines that are considered core disciplines for the chosen study programme, as well as the satisfaction of prerequisites, if they exist. Since 1999, the calculation of the access grade for entering the national competition is based on at least 50% of the secondary school grades, at least 35% of national access exams and, at most, 15% of prerequisites when these apply.

METHOD

Four public higher education institutions – two universities (HEIs α and β) and two polytechnics (HEIs δ and γ) – were selected to obtain a diversified sample in terms of: sub-sector (university and polytechnic); size (HEI α is rather smaller than HEI β; HEI δ is also smaller than HEI γ); and geographic location, since the four institutions cover the north, centre and south of Portugal, while also reflecting the geographical differences between HEIs located on the coastline and those more inland, the former being in the richer and most heavily populated areas (Amaral et al., 2011). Private institutions were left out of this study since they are not under the centralised access placement system used for the public sector.

Table 1 - Faculty/schools and study programmes selected for the study

	Faculty/Schools	Study Programme
HEI α	School of Sciences and Technology	Civil Engineering
	School of Arts (Visual Arts and Design Department)	Design
HEI β	Faculty of Engineering	Civil Engineering
	Faculty of Fine Arts	Communication Design
HEI γ	School of Technology and Management	Civil Engineering
	School of Education	Arts and Design
HEI δ	School of Technology	Civil Engineering
		Plastic Arts – Painting and Inter-Media

Within the four public HEIs selected, two study programmes offered by two different faculty/schools were chosen, corresponding to two contrasting disciplinary areas considered pertinent in terms of comparability of results. Table 1 presents the faculty/schools and respective study programmes. For practical reasons, the references to the specific study programmes are aggregated into the two main disciplinary areas selected for the present study: Engineering and Arts.

The study drew on data deriving both from documents issued by the four sample institutions and from interviews conducted in June 2011 with two distinct groups of actors from each institution. The first group comprised members of the central management and administration of each HEI, namely the Rector/President (or, in their place, a vice-rector/vice-president, or a pro-rector) and the representative of the Quality Assurance structure (or, in their place, of the Senate, of the structure responsible for study programmes, or for the Student Support Services). The second group assembled members of the faculty/schools offering the study cycles in the two selected disciplinary areas, namely the Dean (or equivalent), the representative of the quality assurance structure (at unit level), the study programme director, and two panels, one composed of academics and the other of students (around five participants in each panel). Interviews dealt not only with the provisions of the institutional policy on access and its alignment with the national policy, but also with the access strategies implemented at the level of the faculty/schools and, more specifically, of the study programmes selected. Specifically, the following topics were explored during the interviews: the institutional policy on access; institutional collection of data on vacancies, applications, graduation and non-completion rates; mechanisms and measures to support access and progression for different groups of students (students from economically disadvantaged backgrounds, ethnic minority students, non-native speakers, students older than 23, disabled students, etc.); the most notable changes in enrolments over the last decade and potential drivers; sensitive issues related to access and how access is related with quality assurance. An analytical framework integrating the above-mentioned themes (i.e. the topics covered in interviews) guided the codification of interview data and institutional policy documents, which followed thematic content analysis methods (Silverman, 2001; Tonkiss, 2006). This approach has allowed not only the consideration of formal institutional regulations but also research participants' perceptions of issues related to access. The above themes, which guided both data collection and analysis, are discussed next.

INSTITUTIONAL ACCESS POLICIES AND PRACTICES

In this section we present and discuss the themes as they emerged both from the analysis of institutional documents and interview data: institutional access policies and strategies; HEIs' collection and disaggregation of data; mechanisms to support the admission and progression of distinct cohorts of students; and the major changes in student enrolments and barriers to effective policies and strategies for access.

Institutional Access Policies and Strategies

Public Portuguese HEIs' access policies and strategies are framed by the national policy context, in that these must comply with the national regulations. However, there are some areas where direct intervention is possible: definition of special access exams, the choice of exam disciplines for each study programme, setting the minimum access mark, access requirements for students older than 23 years and study programme transfers. The selected HEIs often seem to develop the strategy for attracting the desired students through the promotion of targeted study programmes.

For instance, HEI α attracts students from all over the country (Continent and Islands) and also foreign students, coming both from Portuguese-speaking countries and other foreign countries, mainly European. However, students still tend to come mostly from the geographical region where the institution is located (HEI α, 2011). Driven mainly by this fact, HEI α fosters a programme of visits to secondary schools to advertise its current study programmes. At this level, some differences emerge between Engineering and Arts. Although both study programmes conduct secondary school visits, these appear to be more systematised and have a bigger impact in Arts. Since this is a recently established programme, it has a proactive policy of visits, its teaching staff making great efforts to advertise it both in the region where the HEI is located and surrounding regions. In Engineering, promotion through such visits, fairs, and other events, is perceived as less necessary, as the study programme has a greater capacity to attract students due to its longer history. However, the intention to promote the study programme more systematically in the forthcoming academic years was reported.

HEI β, currently one of the largest institutions in the country (with around 31,000 students), has a great capacity (greater than, for instance, the previous institution - HEI α) to attract students. In fact, demand is greater than supply in this institution and, since the region where it is located is one of the largest in the country population-wise, student recruitment is mainly local (Teixeira et al., 2009). Within this HEI, dissatisfaction is noted in Arts due to the school's lack of freedom to select the 'best' students (i.e. by portfolio) instead of the students with the best grades and averages selected through the national exams. This is described as contrary to Arts schools' practices around Europe. Some discontent with lack of autonomy is also noted in Engineering. A greater flexibility and possibility of intervention in student selection would be welcome, rather than just receiving students with little saying in the matter. This is despite the fact that Engineering, as it happens in Arts too, claims to attract the best students according to national access criteria. To raise awareness of its offer of study programmes, the faculty/school organises an open thematic week on the Engineering profession, as well as secondary school visits.

HEI γ has witnessed, throughout the past years, an increasing growth in its student population. This is due to an institutional strategy to diversify its offer of study programmes (especially CETs and master programmes), the marketing of this offer, the external promotion of the institution, and the attempt to attract new publics (HEI γ, 2010). Maybe as a result of this, student population is characterised by a strong geographical dispersion concerning its origin, although it tends to come predominantly from the Northern coastal districts of Portugal (HEI γ, 2010). The HEI has a Support Office that promotes the study programmes in different places, such as job fairs, professional and secondary schools. Furthermore, open days take place two or three times a year, giving secondary school students the opportunity to visit the institution. There is also the 'Live Science' project, through which the institution hosts students from the 11th and 12th grades. Through these initiatives all the degrees are advertised, including Engineering and Arts. However, Arts has specific show-casing activities to the outside community (for instance, the presentation of the study programme outputs), with the final goal of attracting students. Besides the national access competition, HEI γ has internal access policies related to the new publics, specifically students older than 23 years and CETs. A Permanent Council, integrated by the HEI's president and the faculty/school directors, is the place where vacancies are discussed and defined, namely concerning technological specialisation and master degrees. This follows a global planning strategy, embodied in the institution's strategic plan, which defines the policies and strategies for attracting students.

Finally, HEI δ is a relatively small institution (about 4,000 students) which offers study programmes that cover a wide range of training areas and aim at giving students a practice-oriented education designed to improve transition to the labour market. Due to the institution's dimension and peripheral situation, students are mainly recruited locally (Teixeira et al., 2009). The institutional access policy is also aligned with the national policy for the majority of students. The access of the remaining students, either at post-graduate level, or students older than 23 years, is regulated by the institution. The Pedagogical and the Scientific Councils determine the access regulations and are responsible for the selection of those candidates. There are specificities regarding different disciplinary areas (Engineering, Arts, Management, Design, Communication, etc.) which are defined by the previously mentioned Councils. In global terms, access to HEI δ requires a minimum knowledge on the part of the candidates in basic areas, defined by the Scientific Council. For instance, in Engineering candidates must have a certain level of knowledge in Mathematics and Physics while in Arts candidates should demonstrate their skills in this specific area. In addition, a certain motivation level among students is expected to enable them to continue their studies (namely in what concerns the access to masters and post-graduate degrees). For instance, in Engineering, mature students have increased substantially in numbers, which translates the institution's ability to attract more graduate students who already know what they want, are motivated, dedicated and committed. This is stressed as an asset for the study programme.

Some actions are developed at the faculty/school level to promote the study programmes and define strategies to attract students. Usually proposed by the programme director, these actions imply resorting to different strategies. That is the case of seminars in which both secondary school students and teachers are invited to learn about the HEI's offer. There is also an annual event, the 'Science Week', which is basically a week targeted at the 10th, 11th and 12th grades students, where the institution presents itself, including the way it functions and its infrastructures and equipment. The 'Science Week' is understood as an important outreach activity and is already on the agendas of many secondary schools. Furthermore, there are other small actions, such as the presentation of the degrees in secondary schools, which, together with the previous initiative, allow for a widespread advertising of HEI δ, at least in the surrounding areas.

In sum, although access to public higher education is centrally regulated, the four institutions have some autonomy to develop strategies in order to attract students and manage the procedures related to the special competition access stream, namely the students older than 23 years and the CETs regimes. Overall, these strategies seem to be much more systematised in polytechnics than in universities, which might be explained by a shortage of candidates especially among the former institutions. In fact, polytechnics constitute, in the Portuguese context, a true second choice, considered less reputable than universities (Tavares, 2011). Furthermore, strategies to attract students are also more noticeable in Arts than in Engineering study programmes. The reason for this may lie in the fact that Engineering is traditionally associated with a high social status and economic income, therefore holding a greater capacity to attract students.

HEIs' Collection and Disaggregation of Data

Another purpose of this study has been to look into Portuguese HEIs' commitment to self-knowledge, signalled by the collection and disaggregation of data (on their offers/enrolments/non-completion/graduates) according to different student cohorts, and by clear assignment of responsibilities for monitoring access within the institution. Self-knowledge has been deemed relevant here because it can inform access and progression policies and strategies.

Globally, the selected Portuguese HEIs tend to collect and disaggregate data according to different cohorts of students. However, not all the data are collected or always systematised and monitored by specific services.

HEI α has published, for almost ten years, a comprehensive annual report which analyses not only the access to higher education, the entrants' profile and the students' academic performance, but also the tendencies conditioning the offer and the demand of 1st cycle study programmes both at national and institutional level. An integrated information system also contains data on the drop-out figures both for the whole institution and at study programme level. Data is also provided on the number of graduates per year and per study programme. The disaggregation of data to give information on different student cohorts occurs only in the case of non-traditional students.

In HEI β data for the whole institution (i.e. on student geographic, educational, etc., background; first and second choices; academic results; graduates), except drop-out rates, are collected and made publicly available. At study programme level a difference emerges between Arts and Engineering. In Arts, no rigorous study is conducted and a clear idea on the above aspects seems to be lacking. Academics report that data are collected at the time of the self-evaluations which are required by the Portuguese agency for assessment and accreditation of higher education. They produce their own statistics on student performance in the curricular units they teach. In Engineering, all the referred data are collected, statistics are produced and used to analyse study programme performance.

In HEI γ data collection is performed under the requirements of RAIDES, a survey on the Registration of Enrolled Students and Graduates in Higher Education, whose indicators are filled mandatorily every year. The monitoring of the data is done by the Academic Services, the privileged locus for database access in terms of entrances, students and graduates. Data analysis is carried out to inform an Activity Report prepared by the Board of Directors. The institution, specifically through the Image and Support Office, also collects data related to alumni, with the aim of following their path.

In HEI δ data collection is managed by the Academic Services which are responsible for the treatment of all statistical data and parameters associated with academic issues, specifically the number of vacancies, students, enrolled students and success rates. All the data are systematised in a single database and are available for each study programme director, so that he/she can know the number of students on the programme and their success rates. There is also a Quality Support Office which collects data concerning student success and drop-out rates. This office prepares a survey for new students, allowing their characterisation as they enter the institution, and produces questionnaires every semester enabling students to assess their respective curricular units and teachers.

Institutional Mechanisms to Support the Admission and Progression of Distinct Cohorts of Students

As mentioned earlier, another aim of our analysis was to look into the existence of institutional mechanisms to support the admission and progression of distinct cohorts of students (lower socio-economic groups; ethnic minorities; non-native language speakers; mature students; students with disabilities) and into the variability of these mechanisms by academic programme.

One can argue that, in global terms, the analysed Portuguese institutions are not concerned with ethnic minority issues, that is, they do not treat these minorities differently from the remainder of the student body in terms of support. However, institutions tend to develop different strategies to support other groups of students, such as students from lower socio-economic backgrounds, non-native language speakers, mature students and students with disabilities. A special concern with students older than 23 years, with foreign students and with students from lower socio-economic backgrounds is transversal to all institutions. In order to ensure these students' integration and further progression, institutions tend to develop initiatives such as flexible and adjustable timetables for working students, English classes, social services, and tutorials to overcome academic difficulties.

HEI α does not disaggregate information on students with disabilities or ethnic minority students. The institution even questions the legitimacy (in legal terms) to oblige students to classify themselves according to specific categories for data gathering purposes. The only strategies aimed at supporting different student cohorts are specifically directed at two particular groups: foreign students and students older than 23 years. Students older than 23 years are generally not perceived as needing special treatment. On the contrary, being mature, they seem more motivated and capable of adapting. Only in some cases (as in Veterinary Medicine) are these students seen as needing extra support. Additionally, some adjustments are made in timetables to facilitate class attendance and examination schedules. As long as they comply with the access requirements, all foreign students intending to attend the institution are treated the same way as the national students. However, being aware of the social and cultural integration difficulties felt by some foreign students, the institution has created support structures, namely the Student Support Office and the International Relations Office. Portuguese language classes are also provided (Erasmus intensive language courses, organised within the Centre for Continuing Education). Students from lower socio-economic backgrounds are supported within the terms defined by law.

In HEI β the Student Support Services offer university-wide support to students with economic difficulties (translated in scholarships) and disabled students. However, a difference is noted between Arts and Engineering in what concerns faculty/programme-level support structures. In Arts there are no formal mechanisms for student support. This is mentioned to happen through the teacher/student relationship, enabling the personalised support and teacher attention to all kinds of student problems, which is facilitated by the 'individualised' teaching in Arts. Students older than 23 years are not deemed to have special needs, thus receiving equal treatment. Interviewed students claim to have requested a Student Support Service for the Faculty, but this has not yet been created. However, there is an Erasmus office to deal with Erasmus students' issues.

Engineering offers Mathematics, Physics and Programming tutorials for students who need extra support to compensate for gaps in knowledge from secondary school. To facilitate Erasmus students' integration a series of curricular units are taught in English (all fourth-year and some third-year units). Academics, in particular, describe a range of broader, forward-looking, proactive measures meant to improve learning and teaching: the design of a new programme timetable with concern for student needs rather than teaching staff preferences; the existence of a teaching/learning lab, a unit meant to improve learning and teaching quality; a pedagogic assessment project comparing study programmes with significantly different results in pedagogic questionnaires and approval rates to understand the reasons behind; an annual pedagogic exchange day for reflection and dissemination of good practices; and pedagogic incentive awards to academic staff with best results in pedagogic questionnaires.

In HEI γ the students' economic and financial problems are managed by a Social Services unit. As regards foreign students, the institution develops various initiatives and activities to attract and to further integrate them, and has created a students' service which provides support at different levels. For the past two years, the institution has also been offering some curricular units taught in English, or in both languages (Portuguese and English), that are particularly aimed at students in the Erasmus and other mobility programmes. In fact, the attraction of foreign audiences is a strategic point for HEI γ, which hosts many foreign students from different countries, coming from Erasmus and Erasmus Mundus programmes and from countries with which it has mobility agreements. For students older than 23 years, as well as for other students, there are additional learning support programmes on the subjects with the highest failure rates. There is also an Image and Support Office which assists students in several different ways. Globally, the institution has been implementing an open strategy, which aims at promoting the proximity and interaction between the institution and students, teachers and students and among students.

In HEI δ a Support Service helps the integration of new students, and different levels of assistance are provided by Social Services, targeting students with financial problems. Students with pedagogic difficulties in the different curricular units, especially those older than 23 years, benefit from additional learning support: flexible timetables and support classes (for example, in Mathematics and Physics, for the case of Engineering). There is also a Language Centre created with a twofold aim: to prepare students for the Erasmus programme, primarily through the teaching of English; and to help foreign students learn Portuguese.

Changes and Barriers

A final aim of the analysis was to investigate the changes which have occurred over the last decade in the pattern of student enrolments as well as the main drivers behind these changes, given the impact they can have on access policies and strategies. Furthermore, we also intended to identify the problematic issues surrounding access and the extent to which these have led to alterations in the institutional approach to quality assurance. One of the patterns which has emerged in the four selected institutions is the influence of the Bologna Process and the consequent increase in mobile students. The participation of foreign students is changing the institutional environment, having a double impact: on the one hand, by providing classes in English, the institutions are explicitly trying to attract foreign students; on the other hand, classes in English are also motivating Portuguese students to go abroad. This exchange is understood as something which promotes quality. Another identified pattern is the growth in regional students, possibly driven by the economic constraints the country is currently facing. This is forcing institutions to develop diversified strategies in order to attract students from other regions beyond the one where the institution is located. Finally, the recent decrease in the numbers of traditional students has rendered institutions more open to new publics, especially those coming through the special competition stream (students older than 23 years and CETs). This phenomenon is perceived as an important change for institutions, since it is forcing the readjustment and development of measures to assure and improve academic quality. Examples of such measures, common to all the four selected HEIs, are additional learning programmes, preparatory programmes in core disciplines, and tutorials.

239

Globally, the difficulty of attracting students, especially felt by the polytechnic institutions due mainly to their geographic location, is identified as the main obstacle to the institutional quality policy. It is held responsible for lower success rates, lower graduation rates and a higher cost of students' education, which are all negative indicators for institutions, despite the number of quality initiatives it might have.

The global analysis of findings has revealed the existence of some barriers to the effectiveness of policy and procedures for access among the four Portuguese HEIs. The national regulations on access represent a first barrier, as the limiting *numeri clausi* system and the fixed number of study programmes (inflexibility to change from year to year) are seen as a constraint. Universities find it difficult to play with *numeri clausi* distribution between study programmes, as faculty/schools are reluctant to give up places. However, not having *numeri clausi* would also constitute a threat to institutions located inland, given student preference for coastal HEIs. Other difficulties are the high costs for students to attend higher education, due to students' low financial resources, especially in peripheral universities.

Another barrier pointed out by universities is the fact that the grades used as selection criteria for HE access under the national access system are 'unreliable indicators of student quality.' Hence the high failure rates in some disciplines despite high access grades, while some study programmes fill up with students who chose them as third, fourth or fifth options, with implications for their motivation. Other obstacles are represented by students' difficulties in adapting to higher education, given the differences in pedagogic approaches between HE and secondary education, or the poor student attendance to classes. Specifically, students identify as an obstacle the assessment which fails to take into account the needs of students older than 23 years. Some teachers expect students to attend their classes, do not make information easily available to students, or resist working with distance teaching and learning web platforms.

Specific obstacles are further mentioned by the actors representing the two disciplinary areas under analysis. In Arts such obstacles include the impossibility of selecting students and the effects of this on quality; the poor educational level of families and a hardly demanding basic education, affecting students' work habits, discipline and success; students' lack of autonomy; or the institution's limited financial and material resources constraining academics' work. In Engineering, especially in polytechnics, the barriers are represented by the attempts to avoid Mathematics as one of the access exams (for instance by changing the study programme name), with negative impact on incoming students' preparation, as well as the existence of study programmes accepting high numbers of students older than 23 years, with negative effects on programme performance, staff motivation, and the training of students.

Specifically in the case of the two polytechnic institutions, one of the most critical barriers identified was the students' increasingly lower educational background. Students are seen as accessing higher education poorly prepared and with limited knowledge in core disciplines such as Mathematics. These deficiencies are even more emphasised by HEI δ since it rarely constitutes students' first choice (rather, it is often the second, third or even fourth choice); therefore, it never ends up having the 'best' students. Another barrier within polytechnics is represented by a certain blurring between the roles of polytechnics and universities, hence the corresponding need to better define the different missions of these two distinct types of institutions. A last barrier is constituted by the geographical location, perceived as peripheral. In fact, the inland location is identified by the polytechnic institutions as the main cause for the increasingly low number of candidates, at least in the first phase of the national competition.

Overall one can argue that the existence of a generalised *numeri clausi* system together with a centralised placement system results in HEIs' low autonomy to select their own students, which constitutes a barrier to the definition and implementation of an institutional policy on access. HEIs are trying to cope with this is by developing strategies aimed at increasing the number of students who access HE through special competition streams: postgraduate students and mature students (older than 23 years). Institutions with high reputation that are able to attract enough traditional students develop strategies to attract higher numbers of master and PhD students, while less prestigious institutions target their efforts at mature students, trying to increase the number of students older than 23 years. This may well explain why Portuguese HEIs are keen to develop measures to promote themselves at regional, national and even international level. The competition for students is indeed a reality in the Portuguese higher education system.

FINAL DISCUSSION

The global results enable us to answer the two main research questions: What is the institutional policy on access? What is the relationship between access and quality assurance processes?

Overall, Portuguese HEIs seem to be developing their own specific institutional policies on access. Although aligned with the national legal framework, institutions have some autonomy to deploy strategies and initiatives to attract students aside the national competition. This is the case, in all the four selected institutions, for the recruitment of students older than 23 years, of foreign students and of students holding CETs. However, resorting to such initiatives seems to be more evident among the institutions with lower demand rates within the national competition, such as those located in more peripheral regions or the polytechnics.

Institutions tend to develop structures and mechanisms, not always formalised or systematised, for the collection of data on enrolments, graduation and dropout rates. Nevertheless, the data collection does not seem to derive from an explicit strategy directed at improving access, but is rather a response to legal requirements regarding the quality assessment of study programmes. However, this seems to enable institutions to be more aware of the potential publics they might attract. Furthermore, one can conclude that Portuguese institutions are developing systems designed to support specific groups of students: students older than 23 years, foreign and CETs students, and students experiencing both economic and learning difficulties. The first three groups currently constitute the major 'new' publics.

It is interesting to note that the tension between quantity (access) and quality (standards) is also evident. Increasing the number of traditional and non-traditional students has led to the admission of more students with lower educational backgrounds than would be desirable. This is especially evident among Engineering where complaints about the lack of prior knowledge of basic concepts and skills (e.g. Mathematics) emerged. This has led to the development of a set of mechanisms and strategies aimed at improving knowledge gaps, in an attempt to avoid excessive failure and drop-out rates and longer times to completion, since these constitute important indicators of study programme and HEI quality.

One can argue that, although not always in a strategic way, the selected Portuguese HEIs are developing information systems enabling the collection and the potential analysis of relevant data. In some cases, this information is used in the management of faculty/school and study programmes. Therefore, compliance with ESG 1.6 seems to be only partial since not all the data are collected and systematised by formal structures specially designed for that purpose. The same can be verified as regards compliance with ESG 1.1. Although institutions strive to assure and improve quality at the level of access, such efforts seem to be in a very early stage and not driven by clearly formulated policies or strategies. In fact, the existence of policies and procedures for quality assurance which contemplate access is not totally clear from the analysed data, neither is the existence of a quality culture in what concerns access. When institutions refer to quality they are addressing much more the academic quality of students rather than the quality culture, procedures and instruments to assure the quality of the institution and of the study programmes.

ACKNOWLEDGEMENTS

This research was undertaken in the context of the project IBAR funded by the European Commission, entitled 'Identifying barriers in promoting the European Standards and Guidelines for Quality Assurance at institutional level', reference 511491-LLP-1-2010-1-CZ-KA1-KA1SCR.

REFERENCES/BIBLIOGRAPHY

Amaral, A., Cardoso, S., Manatos, M. J., Neave, G., Rosa, M. J. (rapporteur WP5), Sarrico, C. (project coordinator), Tavares, O., Teixeira, P., Sin, Cristina., & Veiga, A. (rapporteur WP5) (2011). Survey of Internal Quality Assurance Systems – the Portuguese case.
ENQA (2009). ENQA report on standards and guidelines for quality assurance in the European higher education area. European association for quality assurance in higher education, 2009, Helsinki, 3rd edition. Available at: http://www.enqa.eu/pubs.lasso.
Kohoutek, J. (Ed.) (2009). Implementation of the standards and guidelines for quality assurance in higher education in the central and East-European Countries – Agenda ahead. *Studies on Higher Education*, UNESCO-CEPES.
Land, R., Eggins, H., Gordon, G., Owen, C., & Boon, S. (2011). Quality and access – comparative study,

IBAR Project Work-Package 6.

Magalhães, A., Amaral, A., & Tavares, O. (2009). Equity, access and institutional Competition, *Tertiary Education and Management, 15*(1), 35–48.

MAP-ESG Steering group (2011). Mapping The Implementation and Application of the ESG – final Report of the project steering, Brussels: ENQA.

Silverman, David (2001). *Interpreting Qualitative data: Methods for analysing talk, text, and interaction*, London/Thousand Oaks/New Delhi: Sage.

Tavares, O. (2011). *As Escolhas dos Estudantes no Acesso ao Ensino Superior Português – processos e racionalidades*. PhD Thesis. Porto: Faculdade de Psicologia e Ciências da Educação da Universidade do Porto.

Tavares, D., Tavares, O., Justino, E., & Amaral, A. (2008). Students' preferences and needs in Portuguese higher education. *European Journal of Education, 43*(1), 107–122.

Teixeira, P., Fonseca, M., Amado, D., Sá, C., & Amaral, A. (2009). A Regional mismatch? Student applications and institutional responses in the Portuguese public higher education system. In K. Mohrman, J. Shi, S. Feinblatt & K. Chow, *Public Universities and Regional Development*, Chengdu: Sichuan University, 59–80.

Tonkiss, Fran (2006). Analysing text and speech: content and discourse analysis, in Seale, Clive (Eds.), *Researching Society and Culture*, London, Thousand Oaks e New Delhi: Sage Publications, 367–382.

Legislation

Decree-Law n.º 26/2003. Regulates access to higher education.

Decree-Law n.º 64/2006. Regulates the access to higher education of students older than 23 years.

Decree-Law n.º 90/2008. Regulates access to higher education.

Decree-Law n.º 296-A/1998. Regulates access to higher education.

Law n.º 49/2005. Changes the Fundamental Laws on the Education System and on Higher Education Financing.

AFFILIATIONS

Orlanda Tavares
CIPES (Center for Research in Higher Education policies)
Portugal

Sónia Cardoso
CIPES (Center for Research in Higher Education policies)
Portugal

Cristina Sin
CIPES (Center for Research in Higher Education policies)
Portugal

CPSIA information can be obtained
at www.ICGtesting.com
Printed in the USA
LVOW03s1637050216

473889LV00005B/75/P